THE ABCs OF LITERACY

THE ABCs OF LITERACY

Preparing Our Children for Lifelong Learning

CYNTHIA DOLLINS, EdD

CUMBERLAND HOUSE
NASHVILLE, TENNESSEE

THE ABCs OF LITERACY
Published by Cumberland House Publishing, Inc.
431 Harding Industrial Drive
Nashville, Tennessee 37211

Cover design by Gore Studio Inc., Nashville, Tennessee

Dollins, Cynthia, 1963–
   The ABCs of literacy : preparing our children for lifelong learning / Cynthia Dollins.
      p. cm.
   Includes bibliographical references and index.
   ISBN 978-1-58182-652-4 (pbk.)
1. Oral reading. 2. Children—Books and reading. 3. Early childhood education—Parent participation I. Title.

LB1573.5.D65 2008
372.45'2—dc22

2008025425

Printed in the United States of America
1 2 3 4 5 6 7 8 9 10—12 11 10 09 08

*To my children, Heather and Zack, without whom
this book would not exist. I love you.*

You may have tangible
wealth untold;
Caskets of jewels
and coffers of gold.
Richer than I
you can never be.
I had a mother who read to me.

—STRICKLAND GILLILAN

CONTENTS

ACKNOWLEDGMENTS

This book has been crafted over time through my experiences inside and outside the classroom, as a mother, teacher, principal, and university instructor. It has come to fruition by the love and support of many in my life, including family, friends, and colleagues.

I am grateful to my husband, Mike, who provided me love and encouragement throughout this challenging and exciting adventure. He has been by my side from the roots of this project to its blossoming.

Cara Garcia met with me at the inception of this project and told me, "Keep writing." I heard her voice and repeated those words many times to get me through dry spells, discouraging moments, and those times when I wanted to give up. She has been my mentor and has inspired me to follow my passion.

I am thankful to Kathy Church, self-proclaimed "biggest fan," who has encouraged me and supported me. I am proud to call her a colleague and friend.

To Cumberland House and to its president, Ron Pitkin, who believed in the value of this topic and its potential impact on parents and teachers, I am very grateful. Lisa Taylor, my editor, has been positive and encouraging even during the stressful deadlines.

My friends contributed to this book each time they placed their children's literacy at the forefront. Exchanging children's books, sharing reading and writing endeavors, rejoicing over a new literary selection, and taking pleasure in our children's attempts (and triumphs) at writing are the experiences that inspired me to create this book.

Perhaps most importantly, I must acknowledge my mother, who has been the quintessential reader—a lover of books and all the places they take us, lessons they teach us, and ways they impact us. She introduced me to the world of books and to the power of literacy and knowledge.

THE ORIGIN OF THIS BOOK

I cannot live without books.
—THOMAS JEFFERSON

Since our daughter, Heather, was born, my husband, Mike, and I have tried very hard to read aloud to her every day. We recognized that this practice was an extremely valuable activity that would assist Heather with future literacy success. However, we quickly discovered many other benefits for each of us. It helped establish a sleep routine, as we read aloud before nap and bedtime. We saw that it soothed Heather (and us) as our voices reflected the unique and melodic quality the author created. We got lost in the rhythm and cadence of the stories and experienced the beautiful language of books. Obviously, Heather was too young to understand the plot, identify with the main characters, and focus on the events that unfolded, but we were not. So, while we were laying the foundation of story structure and reading readiness for Heather, we were also re-exploring our own childhood. We were establishing for our daughter, and reinforcing for ourselves, the power of the written word.

As the next few years passed by all too quickly, my husband and I met mothers and fathers who had children close to Heather's age. Friendships developed as we shared and commiserated about the many joys and challenges associated with raising children. Within our circle of friends and acquaintances, I noticed that most seemed to recognize the need to read aloud to their sons and daughters. They were aware that it was an important part of raising a child and were committed to this process. However, numerous discussions with these parents revealed that many were uncertain about the *specific* benefits associated with reading aloud to their preschoolers. They wondered about how this activity could help with their child's future independent reading and assist with later school success. Because of my background experience in education as a teacher, principal, and university lecturer, parents shared with me a desire to understand the detailed benefits of reading aloud. They asked me to help them find books for their children and wanted to know how to select only the best. They told me about the conversations they had with their child when they were reading aloud, how they were unsure whether or not they should point to words or letters while reading, how they laughed or cried at certain literature, and they proceeded to share their frustration at reading the same book over and over at the request of their child. Mothers and fathers invariably asked me what was the *right* way to read to their child.

I found myself giving information about the reading process and the loosely defined developmental learning continuum discussed among teachers and researchers. This continuum includes various labels for the typical stages that readers go through, from pre-reading or emergent reading through beginning reading and finally to proficient and independent fluent reading. Most preschoolers fall within the pre-reading, emergent, or developing reader stages. Visible behaviors are commonly listed within the developmental reading continuum for educators to note and then plan future instruction based on abilities and needs of individual children. Behaviors may include listening to stories, pretending to read books, utilizing illustrations to gain meaning, identifying some letters in print, knowing that print in the English language is read from left to right and top to bottom, as well as numerous other skills that bridge children into eventual independent reading success. One example of a developmental reading continuum is provided in Appendix 1 on page 305. None of the items on the continuum is more important than the others and there is no rush to "check off" the lists prior to entering formal education. It is important to allow our children to grow and discover at their own pace. Just like many other developmental milestones, including crawling, walking, and speaking, most children acquire these skills when they are ready, with the proper support and encouragement.

Discussions about the reading continuum often spurred more questions from friends. I accompanied parents to libraries and bookstores and spent a great deal of time reassuring them about their own read-aloud routines. Throughout my interactions, it became clear to me that there are some parents who want and need more information than can be found in parenting magazines. These parents recognize that being able to read is the key to later success in almost everything we do. Yet the parents who are informed about the importance of reading also seek additional information about exactly *why* we read aloud, what benefits this process offers to our children, and how we can prepare our sons and daughters for future reading success. Some parents are lifelong learners themselves, and they want to understand all that they can about the various aspects associated with the complicated process of reading. It is for these parents that this book is written. I have tried to provide parents with more than simply the knowledge and understanding that we should read aloud to our children every day. Many of us are already aware of this fact. Some parents now want to know why, specifically, we read aloud, as well as what, how, where, and when to do so.

As with so many other aspects of raising children, there is no perfect recipe to ensure that our children will be proficient and avid readers and writers. There is no one right way to draw our children into the reading process. Instead, I have written this book to provide parents with ideas and *choices*. After laying the foundation of the detailed aspects and benefits of *why* we read aloud to our children, I provide options and suggestions for *what* to read aloud, as well as *how, when,* and *where* to do so. You will notice the focus on these options throughout the book with terms like *periodically, sometimes, occasionally*, and other statements that reference paying close attention to your own children's needs and adapting strategies to them. The purpose of these suggestions is to remind parents that the ultimate goal of reading aloud to our children is to invite them into the wonderful world of reading so that they see it as something fun and resourceful. We want our children to be excited about reading so that they are motivated to learn to read on their own one day. Parents want their children to recognize the power of reading for success in life as well as the doors it opens to a world of imagination, beauty, and knowledge.

I felt conflicted as I wrote this book, fearful that parents would see it as a how-to guide for breaking down stories and language into its pieces, thinking they were making it "manageable" for their child. I shuddered to think that parents might begin to "drill and kill" the act of reading by pressuring their children (with the utmost of altruistic intentions) to point to words on the page, locate letters, emphasize spelling, answer numerous questions about the text, and a sundry list of other rote tasks. While I recognized that all these aspects were parts of the reading readiness developmental continuum and were, indeed, necessary for future literacy success, I wanted to be careful not to misrepresent my philosophy about reading aloud. The main goal of reading with our preschoolers should always be simply to bring a child and wonderful literature together. How we, as parents, present the first experiences of reading has the potential to shape our children's lifelong attitudes toward literacy. Through hearing rhythmic language, meeting interesting characters, and discovering the unknown, parents demonstrate how reading can be an enjoyable pastime. Listening to and understanding the story or text material is the most important aspect of the read-aloud experience. In fact, most educators recognize that without comprehension, identification of letters and decoding skills mean very little.

While in the process of writing *The ABCs of Literacy*, I accompanied my daughter, Heather, to a play date at my friend Amanda's house. While the girls played together, Amanda began to discuss with me her concerns about her daughter's progress in reading. She stated that Taylor (then three and a half years old) was becoming increasingly focused on the words in the stories they read each day. Taylor would insist that her mother or father point to each word as they read aloud. Her daughter often imitated the pointing while repeating the title, phrase, or sentence that had just been read. Amanda also confided that Taylor was constantly asking her to spell words while they were in the car, making dinner, or playing together. "How do you spell *mommy*? How do you spell *groceries*?"

During our conversation, I recalled our earlier arrival at their house. The first thing Taylor had done was to bring Heather and me into her bedroom, jump up on her bed, point to the large wooden letters on the wall that spelled her name, and read each of them to us. "I can spell my name. Watch. T-A-Y-L-O-R. Taylor. See?" She was obviously proud of this noble accomplishment. It was true. Taylor was indeed noticing letters and words and demonstrating a great interest in this aspect of the reading process.

I could not help but smile as Amanda continued to relay her interactions with Taylor. I thought it was wonderful and wondered why she was having concerns about it. I had always thought of Taylor as a bright, talkative, creative, and inquisitive girl. Her latest interests and behavior were certainly in line with this. Amanda felt this was happening too soon and that her daughter could not possibly be ready. She worried that she was just memorizing the words and asked me my "professional opinion" of how Taylor *should* learn to read. "Isn't it too early?" she queried. After some probing from me, Amanda confessed that she felt Taylor was focusing too much on the mechanics of reading and might lose her sense of imagination and wonderment. After all, "She's only three and a half."

This interaction led me to think of Linda, another friend of mine, whose son could track words and "read" simple texts by the age of four. I contrasted both of these stories with those of some of my other friends whose children of similar age had shown little or no such interest in the details of words, spaces, or spelling. These children, too, certainly appeared to be bright and articulate and loved to have their parents read aloud to them. However, their focus at age three and a half was not on the parts of the words or on tracking them. I knew that would come. One was not necessarily better than the other. It did not mean that one child had a higher I.Q. than the other or even that one would be more successful upon entering formal classroom instruction. All of these children were still young, and they were merely showing that they had different interests in the varied and multi-layered aspects of the reading process. Many educators believe that each child's growth can be found on a loosely defined developmental continuum of reading readiness skills. Some preschoolers know all the names of the letters and their corresponding sounds. Others actively engage in conversations about stories and their characters and plots. Still others enjoy chiming in with repetitive phrases and rhyming words. Additionally, some three- to five-year-old children love to merely look at the pictures and snuggle next to Mom or Dad, just listening as they wind down.

Because of Amanda's concern, she had even taken measures to counteract what she viewed as the potential loss of creative thinking by specifically purchasing books about fairies and other imaginary characters in an attempt to keep the whimsy of books alive for her daughter. This time I laughed at myself, reflecting on the irony of my concern that parents may forget about the story for story sake and focus only on the parts of sentences and words. I wanted my message to ensure that the pleasure of story time would not become a classroom lesson where our children started to associate reading with skills, flashcards, and accountability. Instead, my goal in this book was to make it clear to parents of preschoolers that the main goal of reading aloud was to ignite the spark of curiosity, imagination, and knowledge through the world of books.

Talking with Amanda reminded me of what I had witnessed in the classroom time and again as an elementary teacher and principal. Children are ready when they are ready. And when they are ready, we must look closely and seize the opportunity. Rather than forcing them to read the title and author after we have done so, point to the first word on the page, or locate a letter on the page that is the same as the beginning letter of their name, we model, and read, and praise, and enjoy. Yet, in the same respect, we capitalize on their interests and their intrinsic motivation to learn more. When our children show signs of curiosity about the letters within words or the spaces between these words, we answer their questions. Then we read some more. Preschoolers have a wonderful way of showing us when they are ready to learn more. They ask.

The perfect scenario is to build on learning at the point that our child is ready. Teachers look closely at their students in an effort to find this "perfect" time. They observe, take notes, and assess, all in attempt to find when it is just right to introduce new concepts. Lev Vygotsky, a developmental psychologist well-known in the field of education, refers to this as teaching within a child's zone of proximal development or ZPD.[1]

The ZPD is the range between a student's actual developmental level and their potential developmental level, the period when they are ready to take in the information presented to them. With the help of a significant and caring adult, be it a parent or a teacher, the child is supported through the learning process. They ask questions to clarify their understanding of the new knowledge and then typically want to put that new knowledge into practice. Taylor was clearly signaling to her mom and, in essence, saying, "I am interested in letters and words. I have noticed that what you say when you read to me corresponds with what is on the page. Tell me more. Teach me more. I am excited and ready to learn."

After reassuring Amanda that periodically focusing on skills did not necessarily negate the love of literature, I discussed with her a compromise to ensure that Taylor would not lose sight of the beauty that is found in books. After all, both aspects of reading aloud are important to future reading success. Together with Taylor, Amanda or her husband would select one of the three books they read aloud and would focus on word tracking, alphabet knowledge, repetition, or whatever Taylor was interested in doing. The two other books would be read aloud without highlighting the parts of the printed words. Discussions could evolve from these two books, but the main focus would be listening to the rhythm of the language, the wonderful vocabulary, and the story or information as a whole, instead of the specific concepts about print and word detail. A balance was reached to continue Taylor's progress related to the parts associated with reading without losing a sense of the whole of the book.

Throughout the raising of our children, parents are constantly reminded of the importance of considering our children's needs, our goals for them, and their developmental readiness. This fine balance requires careful observation of our children, a quest for knowledge from outside resources, and most importantly, a trust in our children and ourselves. Working together, parent and child will guide each other.

INTRODUCTION

Read to me so that I may learn.

We read to our daughter, Heather, so that she can build background knowledge about dinosaurs, trees, butterflies, seahorses, penguins, and all the living things our world has to offer. We read to her to build background knowledge about the conventions of how print works and how book language differs from other forms of communication.

We read to Heather so that she may learn phonemic awareness, fluency, sounds and letters of the alphabet, new vocabulary, comprehension of story structure, and other key preliteracy skills. We read to her so that she will have the necessary tools to become an independent reader and writer.

We read aloud fiction, nonfiction, poetry, recipes, and magazines because research tells us that readers need to understand and implement different strategies for each genre.

We read to Heather so that she may listen and understand, so that she may imagine and create. We cook, draw, sing, dance, and write after reading books because research has shown that a multimodal approach helps children comprehend text more thoroughly. More importantly, perhaps, we do this because we want our daughter to know how truly fun the world of books can be.

We read to her and sometimes ask questions so that she may grow into a critical thinker who also asks questions, seeks answers, and makes educated decisions.

We read to her so that she may become wiser.

We read to her so that she may become better.

I invite you into this book to learn the power of the written word for our children. Let us explore together the rhythm and cadence of language. Let us learn how it helps bring us closer to our children in a unique and pleasurable way, how it helps them develop reading and writing readiness skills, and how it promotes exploration of the world. My goal is to help parents build a better understanding of why reading aloud to our preschool children is so valuable. I discuss the best times, places, and approaches to reading with your child. I provide guidance on how to select quality texts to lay the foundation for future reading success, and I also give ways to extend the read-aloud experience to promote higher-level thinking through questions and discussion before, during, and after a great book. Additionally, I offer ideas for including writing, art, music, and crafts as part of the overall literacy experience with our children.

My hope is that you will come away from this book with a passion for children's literature, a love for reading aloud, and an ability to look more closely at your child's steady developmental progression as a natural and authentic experience. Perhaps both you and your child will benefit from the information in this book by coming closer together and by sharing the excitement, charm, magic, silliness, and newfound knowledge available in books. Ultimately, my goal is for families to enjoy the process of exploring all that books have to offer and to know the joy of lifelong learning. To that end, let us turn the page and begin.

Part **A**

Why We Read Aloud to Young Children

CHAPTER 1

Pull Parent and Child Closer:
The Affective Domain

Little Nutbrown Hare,
who was going to bed,
held on tight to Big Nutbrown Hare's
very long ears.
He wanted to be sure that
Big Nutbrown Hare was listening.
"Guess how much I love you," he said.
"Oh, I don't think I could guess that,"
said Big Nutbrown Hare.

As Sam McBratney's *Guess How Much I Love You* proceeds, father and son Nutbrown Hare compare all the ways they love each other, as high as they can reach and hop and see. Sharing books like this gives parents an opportunity to snuggle up, get cozy, and *show* their children how much they mean to them. The powerful draw of the written word can bring us closer to our children. Giving undivided attention and actively listening as you embark on the adventures that unfold in books builds a sense of community and togetherness. Creating a ritual of reading aloud before bed, naptime, or some other special time each day helps build a family tradition that can be handed down from generation to generation.

I invite you to think about your own early childhood experiences with read-alouds. Some of us can recall the warm feeling of being read to by our parents before bedtime. My friend, Megan, relayed to me that her favorite part of first grade was just after lunch when she would put her head down on the desk and listen to her teacher read. Others of us have fond memories of being read to in our place of worship, feeling close and connected to our religious community. My friend, Mark, reminisced about the entire family bringing books on all their outings. Sitting around a campfire, a flashlight was passed around and different family members read poems, quotes, or special paragraphs. Some passages made Mark laugh; others were meant to frighten and heighten the camping fun. You may choose to continue your family practices, or perhaps you will create your own literacy traditions.

Bedtime story reading is a natural activity for parents to interact with their children. It taps into the affective domain because it brings child and parent closer together in an authentic, unforced way. Educational psychologists divide learning experiences into three interrelated and overlapping domains: psychomotor (skills), cognitive (knowledge), and affective (attitude). The psychomotor domain refers to the use of basic motor skills, physical movement, and coordination. The category involving knowledge and the development of intellectual skills is the cognitive learning domain. The affective domain addresses a child's emotions, attitudes, and interest level toward a learning experience. All three domains work together to create a complete learning experience.

Reading with our own children can impact the affective domain by furthering the emotional connection we have together. Sharing books with them, affectionately referred to as lap reading, creates a safe and warm environment that can lead to a lifetime love of reading and learning. By sitting on a parent's lap or next to someone special, children receive focused attention and begin to associate reading with pleasure. Edward J. Dwyer and Evelyn E. Dwyer state, "The foundation of any learning environment is a warm invitation to learn."[1] The read-aloud experience provides this invitation. Through a loving interaction, books are seen as sources of valuable and exciting experiences. Parent and child laugh together, wonder together, and learn together. Parents serve as role models as they read aloud, showing that reading is useful, relaxing, and enjoyable. When children see their parents excited about reading, they will catch their enthusiasm and will be motivated to one day read on their own.

Several years ago, prior to having children of my own, I stopped by to visit my friend Becky and headed upstairs where she was getting her two daughters ready for bed. I expected to see them finishing baths, brushing teeth, or putting on pajamas. Instead, I walked in and saw three sets of eyes peering over blankets, Becky sandwiched between her then three- and six-year-old daughters. Their heads were snuggled tightly together on one pillow, bodies buried beneath the covers. All were engrossed in the story of the night, smirking as they caught a glimpse of me invading their special time together. I smiled and excused myself back downstairs so as to not interrupt any more of this obviously intimate moment.

Later I talked to Becky about what I had seen and marveled over the fact that she found time in her busy schedule to stop and place a priority on reading to her daughters. Becky lived a seemingly hectic life, working full-time, being involved with numerous other projects within her field, and, like so many parents, carting her girls to soccer, dance, horseback riding, and the like. I thought of the proverbial modern household filled with chaos to get the kids in bed, then quickly prepare for the next day where the busy-ness of life would no doubt start all over again. How could Becky slow down each night and take the time to read to her girls? I wondered why she placed so much value on this experience. She told me simply that this was her special time to bond with her girls in a way unlike any that they had throughout the day. Although there were obviously other times in the day where she offered undivided attention, hugs, snuggles, and love with her girls, she said that reading to them was nonetheless unique. It closed out their day. It calmed down their night. Reading aloud gave them a common language as a family where they could travel to other places and visit other cultures. The nighttime ritual was a way for Becky, Audrey, and Rae to discuss, giggle, and ponder together over the books they shared. They shut out the rest of the world, created their own, and ended the day on a positive note. "Wow," I thought. "What a wonderful way to wind down the day with our children."

Several of our friends have chosen to read aloud with their children in bed. When Heather first came home from the hospital, Mike and I rocked her in the glider from our den. We used the same pillow to prop up our arm that now serves as a place for her to lay her head down in the midst of reading if she chooses. We sometimes still sit her in our lap and always hold her close, positioning the book so that she can see the pictures, the letters, the words. We used to wrap a blanket around her during our read-aloud time, but now that she has grown to be a preschooler, we may drape one over our legs. No TV. No radio. Just Heather and her daddy or Heather and her mommy. When Heather's little brother, Zack, was born, the read-aloud routine became even more of a family event. The four of us now gather on the couch and Mike and I switch places each night, giving our children an opportunity to hear each of us read aloud. As Heather has caught on to the predictability of some books and learned more and more words, she sometimes chimes in and even reads to us some things on her own. This has become a special nighttime ritual that helps us all unwind and be together as a family. I think it is important to select a special place and time to share books together, be it huddled in bed, on your favorite rocker or couch, or in the backyard swing.

When I was an elementary school teacher, I was a strong advocate for reading to my students every day. I used read-alouds to teach about writing styles, add to class knowledge of a particular unit of study or content area, expose them to classic and great literature, prompt thoughtful discussions, and set a calming tone after lunch recess. However, I learned something new from Becky that night. I received a glimpse into the greatness of the read-aloud experience for the family. I was reminded that reading a wonderful book is twice as much fun when you can share it with someone you love. I believe it is one of the special gifts we can give to our children.

While it is the *act* of reading aloud that brings us closer to our children, regardless of the actual book we share, I have nonetheless compiled a list of titles that I feel exemplify this unique connection. Since books afford us a special way to express our feelings, I have specifically looked for ones that reinforce the deep love between parent and child. These evoke a sense of warmth and closeness. They are books about reassurance and comfort. Maryann Cusimano delightfully describes the beautiful way that a parent and child complement one another in her book *You Are My I Love You*.

> I am your parent; you are my child.
> I am your quiet place; you are my wild . . .
> I am your lullaby; you are my peekaboo.
> I am your good-night kiss; you are my I love you.

The books I have chosen to include in the affective domain booklist (see page 245) are snuggly and cuddly and gentle and peaceful. They are lullabies and bedtime stories. Some are poetic and soothing. Others are quiet and restful. They are tales of kisses and hugs and "I love yous." They are the soft and serene stories that remind both parent and child how valuable each is in this special relationship.

CHAPTER 2

Build Background Knowledge

There are many little ways to enlarge your child's world.
Love of books is the best of all.

—JACQUELINE KENNEDY

In Leo Lionni's *Fish Is Fish* a tadpole and minnow are inseparable friends until the tadpole becomes a frog and leaves the pond. He finally returns one day and describes all the extraordinary things he has seen on land, including birds, cows, men, women, and children. In an attempt to help the minnow visualize the animals he has never seen before, frog provides a detailed description of each. He tells about wings, two legs and the many colors of birds. He offers horns, four legs, eating grass, and carrying milk in a pink pouch to describe a cow. Because of the minnow's limited experience and background knowledge outside of pond life, he incorrectly pictures each animal looking similar to a fish with the specific details the frog states. In his mind, the birds resemble large colorful feathered fish "swimming" through the air. Even the people are pictured as large fish with clothes. Clearly the minnow had no background knowledge of life on land. Therefore, his views were generated from existing and skewed information that he applied to all forms of life.

Just like the minnow, we all use our prior knowledge to help make sense of new information and the world. The more experiences and knowledge we have, the more readily we can apply them to help understand new information. Prior knowledge is a critical factor for proficient literacy development. Our background knowledge is the accumulation of all our life experiences up to this point. Each of us has a unique set of background knowledge based on all our experiences with travel, people, books, movies, and conversations. It includes everything we have seen, tasted, touched, smelled, and learned. The term *schema* is used by educators to mean the same thing as background knowledge. In order to provide you with a visual to better understand schema theory and how background knowledge is organized, think of the brain as a large file cabinet. Schemas, or schemata, are the individual file folders in our brain on each topic that we have created from diverse experiences in our lives. We have schema for animals, deserts, restaurants, flying, grammar, driving, and trips to the pediatrician. Each time we learn more about a particular topic, our brain quickly accesses the corresponding file folder and we add the new information to it.

Since parents are children's first teachers, one of our goals is to help them learn and grow cognitively. We want them to have many file folders, filled with information from numerous resources. Perhaps if we lived in a perfect world, our children would experience everything it has to offer. They would travel the globe and learn about other cultures; hear other languages; taste authentic Chinese, Italian, and Peruvian food; ride trains; meet artists; climb mountains; feed lions; throw snowballs; hold spiders; listen to African drums; and make friends with children from different walks of life. If money and time were no object, perhaps our children could see firsthand the diversity and the similarities of our world. They could actively build schema directly through hands-on experiences. Unfortunately, most of us cannot provide our children such indulgences. We can, however, help them begin to build file folders by inviting them into this learning process through a different experience, the experience of books. While there are many ways to build schema, one that is readily available to us and can be accessed on a daily basis is reading aloud.

The ability to understand something we hear is usually at a higher level than our own reading comprehension. Therefore, reading aloud to our children helps them develop schema about a variety of topics. When preschoolers listen as their parents read to them, they begin to create little "files" of information that can be retrieved when needed. Reading aloud helps build background knowledge in three key areas: subject matter, print conventions, and book language. I have elaborated on these in the following sections to provide you detailed information on each. I hope that you will clearly see the benefits reading aloud offers our preschoolers in building background knowledge, one of the key literacy skills for vocabulary, spelling, reading, and writing development.

Background Knowledge on Subject Matter

By reading nonfiction books such as *Frogs* by Gail Gibbons, our children learn details about the life cycle of the frog. Children also learn numerous interesting facts about these animals. They discover that frogs do not hunt for food, but rather wait patiently for something to cross their path. Most frogs can jump ten times their body length and have two sets of eyelids, one of which is transparent, to protect their eyes in water. If we skim through the latest issue of *Your Big Backyard*, published by the National Wildlife Federation, and select an article here or a caption there to read to our children, they may learn one more fact about giraffes, butterflies, polar bears, wolves, or ring-tailed lemurs previously unknown to them.

> Ring-tailed lemurs live in large groups called **troops**. Troop members spend most of the day on the ground, looking for food. As they walk along, they raise their tails in the air like flags. These "flags" tell other lemurs to "follow me!" (*Your Big Backyard*, August 2005, p. 5)

Books afford preschoolers the opportunity to learn about children in diverse parts of the world who may have different experiences from them. Preschoolers can almost see the tiny lights flickering on and off when they sit closely next to their mother or father reading *Fireflies!* by Julie Brinckloe. They learn that on summer nights in certain parts of America, children excitedly find a jar, punch holes in the lid, and run outside to capture fireflies with all their friends.

When parents read aloud Ina R. Friedman's *How My Parents Learned to Eat*, children see that some people eat with chopsticks and drink soup from a bowl, while others eat with a knife, fork, and spoon. They hear words like *kimono* and *sukiyaki* and compare different greetings like shaking hands and bowing.

Through books, our children can gain background knowledge about places around the world. They are provided a glimpse into a Tanzanian village in Stephanie Stuve-Bodeen's *Elizabeti's Doll*. They see lifestyle differences such as food being cooked over an open fire in a separate hut from where the family sleeps. They hear words like *kanga* and learn that babies are carried on their mother's backs in these brightly colored cloths. Children notice that Elizabeti brings water in a large jug atop her head for her family to use. They witness that not all children have access to the same resources. They see that imagination and love can create something special, and that even a rock can become the perfect baby doll in the creative mind of a little girl. And, it is hoped, they also learn that themes of family unity, friendship, and love are universal.

Background Knowledge About the Conventions of How Print Works

By listening to quality literature that includes stories, nonfiction, poetry, and other genres, our children begin to develop unique background knowledge separate from the specific information provided in these texts. Preschoolers build awareness about how print itself works. As they snuggle next to us for the read-aloud experience, they notice and learn that the English language is read from left to right, top to bottom, and front to back (unlike some other languages). They begin to see how books are read in order from the first page, whereas magazines or newspapers may be skimmed until an article of interest is selected.

As we read aloud children's magazines like *Ladybug*, our preschoolers see how stories, comics, songs, poems, and nonfiction can be combined into one type of print, minus all the advertisements from many magazines for older audiences. They learn about options in magazines to read a story here and a poem there, skipping and selecting based on the reader's goals and moods. When parents read aloud comic strips, our preschoolers see this format of print laid out quite differently from other genre of writing, and thus they become more accustomed to navigating through brief scenario set-ups and dialogue bubbles, figuring out the humor as they go.

Preschoolers begin to notice and learn how poetry is distinguished from prose through the author's attention to spacing, line, and punctuation. They become aware of the print differences seen in verses and stanzas from poetry compared to sentences and paragraphs in prose. Careful attention to length of line creates a visual for our children that will assist them in deciphering the poet's message. When we read poetry to our children, they see the subtleties of word placement and come to recognize how many poets manipulate the structure of grammar to create a certain feeling. Nouns, verbs, adjectives, and adverbs may not follow the traditional structure found in prose, but selective placement of each is heard to contribute to the author's intent.

Since nonfiction houses a unique set of print conventions, we are helping our children become familiar with these and build schema each time we read aloud this genre. They see us skipping around to different pages in nonfiction instead of reading everything in sequential order like in narrative texts. They become accustomed to captions, labels, and diagrams as parents direct them to read additional information. Referring back to the example of the book *Frogs*, children learn more than just facts about this animal in experiencing this book. They see how the layout of the text itself is different from most stories that have been read aloud to them. They notice tables, charts, and diagrams that clearly distinguish the text from narrative. In *Frogs*, preschoolers see an illustrated diagram of the frog with body parts (webbed feet, skin, teeth, nostril, etc.) clearly labeled. Two full-page charts list the differences between frogs and toads. From experiences like this, preschoolers learn that details in nonfiction are provided in both the text and the accompanying photographs or illustrations. Chapter titles, article headings, and the use of bold print are noticed by our children as distinguishing features of nonfiction. (Many other features about how print works in the English language are discussed in chapter 3, "Connect to the Concepts About Print.")

Background Knowledge About Book Language

By reading aloud to our children, we are building background knowledge about the language of books, a language different from oral speech, conversations with friends or family, or that which is heard on television. Conversations are often reserved for communication between two or more people where turns are taken. They may involve asking or answering questions, giving commands or directions, or pausing and listening. Spoken language often uses contractions (*it's, she'll, can't, we're*) and brief sentences, many of which may not be complete. Written language, on the other hand, usually consists of complete sentences and uses words like *it is, she will, cannot,* and *we are.* Daily oral interactions involve numerous commands. In books, dialogue is denoted by quotation marks, and the text specifically states who is speaking and often includes additional information about what, how, where, or why they are speaking. Spoken language is often brief and direct, whereas written language focuses heavily on careful word choice and attention to descriptive phrases that add depth to the text. Take a moment to compare the sentences below to illustrate the contrast between spoken language and its more formal written language counterpart. It is not surprising to see why children who have had only limited (or no) exposure to written language could have great difficulty understanding it. Notice the differences between what might be spoken and what is actually written in the following excerpt from *The Scarecrow's Hat* by Ken Brown.

> **Spoken:** He's happy because he traded his hat for a stick.

> **Written:** With a grateful sigh of relief, he leaned his tired old arms on the stick and gladly swapped it for his battered old hat.

Background Knowledge on Different Genres of Writing

Through numerous read-aloud experiences, preschoolers begin to make generalizations about different types, or genre, of texts. They hear how stories often have a clear beginning, middle, and end and usually contain a problem and resolution. They notice that colorful words and play-ful language enhance the story or help to embody the theme. Preschool-ers begin to recognize that most fairy tales start out and end in a very specific way, unique to this type of story. "Once upon a time" and "they lived happily ever after" become part of our children's own language as they pretend to read by themselves.

As parents read aloud poetry with expression, we provide back-ground knowledge of yet another type of text language. We help them recognize the flow and musicality of this special genre. Children begin to experience the rhythm, mood, and feeling of the writer. The brevity and careful selection of precise and beautiful words set poetry apart from other genres. Preschoolers begin to understand that this minimal-ist approach to writing can still tell a humorous or profound story. Our children discover that similes, metaphors, and imagery are key elements of poetry. Like adults, preschoolers can be moved by the power of po-etry. They begin to understand that careful attention to every word, every phrase, and every pause leads the listener to a feeling of silliness, sadness, or contentedness.

Through their experience with hearing nonfiction read aloud, chil-dren begin to notice the nuances of how authors approach text. When we are interested in finding out facts, getting questions answered, or having something explained, we turn to nonfiction. The sentences are often brief and the style is clear and direct. Through quality read-alouds, children begin to hear the differences associated with nonfic-tion text.

The Power of Prior Knowledge

So why is background knowledge so important? The prior knowledge children gain through the read-aloud experience actually aids them in becoming independent readers themselves. Consider the sentences below:

- Mommy *wound* a Band-aid around the *wound* on Madeline's finger.
- Unfortunately, Noah had to *desert* his ice cream *dessert* after it melted in the hot *desert* sun.

- Emma asked her dad to *wind* the string tightly around his hand so the *wind* wouldn't blow the kite into the tree.

It was not your ability to decode these words using phonics that helped you read each sentence. On the contrary, it was your background knowledge of the words that allowed you to read and correctly pronounce each homograph (words that look the same but have different meanings and are sometimes pronounced differently). You had to have prior experience with these words, having previously heard them used in different contexts. Reading aloud to our children helps provide them with this essential prior experience. They hear the words first. Then, when they come across these same words in future independent reading, they are able to identify them more easily and read them on their own.

The more vocabulary they have heard and know and the more information they have about a particular subject, the better they will be able to read and understand a passage or book about the same topic. When children hear stories read aloud, they retrieve the mental file folder, or schema, that contains information on the particular topic and use it to understand the new information presented. If they already have a folder on dinosaurs, they can access it to help them understand the new information being presented in the next book. It is easier to understand that some dinosaurs were herbivores and some were omnivores if you have previously been exposed to the fact that tyrannosaurus rex was a carnivore who ate other dinosaurs. Consider, also, how much easier it would be to understand new information about golf if you have already heard the words *birdie, bogie, fore, drive, wedge,* and *eagle* in context. We use the information we already know from books to help us read and understand new information in texts.

When preschoolers see how print works and have been shown how to navigate through a particular type of text (prose, nonfiction, poetry), they are better prepared to do so themselves. As we share the cadence and beat of each type of text, our children begin to hear and expect a certain flow of language when they approach texts on their own. Their background knowledge of the subject matter, how print works, and how book language flows become key factors when they tackle text independently in the future. It becomes a circular process. The prior knowledge that children gain through hearing texts read aloud assists them in acquiring more knowledge from future texts. Background knowledge helps us become better readers and this enables us to read more, thus increasing our background knowledge so that we continue to learn and grow.

CHAPTER 3

Connect to the Concepts About Print

There is no substitute for books in the life of a child.
—MARY ELLEN CHASE

In *Tops and Bottoms,* by Janet Stevens, Hare is poor and desperate after selling his land to pay off a debt to Tortoise. He and his family partner up with Bear down the street in this hilarious story. In a clever deal about "tops and bottoms" of vegetables, Hare outsmarts the lazy Bear and comes out on top in the end. This trickster tale has roots in European folktales and slave stories and proves that an energetic and hardworking Hare is smarter and more profitable than a rich, lazy Bear. Both the story and the comically drawn illustrations make this book a wonderful read-aloud for all preschoolers. Additionally, I use the book to reinforce the concepts about how print works in the English language.

"Concepts About Print" (CAP) refers to the understanding of how print works. It is the knowledge that reading and writing are performed for various reasons and have many different purposes. We read signs, menus, invitations, recipes, dictionaries, and stories. In order to perform these tasks, children must first understand how the English language works in printed form in order to be able to decode and comprehend the text. Children need to be able to identify the front cover of a book and know how to turn the pages in consecutive order. They need to understand that print is read from left to right and from the top to the bottom of the page. In order to be successful in independent reading and writing, they must understand terms such as *letter, word, sentence, paragraph,* and *question mark.* Reading books aloud to our children can introduce them to all the unique ways that text works.

Tops and Bottoms has a unique format that deviates from most books in the English language. To correspond with the title, the book's format is vertical instead of horizontal. It opens to the "top," with each subsequent page repeating this pattern. When I read this book aloud, I point out how silly the author was to create a book like this. I emphasize how it contrasts with other books, thus helping children remember the way books work. It is helpful for parents to use informal settings like the read-aloud experience to introduce and teach preschoolers about CAP.

While we may take for granted the concepts about how print works, these are learned skills. Contrast this knowledge of concepts in English with the Chinese, Korean, or Arabic language, which is read in the opposite direction, from right to left. Children do not instinctually know that print carries meaning and that there is a connection between our oral speech and what is written on the page. Through frequent read-aloud experiences, our children gain the knowledge of how print works in a natural and non-threatening setting. They see us open the front cover of a book and turn the pages. It is through interactions like these that children begin to recognize the difference between a book that is held correctly and one that is upside down. Preschoolers eventually begin to understand the nuances of written text. As they become ready, children learn that print is spoken words written down, letters in words are written in a certain order, and written words are separated by spaces. They notice that different types of punctuation direct the reader to read in various tones and expressions.

Children who are emerging into reading, have been read to often, and have had opportunities to explore a variety of print, enter school with a basic understanding of the concepts about print. Those who have had limited experiences with the written word may struggle with this. It is important that parents assist their children in developing an understanding of the following concepts:

- The purpose of print—that it carries meaning
- The parts of a book—front cover, back cover, title page, illustrations, etc.
- Directionality—readers and writers move from left to right and top to bottom
- Spacing—the concept of an individual word and word boundaries
- Recognition of words and letters—distinguish between upper and lower case letters
- The relationship between print and spoken language; there is a one-to-one correspondence between spoken words and individual words in the text
- Book handling—how to hold a book correctly (upright) and turn the pages one at a time
- The idea that most stories have a beginning, middle and end
- The idea that sentences are comprised of words and words are comprised of letters
- The function of punctuation—it affects meaning and expression in reading
- The role that illustrations play in reading—they support the message of the text and can be used to help predict its meaning

Putting CAP into Practice

While reading aloud, periodically draw your child's attention to the fact that what you are saying is connected to the print on the page. Focus on the cover of the book and point to it, as well as paying respect to the author and illustrator by reading their names. Literacy expert Marie Clay suggests that parents of preschoolers occasionally point to the print in the book and run a finger beneath the text while reading to assist in connecting the spoken word with the letters on the page. This is known as "tracking the print," and it helps children focus on each word. However, this process can sometimes slow down the ability to read aloud in a natural and authentic way. Therefore, it is recommended that you balance tracking with fluent reading of the stories that does not impede the flow of the words. Use your judgment as to the amount of time you spend on tracking and focusing on other skills to be sure that the fluency of reading does not become artificial and controlled. Making reading a pleasurable experience should continue to be the primary goal of parents.

The Value of Understanding CAP

Knowledge about how print works is dependent on the type of text that we are reading. When reading nonfiction, we do not always read each page consecutively and do not always follow the left-to-right, top-to-bottom routine. Think about how you read the newspaper. You may scan the titles and then select the article that interests you the most. Consider phone books, directions, maps, and encyclopedias. Sometimes readers skip around to focus on an illustration, table, or graph that helps make the information more comprehensible. When I was reading aloud to Heather an issue of the children's magazine *Your Big Backyard*, it directed us to page twelve to learn more about the northern pintail duck. We counted the pages and turned to the appropriate one, viewed and discussed the illustrations on that page, and then flipped back to page three to continue with the next story. Without "teaching" the concept, I was demonstrating to Heather how a reader uses texts in different ways. Unlike a story, we did not read the pages in consecutive order, from front to back. We skipped around, gaining more information as we went. I then read the table of contents and asked her which article she would like me to read next. Again, this showed the options provided with a different type of text.

Reading aloud a variety of genres helps our children see how our process varies based on our purpose in reading. We demonstrate how the table of contents, an index, or a map can aid our reading. Thus, we are teaching our children how to look all around the text to gain insight and assistance into the meaning. Regardless of the type of text we read aloud, we continue to reinforce the connection between spoken word and text. Our children begin to understand that the words we say are written down, that each of these words is comprised of letters, and they begin to recognize common words as well as individual letters. They grasp how print works and they begin their journey to future reading and writing proficiency.

CAP: An Example at Home

Consider the interaction recorded below between Lucy and her four-year-old son, Adam, as she reinforces the concepts about print during a read-aloud.

> Adam is listening to his mom read *If You Give a Pig a Pancake*. She has read it to him numerous times before and he always enjoys the silliness of the story as a piglet first asks for a pancake and then wants syrup to go with it. The piglet makes increasingly elaborate demands until the story comes full circle back to wanting a pancake. Lucy has told me that both she and her son laugh and enjoy the illustrations each time it is read. Lucy has been sure to expose Adam to the entirety of the story so that he can see its progress from beginning to end. Adam can appreciate the humor and ridiculousness throughout each cause and effect from pancakes to stickiness to baths to bubbles to rubber ducks. She is confident that he has a sense of wholeness for the story, so she has now decided to focus on reinforcing some of the concepts about print during this reading aloud experience.
>
> Lucy reads the title page and states, "Written by Laura Numeroff. That's the author, the person who wrote the words in the story. It's been illustrated by Felicia Bond. What does that mean? What is an illustrator?"
>
> "Drew the pictures," Adam responds.
>
> "That's right. Felicia Bond did the artwork. She drew the pictures. Let's open to the first page and begin reading it. I can't wait to visit this funny piglet again. Will you help by turning the pages for me?"
>
> Lucy reads the first, second, and third pages from the book, sweeping her finger under the words as she does so. She points out the placement of the words on the pages. "Notice how the writer puts the first line on the top of the page. The second line is on the bottom of the second page and the third line is back up top on the third

page. Remember how we've noticed before that our books are written top to bottom and left to right?" She briefly turns the pages back and points out the top-to-bottom, left-to-right word progression.

Adam nods. She continues to read and they both laugh throughout different parts of the story. [Notice that she returns to reading at a normal pace and brings the focus back to the enjoyment of the story rather than only drawing attention to skill development.] After several more pages are read without interruption or her tracking the print, Lucy pauses once again.

"Hey, let's play *I Spy* on this page. I spy the letter *a*. I don't see an *a* that starts like the beginning of your name, *Adam*. But I spy a lowercase *a*, a small *a*. Do you see it?"

Adam leans forward a little and looks. After a moment, Lucy assists him by pointing to an *a* and asking, "Is that a lower case *a*?" Adam smiles and says yes.

"Wait. I see more *a*'s. Can you help me find them? I spy another *a*. Where could it be?"

Adam looks at the text again and finds the correct letter in the middle of a word, points to it and says, "There!"

"Yes! Wow! You're good at this. Hey, look there's another one. (She points to another *a* on the page.) Do you see any more? No? Well, I don't either. Let's read some more and maybe we could play a different *I Spy* game to look for something else."

Lucy once again resumes the read-aloud for a few additional pages and then stops. "O.K. Your turn. You tell me what to find."

Adam gleefully obliges and tells mom, "I spy a letter that starts with your name. Do you see it?"

"Oh. You mean an *L*. My name, Lucy, begins with a capital *L*. I don't see a capital *L* on this page, but I do see a lower case or small *l*. It's right there. Hey, and there's another one. See it? That was a good game. Thanks for helping me focus on *l*'s Now it's my turn again. I spy . . . let's see. Here's a tricky one. I spy a space. I spy a space between words."

It seems obvious that Adam has played this game before. He points to a space between words. He then points to several others. Lucy reinforces and tells him, "Oh, I can't trick you."

They continue the *I Spy* game, asking each other to find a word, a sentence, and selective lower and upper case letters.

Lucy stops just before reading the last three pages of the book. She points out how the author has once again emphasized the top-to-bottom pattern of reading in the English language. She turns the pages to the end and shows Adam how the print is placed on only the top of the first page, bottom of the second page, and back to the top on the last page. Then she goes back and reads them.

"The end. The book ended with a certain punctuation mark. Do you remember what we call that?"

Adam does not appear to recall the correct term.

"It's a period," Lucy reinforces. "That ends the sentence. We call that a punctuation mark and its name is a period. Remember how I told you that punctuation marks give us, the readers, signals for how to read the book? The period tells us to stop or pause ... or take a breath. Then we can read the next sentence. It helps the reader with the pacing of how they read. Thank goodness. Could you imagine if the author didn't do this? I'd be reading and reading and couldn't pause or stop, and I'd be all out of breath." Lucy exaggerates as she reopens the book and reads a few pages without pausing. "Whew! I can't do it. I need some periods. Thank you, author, for giving me periods."

Adam laughs. Lucy selects yet another book from the basket and tells her son that they are not going to stop during this one to play *I Spy*. Instead, they are just going to read it and see what happens. She reads the title, author, and illustrator and wonders aloud what the story will be about.

Formalized Instruction and Concepts About Print

Teachers understand the importance of children acquiring concepts about print as a reading readiness skill. Many teachers of the earliest grades (kindergarten through second) will emphasize CAP during read-alouds in the classroom. They will read the title, author, and illustrator for each book. The teacher will often run her finger beneath the text as she reads, helping to highlight the connection between spoken and written words. Discussions may surface about spaces between words, punctuation marks to assist with reading, and various letters within the text. Typically when children enter school for the first time, they are assessed on the concepts about print. The teacher may purposely hand a book to the child upside down and turned backwards. They are looking to see if the child has been exposed to reading. Those children who have had the read-aloud experience will know to turn the book around the right way. The assessment will continue as the teacher asks the student to tell her where she should begin reading. Those children who have been read to before entering school will know to point to the words on the first page. Those who have not had these experiences may point instead to one of the illustrations, not understanding the idea of words. The teacher may also ask the child to point to a word, a letter, and a punctuation mark. Parents who have read aloud to their preschoolers on a consistent basis can be confident that they are helping their child to naturally develop concepts about print.

CHAPTER 4

Foster Phonemic Awareness

"I think," said a little boy, "you're all very silly.
Shmancakes . . . sound like
Fancakes . . . sound like . . .
Pancakes to me."

In *The Hungry Thing*, by Jan Slepian and Ann Seidler, a large, demanding creature comes to town wearing a sign that reads, "Feed Me." A little boy seems to be the only one who can understand what he wants to eat. The Hungry Thing requests a variety of foods, including shmancakes, feetloaf, and hookies, which turn out to be pancakes, meatloaf, and cookies. This book engages our children's natural urge to play with the English language. Preschoolers like to change the beginnings of words and laugh at how they sound. They try to stump us with their creativity and also like us to join in with their antics. "Mommy, I want some snicken. Some sticken. Some flicken . . . I mean chicken." At the preschool stage of development, children have begun to acquire some mastery of language and delight in their ability to get it right, and then purposely manipulate words to make them "wrong." This ability should be encouraged and fostered by parents as it has been shown to be a helpful skill to future reading success.

Children need to know that words carry meaning. However, separate from this skill, they must also understand that words are made up of a series of distinct sounds. The ability to hear the individual sounds found in words is called phonemic awareness. When a child is able to discern the three sounds in the word *cup*, /c/, /ŭ/, /p/, for example, they are beginning to develop an awareness of how words are created from separate sounds. Other skills associated with phonemic awareness include the ability to rhyme, as well as notice similar sounds in the beginning, middle, or end of words. Reading aloud can support the development of phonemic awareness for our children, which is a powerful predictor of later spelling, reading, and writing success.

In order to assist our children in developing this key skill, we can read aloud books that specifically focus on playing with words and language. Parents can delve into books that emphasize speech sounds through the following elements.

- **Rhyme**: a word that corresponds with another in the ending sound (*night, spite, fright, kite*)
- **Alliteration**: repetitive beginning sound (the *l* sound in the sentence *Lily Lizard likes licking lots of luscious lollipops.*)
- **Consonance**: the repetition of similar consonant sounds, usually at the end of words or accented syllables within a word (the *k* sound at the end of *bark, lick, ache, snack* or the *d* sound in the middle of *puddle, ladle, pudding, rudder*)
- **Assonance**: resemblance of sound in the middle of words, usually corresponding to the vowel (the long *a* sound in *pain, break, flame, stay*)

Texts with these elements provide children opportunities to listen carefully to language and play with the various parts that make up words, phrases, and sentences. Phonemically aware children enjoy the rhythms of poems, silly songs, and books that focus on the nuances of sounds. Mem Fox, the children's author and internationally respected literacy expert, once wrote about the power of rhyme and the lyrical language found in many books. "They are a natural extension to the heartbeat of the mother and the rhythmic rocking of a child in loving arms or in a cradle."[1]

Consider how an author's use of playful language supports the development of phonemic awareness. For example, in *I Love the Alphabet*, author Dar Hosta uses alliteration and rhyming to teach letters and sounds within an animal alphabet adventure. These bouncy rhymes help keep a child focused, but they also serve the purpose of teaching and reinforcing the key preliteracy skill, phonemic awareness.

> Giggly goats ride sailboats
> out on a moonlit sea.
> Hippo's feeling happy
> underneath the apple tree.
> Two mischievous monkeys
> mambo on the moon.
> Nine hungry newts
> are looking for a spoon.

In addition to rhyming lines, Nancy Shaw's *Sheep in a Jeep* emphasizes assonance, using the repetitive medial sound /ē/. A minimal text tells the story of a group of sheep who head out on an adventure, only to have one silly mishap after another occur. Shaw cleverly highlights the long *e* sound, incorporating words in the book that include *sheep, jeep, steep, leap, heap*, and *weep*. Also note that the sound is spelled in more than one way, *ee, ea*, helping children transition into associating the sounds with letters, which is phonics. Children's poems, too, such as this one from Mother Goose, often house rhyming schemes, a key skill for the development of phonemic awareness.

> Once I saw a little bird
> Come hop, hop, hop;
> So I cried, "Little bird,
> Will you stop, stop, stop?"
> I was going to the window
> To say, "How do you do?"
> But he shook his little tail,
> And far away he flew.

These texts foster phonemic awareness through their use of rhyme, alliteration, assonance, consonance, and language play. Children are drawn to the lyrical sounds and therefore focus on the patterns heard at the beginning, middle, and end of words. By carefully selecting books that focus on word play, parents help lay the groundwork for their preschooler's development of phonemic awareness. Numerous children's books offer an authentic context for building this skill.

Look for opportunities to build your child's phonemic awareness at key and natural points in the read-aloud experience. While in the midst of reading aloud Robert McCloskey's *Make Way for Ducklings*, I stopped to point out and focus on the hilarious names of the baby ducks. I had read the book numerous times before to Heather, and we had enjoyed the darling story of Mr. and Mrs. Mallard looking for the perfect spot in Boston to raise their family. On this reading, I emphasized the ducklings' names, *Jack, Kack, Lack, Mack, Nack, Ouack, Pack*, and *Quack* by repeating them. Heather and I giggled. We decided that we especially liked the name *Ouack*. Then I pointed out how all the names ended the same, making them rhyme. I asked Heather if she could think of other words that ended in the *-ack* sound. We came up with *snack, smack, black*, and *attack*. Although I never want to take away from the beauty of the story, I chose to take a brief moment during this reading to highlight the skill of rhyming, knowing that I was helping Heather develop phonemic awareness. While we need to be cognizant of maintaining the essence and rhythm of the text, parents can look for ways to teach and reinforce phonemic awareness. We can point out how many of the words in a certain book begin the same way or end with the same sound. We can extend this learning as well by asking our child to think of additional examples that focus on the same phonemic element presented in the book. "Let's think of other words that begin with the *s* sound." "What other words end with the sound, *-at*?" Then we can praise our child and continue the story, enjoying it for all the author has to offer.

Another way to foster phonemic awareness is while reading aloud poems and books that rhyme. My friend Laura strategically paused when reading aloud the nursery rhyme *Twinkle, Twinkle Little Star*.

Twinkle, twinkle little star,
How I wonder what you are!
Up above the world so high,
Like a diamond in the _____.

She wanted to see if her daughter could fill in the missing word, *sky*. This is a perfect example of how a parent can incorporate the skill of phonemic awareness within the reading of a text. Of course, if the child does not know the "answer" and cannot think of the correct rhyme at that moment, we do not insist she keep trying or wait a ridiculous period of time. We simply provide the answer, *sky*. Then we read on. We want our child to hear the sounds of language and develop the key skill of being phonemically aware. However, we always want to do this in a comfortable and supportive way. Undoubtedly a child will pick up on the idea of attending to sounds the more she is exposed to texts that emphasize this type of language. When a child is ready, it will click and she will become phonemically aware. Give her time. Read aloud a great deal. Celebrate the power of beautiful and luscious language.

Laura paused during the reading of *Twinkle, Twinkle Little Star* because she realized that the ability to rhyme is a strong indication of future spelling, reading, and writing success. The process of rhyming words may seem quite simple to parents. However, it actually requires complex thinking strategies. In order to rhyme, a child must be able to hear the similar ending sounds in words. She must be able to separate the initial sound, or consonant(s), and replace it with another one. Consider the word *rat*. In order to think of words that rhyme, a child must first remove the /r/, recognize the leftover /at/ and then add a new sound to this ending. She can then create *cat, mat, splat, flat*. Whether or not your child can label or identify the term *rhyme* is not important. The fact that he or she is able to say words that end the same—*snug, bug, hug, plug*—is the skill that is valuable for future success in literacy and in school.

The Importance of Phonemic Awareness

Many preschoolers do not recognize that spoken language is made up of individual words, which are made up of syllables, which, in turn, are made up of the smallest units of sound. These smallest units of sound are called *phonemes*. Think of the word *phone*, which we use to *hear* someone, to help you remember *phoneme*, the individual sounds that we can *hear* in a word. A child's ability to hear sounds in language and do different things with these sounds, like break them apart from words and blend them back together, is phonemic awareness. Reading aloud books that highlight alliteration or rhymes helps our children begin to focus on the separate sounds in words. Parents can support their child's phonemic development by noting, "The author starts almost every word with the same sound." We can engage our child to see if they noticed the creative use of language by the author and then we see if they can offer additional examples of a particular beginning sound or rhyming pattern.

Since English is an alphabetic language, one that associates a letter or letters with each sound in a word, it is imperative for children to recognize each individual sound. (This is not true for all languages.) This recognition lays the foundation for "sounding out" words in future reading as well as figuring out how to spell words in their writing. Once children can distinguish one sound from another within words, they can begin to associate speech sounds with a letter or letters that represent that sound. If one cannot hear the three sounds in *hot* (/h/, /ŏ/, /t/), for example, then it will be nearly impossible to decode this word in reading or spell it in writing. Perhaps a preschooler was only able to identify the beginning and ending sounds (a very common issue for young children). He would logically also have difficulty later identifying the word in print or correctly using three letters to spell it.

The ability to hear and manipulate sounds within words is a skill that has been shown to be a powerful predictor of later reading success. Preschoolers who are aware that phonemes form words will have an easier time learning to read. Over the past two decades, phonemic awareness has received increased attention because long-term studies have shown its connection to reading success.[2] Research indicates that it is the best predictor of the ease of early reading acquisition, better even than IQ, vocabulary, and listening comprehension.[3]

Most parents are familiar with the term *phonics*, which may sound similar to phonemic awareness. It is important to make clear that phonemic awareness and phonics are *not* the same thing. Phonics involves *written* letters and letter combinations. It is the association of a letter or letters with each sound. Phonemic awareness, however, does not attach a visual letter symbol. Rather, it works only with the *sound* created by an individual letter or group of letters. Phonemic awareness is a foundational skill to phonics, and it is a skill that children should acquire for the process of learning to read. If a child cannot hear and distinguish sounds, she cannot relate these sounds to the respective letter(s).

Table 1: Compares phonemic awareness and phonics.

Phonemic Awareness	Phonics
The ability to **hear** sounds in words.	The ability to see or recognize the **letters** in words.
Knowing that *ribbon*, *rake*, and *run* begin with the same **sound**.	Knowing that *ribbon*, *rake*, and *run* begin with the same **letter**.
Hearing the words *dark*, *pat*, *dish*, and *doll* and knowing that *pat* doesn't belong because it begins with a different sound.	**Seeing** the words *dark*, *pat*, *dish*, and *doll* and knowing that *pat* doesn't belong because the first letter looks different.
Knowing that *eye*, *pie*, and *sky* have the same ending **sound** and therefore rhyme.	Knowing that different **letters** are used for the endings of *eye*, *pie*, and *sky*.
Knowing that *cape* has three **sounds**, /k/, /ā/, /p/.	Knowing that *cape* has four letters.

Author Jane Bayer reinforces phonemic awareness and seamlessly bridges it to phonics in her book *A, My Name Is Alice*. A funny verse is provided for each letter of the alphabet. Phonemic awareness is still heavily supported through rhyme and alliteration, but Bayer also directly connects the letters to the corresponding sounds.

D my name is Doris and my husband's name is Dave.
We come from Denmark and we sell dust.
Doris is a DUCK.
Dave is a DACHSHUND.

Learning Phonemic Awareness Through Play

Learning phonemic awareness does not require that parents quiz their children on the number of sounds they hear in spoken words or ask them to rhyme words in a rote manner. Parents need not spend time each day drilling their child on beginning and ending sounds and breaking apart words into phonemes. These interactions can be boring and quite frustrating for both of you, feelings that we do not want children to associate with reading. On the contrary, one of the best ways to foster phonemic awareness is reading aloud literature that focuses on language play. The vast majority of children who enter the school system with phonemic awareness have been read to by their parents. Young children who are exposed to an environment rich with language play from books, songs, poems, and nursery rhymes usually develop phonemic awareness with relative ease.[4] Reading aloud provides natural opportunities for you and your child to experiment and have fun with language. Through careful selection of books, children hear words that seem to bounce, roll, and glide off the tongue. They enjoy the process of language exploration as they hear and attend to individual phonemes without the need for a formal "instructional" session.

Because acquiring phonemic awareness is an auditory skill, parents are laying the foundation for success by reading aloud to their child, especially those books that purposely play with language. Reading aloud can draw a child's attention to the sounds within words. Parents can support their child's development of phonemic awareness within the natural context of a book.

As discussed earlier in this section, parents can foster phonemic awareness by engaging their child in manipulating the sounds in words. Encourage your child to make up silly rhyming "words," real or even made up, such as *pickle, tickle, nickel, shmickle*, and *fickle*. Using the author's words as models, the child can begin to explore his own rhymes or additional words that begin or end with a certain sound. It is not necessary for a child to recognize that these fun games are also purposeful activities that help with literacy development. It is more important to know that he is enjoying the process of learning, growing, and eventually moving into reading success. A list of books that build phonemic awareness is included in the booklist that begins on page 273.

While phonemic awareness is a strong predictor of future success in reading, spelling, and writing, please be mindful that books that reinforce this concept should not be read aloud at the exclusion of other quality literature. It is important for us to recognize that our children need to hear different types of stories and text. Books with rhyme, alliteration, and other language play should be read as one part of an overall comprehensive literacy experience for our children that includes fiction, nonfiction, and texts that serve a variety of purposes. Part B of this book discusses the various types of texts that parents should include in their read-aloud repertoire.

CHAPTER 5

Venture into Vocabulary Development

Once upon a time it was night. It was a perfectly perfect time for becoming still and quiet, for making up a good dream, and for floating off to sleep.

But, as the sky began to dim, there was a stirring and a scurrying, a wiggling and a waking; and a whisper on the wind called out, "*I love the night . . .*"

And the nocturnal adventure began.

In her "perfectly perfect" tribute, *I Love the Night,* Dar Hosta lulls your child to sleep with lyrical words and gorgeous illustrations. As each of the nocturnal animals wakes from a lazy day, they celebrate the wonders, sounds, and beauty of the darkness. Crickets chirp, fireflies twinkle, and the octopus unrolls himself and wanders through the waters, "hoping to scare up a delicious dinner." Through the use of exceptional adjectives and adverbs and the inclusion of alliteration and rhythm, *I Love the Night* beautifully captures the world that awakens after the sun has set and the moon comes out. Meticulously selecting words like *graceful, dainty, snugly, shimmering, relishing,* and *glorious,* the author establishes a gentle, quiet mood that whispers all to sleep.

I Love the Night and other quality books distinguish themselves with their melodious text, crafted from carefully selected words that the author has woven together with precision. Picture books that include exceptional language serve as models for our child's vocabulary development. They build background knowledge for future reading endeavors and become springboards for the child's own speaking and writing. As parents select books to read aloud to their children, it is important to look for those with wonderful words.

In addition to providing children valuable information or housing stories with silly or moving plots, books can provide access to new vocabulary and exemplary language structure. Hearing words like *rousing, coursing, mottled, wily,* and *relishing,* all part of the gorgeous language found in *I Love the Night,* within the context of a story, provides our children a head start on building an extensive and varied oral vocabulary. It also establishes background knowledge for future independent reading and writing success.

As parents of young children, one of our goals is to expand and enrich their life experiences through books. We want to promote oral and listening vocabulary and lay the foundation for comprehension of text. In the book *Improving Literacy in America,* the authors clearly state that vocabulary development predicts later reading and academic achievement.[1] Parents can support their children's vocabulary expansion each time we read aloud the best, brightest, most colorful and creative language we can find. Children's books are excellent sources of sophisticated words.[2] As our children hear and attend to the beautiful words authors have selected, they too begin to hold a high standard of word choice for themselves. Therefore, parents need to select special books that provide appealing stories with exquisite language to read to their children.

During a conversation with my friend, I asked if she had noticed her son, William, using new vocabulary they had found in books she read aloud. She was quick to tell me that she had not seen any words that were particularly noteworthy. "After all," my friend Joyce boldly stated, "They're picture books. There really aren't any great sentences or words in them." Since she and her husband were both English majors in college and were avid readers themselves, I knew that she valued the read-aloud experience. She had previously shared with me that she read to William in the morning and after nap, as well as numerous other spontaneous times throughout the day. Given her family's background with reading, I was puzzled as to why she did not recognize the exceptional vocabulary contained in many picture books for children.

While it is obviously true that many books for children cannot compete with novels and classic literature for adults, I wanted Joyce and other parents to appreciate the relatively complex language structures available to our preschool children. Although some children's authors create wonderful stories that delight us with each reading but do not necessarily include vocabulary that is outstanding, careful attention by the reader can uncover how many others choose rare words. As parents become word detectives, they will begin to see opportunities to highlight unique and unknown words for their children even in some of the simplest texts. In *The Very Lazy Ladybug*, for example, author Isobel Finn uses a minimum number of words. In this humorous story, a ladybug sleeps all day and refuses to learn to fly. She decides to take a ride on several other animals to get to a new location, only to find that each mode of transportation does not allow her to sleep soundly on the way. Because of the story's brevity, parents may initially dismiss its potential as a vocabulary builder. However, upon closer inspection, one finds that the story contains words that invite parent and child to learn, discuss, and act out. The animals *bounded, padded, ambled, plodded* by. In addition to enjoying this humorous tale with a clever ending, parents can take note of the uncommon words that appear in the book. We can use the read-aloud experience as an avenue for word exploration and vocabulary building.

As I reflected on the word opportunities children's books afford, I wondered if my friend Joyce just had not taken note of the magnificent language or simply was not selecting the books that were models of rare words and sentence structure. Perhaps she was focusing on a different aspect of reading, such as the overall appeal of the story, the connections to William's life, or the pleasure of the read-aloud experience itself. All of these were obviously extremely valuable and key elements of future reading success. Perhaps exceptional words had been overlooked.

Regardless of the reason why vocabulary was not noticed by Joyce,

I recognized at that moment the need to highlight this aspect of children's books for parents. I want everyone to see the value found in the words of these books. Through careful selection of children's texts, parents can support their preschooler's vocabulary development and future writing. I felt compelled to include a chapter in this book that addressed how authors often provide exposure to unique words, phrases, and sentences that are meticulously strung together in rhythmic and poignant ways.

Reading aloud introduces children to the language of books, which differs from language heard in daily conversation, on television, and in movies. A common myth is that authors of picture books use limited vocabulary, as well as simple grammar structure, so that young children are able to understand it. Many parents believe that complex sentences and challenging words will confuse preschoolers, leading to boredom with the book and an inability to comprehend what is taking place. On the contrary, numerous picture books contain exceptional sentences, words, and phrases, and serve as models of exemplary speech. Authors of children's books are able to expand vocabulary and language style while ensuring understanding through the use of other tools such as illustrations and content appropriate to the age and background experiences of preschoolers. Consider Patricia Polacco's use of words and complex sentence structure in just a few lines in her book *Thunder Cake*. The grandmother in this story helps her granddaughter deal with the fear of thunder by working together to gather all the ingredients and bake a special treat.

> Her eyes surveyed the black clouds a way off in the distance. Then she strode into the kitchen. Her worn hands pulled a thick book from the shelf above the woodstove.
> "Let's find that recipe, child," she crowed as she lovingly fingered the grease-stained pages to a creased spot.

Because the best books for children offer a variety of clues to support meaning, authors can introduce exceptional words and sophisticated language structures to bridge children into more complex text. In this way, children hear and eventually begin to use new vocabulary and complex grammar structure.

Wonderful Words to Use in Writing

One of the tasks for nearly all writing instructors is to help their students use more descriptive words within dialogue. The goal is to abandon the overused and tired word *said*, replacing it with a more precise word that captures the essence of the characters and the situation taking place. Many teachers will ask students to generate a list of alternatives for *said*, and some will even go so far as to forbid children from using it in their writing just to make a point. I have found that children often have a difficult time thinking of other words to clearly describe the interactions of characters in a story. Therefore, I have turned to picture books as treasure troves for ideas of extraordinary and interesting words. When I am teaching students how to improve their writing, I pass out picture books to young children, high school students, and even adults in graduate courses. They are asked to read a story (or listen to one if more appropriate) and then work as a class to brainstorm a list of alternatives for *said* found in the books they've read.

To illuminate how worthy a resource picture books are for exceptional words, I have compiled a list of different words used in dialogue from just one picture book, *Stellaluna*, by Janell Cannon. The results are showcased in Table 2. During an owl attack, a young fruit bat named Stellaluna is knocked out of her mother's loving grasp and falls into a bird's nest. The bird family adopts her but she must adapt to their unique ways, including eating awful tasting bugs, flying in the daytime, and sleeping right side up. Stellaluna is finally reunited with her mother and resumes her natural bat habits, but she still appreciates the different ways of her new friends. The darling premise of the story will delight preschoolers, but the excellent use of language is noteworthy as well. The author includes twenty-two alternatives to *said*. This example from *Stellaluna* clearly demonstrates the vast opportunities for vocabulary development available in children's texts.

Table 2: Alternative Words for SAID found in *Stellaluna*

crooned	whispered
squeaked	cheered
cried	agreed
chirped	explained
hissed	yelled
warned	howled
sighed	shrieked
stuttered	gasped
gasped	replied
murmured	mused
asked	wondered

Contrasting Speech with Picture Books

Imagine for a moment how potentially limited our child's vocabulary would be if their only exposure to words was through conversations with family and friends. Hayes and Ahrens, in their article entitled "Vocabulary Simplification for Children: A Special Case of 'Motherese,'" contrast book language with the interactions of parents and children during everyday conversations. They found that adults tended to simplify their grammar and use common, instead of exceptional, words in their speech with children. Additionally, they noted that adult family members and friends tended to interact with children in ways that were "lexically undemanding." Adults focused on mundane topics and utilized informal speech.[3]

I recognize that many conscientious parents pride themselves on the special focus they give to their verbal interactions with their children. Through attention to personal word choice and reinforcement of selected words by our children, parents can increase their children's depth and breadth of new words. Parents can, indeed, strongly influence the expansion of children's vocabulary. However, conversations between parent and child still differ from those found in texts. Even though careful forethought and calculation while speaking with our children may take place, parents have a different purpose in their exchanges with family. Day to day interactions warrant a different type of speech than is typically found in quality read-alouds. We use contractions and abbreviations and typically leave out implied nouns when talking to someone we know. For example, book language may state something in this way: "*Is your shoelace too tight? I will loosen it for you.*" Someone speaking may state this same thought like this: "*Too tight? I'll loosen it.*"

Authors are often more precise, specifically naming nouns and speaking in complete thoughts and sentences. Consider the contrast between the words that may be said in a conversation between parent and child and the language found in books. Parents may put a child to bed and say, "Night night, sweetheart. Sweet dreams. I'll see you in the morning." Angela Medearis, author of *Snug in Mama's Arms*, says goodnight in this rhythmic and beautiful way:

> In igloos and on sampans,
> in hogans and on farms,
> children all around the world
> are snug in mamas' arms.
> Someone's sleeping soundly
> with dreaming eyes closed tight,
> safe and snug in mama's arms.
> Sleep well, my love. Good night.

It is not often that parents carefully use metaphors, similes, personification, and rhythm while talking with their children. Because authors specifically select their words based on the purpose of their story or the mood they are trying to elicit, book language is often more descriptive and uses more formal grammatical structures. The books we read aloud are often the best sources of new vocabulary for our children. Therefore, they serve as models for our children's speech, their vocabulary, and their future reading and writing endeavors.

Jane Yolen, in her book *Owl Moon*, makes use of numerous comparisons like the simile below to establish a beautiful melodic tone.

> Somewhere behind us a train whistle blew,
> long and low,
> like a sad, sad song.

Owl Moon is a quiet and sentimental tale about a daughter who accompanies her father for the first time on a late night owl search. The author uses descriptive, poetic language to evoke a calm feeling. Beautiful similes like the one above are combined with metaphors, personification, and other literary tools to transform an ordinary activity into a magical adventure. Similes, the art of explicitly comparing two dissimilar things using the word *like* or *as*, build a unique visual experience for all readers and listeners. Understanding and emulating great writing like this are the tools we want to instill in our children as they emerge into their own reading and writing.

Where in the World Do We Learn Words

I once heard a teacher speak to a group of peers about how she helped her fourth-grade students expand and use quality vocabulary in their writing. She discussed ways to allow children to participate in experiences that accessed the five senses in order to help them think of descriptive words. The teacher relayed an activity she had done in her classroom where raw ginger was tasted by each of the students. The fourth graders had exceptionally strong first impressions of the ginger, and they used these reactions to create a class list of words to describe the experience. During the presentation, the teacher showed the audience the generated list of words, which included *bitter, delicious, tart, pungent, aromatic*, and *despicable*.

Reflecting on this extensive list, I could not help but think that it was not the tasting of the ginger that invoked the descriptive words. The children must have already had a large word bank from which to draw upon. If not, they could easily have slipped into the familiar and ordinary descriptors encompassing *good, yucky, icky*, and *nice*. So where did they get the words they accessed to directly portray their experience with the ginger? I would hypothesize that many were learned through conversations and, most significantly, through books. It is because of the language learned from books that the children were able to pinpoint the best descriptor. It was not the experience of tasting the ginger itself that magically created an exceptional list, but rather the words already existed in their working vocabulary, previously compiled through their interactions with books.

It is no surprise that authors themselves get much of their extensive vocabulary from their own reading experiences, highlighting the true power of books to increase our reservoir of words we may draw upon during speaking and writing. While attending a children's literature conference, I had the wonderful opportunity to informally speak with several different authors. I asked them where they found inspiration and how they selected their words. Each mentioned the value of reading. Denise Fleming, author of numerous children's books including *In a Small, Small Pond*, *The Everything Book*, and *Mama Cat has Three Kittens*, talked about being a "word collector." She said she was constantly looking for words to add to her collection: words that moved her, words that were intriguing, and words that sang to her. As she read for pleasure or information, her secondary agenda was to scour the newspaper, novels, journals, and the like in search of irresistible words. I, too, find word inspiration from books whenever I am writing. If I feel empty of ideas or am looking for that "perfect" word, I have repeatedly turned to other authors. Hearing the rhythm of their words and how each is used in beautiful, engaging, and powerful ways helps focus me back on the task at hand. I am renewed through their fresh use of language. I believe that if authors turn to books as resources, it only makes sense that we, as parents, should follow their lead. Books provide models of the artful process of choosing the richest words.

If picture books are to serve as models of effective language use, then their texts must be well written. The brevity of picture books dictates that the text must often be concise, conveying a good deal of meaning with a few well-chosen words, imaginatively used.[4]

It is hoped that through repeated exposure to a high standard of word choice and correct grammar, children will adopt these practices in their daily interactions. Once they begin reading independently, they will have a reservoir of story structure, unique words, and stylistic sentences. If they encounter unfamiliar vocabulary, it can be deciphered and defined more readily because they have some background knowledge related to the word or concept. If children have previously *heard* the word read aloud and can place it in some context from that experience, they are better able to access it in their own reading and thus understand its meaning. Without this information, new words exist in a vacuum and our child's brain searches randomly to make sense of them. Reading aloud provides the background knowledge that serves as a powerful tool to familiarize preschoolers with new vocabulary.

Parents sometimes ask if watching television does not help in the same way to expand a child's vocabulary and serve as a model for grammar and sentence structure. Hayes and Ahrens found that television was a poor source for quality vocabulary and noted that children's books were better resources for introducing relatively rare and sophisticated words.[5] In addition to being a language model for our children, the read-aloud experience is unlike television because it provides opportunities for interaction. Parents can immediately reinforce and expand language by capitalizing on a child's curiosity about what is taking place in books and can echo and clarify new vocabulary. We can anticipate misunderstandings in the moment and help define unknown words for our children within the meaningful context of a read-aloud. Children who listen to read-alouds from a parent or other important adult have opportunities to ask questions and discuss elements of the literature. They experiment with language, practice negotiating meaning with someone else, and begin to implement the unique vocabulary they are hearing. These skills are all preludes to becoming independent readers.

Noticing the Newfound Words
As you reflect more closely upon your own child's direct transference of language and "book talk," I am confident you will begin to recognize the endless learning possibilities that books afford. Seeing our children in-

fusing language from books into their everyday experiences, we recognize that they have taken ownership of these words. They have incorporated them into their speech, and have therefore expanded their personal vocabulary. This is such an exciting time for all of us. Let's support their literacy adventure with fabulous books that contain awesome adjectives, vivacious verbs, sensational similes, magnificent metaphors, powerful personification, and simply luscious language.

Part **B**

What to Read Aloud
to Young Children

CHAPTER 6

Selecting Quality Literature

The man who does not read good books has no advantage over the man who cannot read them.

—MARK TWAIN

Parents often ask me to provide suggestions for books they should read to their children. They question whether or not reading aloud *any* book will help bridge their child into independent reading. Parents further the discussion by wanting to know how to distinguish quality books from those that should be left on the shelf at the library or bookstore. While there is value in exposing your child to any text that she finds enjoyable, it behooves parents to include the highest quality texts in the read-aloud experience. After all, childhood is too short to waste time on mediocre books.

Periodically our daughter, Heather, will ask to have books read aloud that I do not consider quality texts. However, she enjoys them for a variety of reasons. They have familiar characters, or they may have interactive elements such as lift tabs, pop-ups, or something else that draws her in. While I am quite cognizant of the fact that these particular texts do not necessarily house well-written language or even captivating illustrations, they do prove enjoyable to her. Since we want Heather to associate reading with pleasure, Mike and I gladly read these texts. However, we strive to balance (and outweigh) these more trivial texts with quality literature. The books that we select to read to our children have the power to shape their lifelong tastes and attitudes toward reading. In their book *Essentials of Children's Literature*, Carol Lynch-Brown and Carl Tomlinson have captured the essence of this process well. "Over a period of time, evaluation and selection of picture books become a matter of achieving a good balance between what children naturally enjoy and what you want to lead them to enjoy."[1] It has been suggested that the caliber of books read aloud can greatly impact children's learning. Therefore, parents need some criteria by which to measure the best books to read aloud that will promote skills for lifelong reading success.

It is sometimes difficult to pinpoint what makes a literature selection quality, since it can be dependent upon the perspective of the reader. However, most of us remember books from our childhood that we wanted to read again and again. These books resonated with us for some reason and stayed with us into adulthood, evoking positive memories. Surely we can point to many of the books considered classics and understand why they have been so designated. They may contain a universal theme that is uniquely human to all of us, or they may tug at our heart or emotions. The author's words may be so carefully chosen that we find ourselves quoting them in conversation to make a point. Picture books, too, distinguish themselves through the feelings they evoke and the themes they hold. They also contain exemplary use of language as evidenced in examples listed throughout this book. Books from our childhood remain with us because of our reaction to them, the reaction that made us laugh, cry, feel deeply, or just think.

So how can parents determine quality in children's books and what distinguishes a magnificent book from a mediocre one? When previewing a book to read aloud to your child, look for those that contain all or most of the following elements:

- Illustrations that are beautiful, captivating, or unique
- Exquisite and exceptional language
- A main character to relate to and love
- Emotional impact; they make you laugh, cry, sing, smile, think, feel

- A universal theme, be it love, friendship, honesty, or growing up
- A text that is unique in some way, clever, or offers a surprise or twist for the reader

Each of these criteria is covered in the following chapters, which focus on the various types of books suited for preschoolers (predictable books, books featuring diversity, informational books, etc.). I have provided specific examples from children's texts to help you clearly see how the criterion manifests itself in quality books on a wide range of topics.

There are many reasons that certain books appeal to me. I look for ones that sing to me and are exceptional in some way. Read-alouds are often the first books that children are exposed to and therefore must charm and invite them into a lifetime of literacy. Picture books should entertain the child and the adult who reads them aloud. The illustrations should be fetching, and the words should dance on the page. The story should be memorable and should invite the reader to revisit it again and again. The best books evoke emotion so they stay with you, warm you inside, put a smile on your face, make your heart sink in sadness or leap for joy and surprise; for these are the *real* experiences of a child.

Unique Illustrations

When selecting the best of the best to read to our children, I look first at the illustrations. As I pull a book off the shelf and thumb through it, I am drawn to artwork that is unique, captivating, and beautiful in some way. It may be lively, lovely illustrations that capture my attention, vivid colors that jump from the page, or soft hues that seem dreamy and whimsical. Simple black and white charcoal drawings may strike me, just as photographs or rich oil paintings can. Colorful and intricate collages like those found in *I Love the Alphabet* and *If I Were a Tree* by Dar Hosta, invite children back time and again to pore over them looking at every detail. The watercolor paintings by Jon Muth from such texts as *I Will Hold You 'til You Sleep* by Linda Zuckerman and *Come on Rain!* by Karen Hesse are remarkable. He has a wonderful talent to perfectly mirror the tone of the book and extend the text. Whether playful, sentimental, or soothing, Muth's art tells its own story. The common thread of wonderful books is interesting artwork that is visually appealing and delightful.

Exceptional Language

Of course, the artwork is only part of the criteria I use to select a good book. Exemplary art may invite me in, but it must serve as a complement to the words on the page. Once the illustrations have caught my attention, I focus very closely on the author's words. I am enchanted by beautiful language. Language that is rich and mesmerizing and can be savored holds my interest. Listen to the wonderful words Patricia Thomas uses in *Firefly Mountain* to describe nightfall.

> An orange ball of a sun dipped down behind the orchard,
> painting the sky pink and red behind it.
> One sleepy bobwhite whistled out his name—
> so we wouldn't forget it I guess.
> Then he went to bed.

Words like these reflect the language parents should look for in quality literature. They appeal to the senses and clearly allow the child to hear, touch, taste, smell, and visualize what the author is saying. I avoid contrived text where dialogue appears forced and sentences seem strained. Contrast this with how Lester Leminick uses dialogue to help the reader clearly see the setting in *Saturdays and Teacakes*.

> Then Mammaw looked at me sort of sideways and said, I reckon I know a boy who'd like something sweet to eat.
> And I grinned.
> Yes ma'am, I reckon you do.

Simple words such as *pretty, nice, good,* and *bad* are lukewarm to me. I prefer spicy words that invoke one's imagination, that are clear and precise and ... perfect in the context of the story. Vocabulary that is fresh and words that are obviously carefully selected by the writer will be remembered by our preschoolers.

I believe that authors should not talk down to children, so I choose books where words are used naturally and are sophisticated enough to challenge children and expand their vocabulary without being too far beyond their experience and comprehension level. Reading aloud is an aural activity, so I think children like to hear words that are lyrical or have silly sounds. Words like *vroom, swoosh, lollygag, kumquat*, and *trotted* tickle the tongue and invite children to repeat them. Books with rhythm and rhyme are playful to our children, and those with repetitive phrases encourage participation, making the story less of a passive experience for the child and more of an active one.

Relatable Main Character

Through the development of a compelling and lovable main character, children can act out numerous thoughts, feelings, and situations. If a character is strong or smart or brave, the child can be strong and smart and brave. Preschoolers identify with Louise, the little sister from Kevin Henkes's *Sheila Rae the Brave*. Big sister Sheila Rae is admired for growling at stray dogs, stepping on every crack in the sidewalk, attacking monsters in the closet, and riding her bicycle "no-handed with her eyes closed." But when Sheila Rae takes an alternate route home from school and gets lost, it is little sister Louise who bravely helps them both find the right way back. Through great literature a child can be comforted, supported, and reassured. They can recognize that everyone gets angry, frustrated, tired, and grumpy. Books like *Alexander and the Terrible, Horrible, No Good, Very Bad Day*, by Judith Viorst, remind children that we all have bad days. In this story, the main character goes to sleep with gum in his mouth and wakes up with gum in his hair. And the day only gets worse. Alexander is "smushed" in the car on the way to school, his mother forgets to pack him dessert in his school lunch, and the dentist discovers a cavity. Books like these allow children to recognize that they are not alone, even in a day where nothing seems fair and everything and everybody seems against you. Viorst humorously reminds the reader that some days are like that for other people too.

Emotional Impact

Stories that have an emotional impact are the ones that we tend to remember and love. Books where joy, anger, sorrow, and wonder are communicated through the experiences of a young character pull a child into the story. Children make connections to the rawness of emotion and associate these books with their own experiences and their own world. Preschoolers enjoy books with happy endings, where good triumphs over evil, and where even the scariest of monsters are conquered and everyone sleeps well at night. Books like *There's a Nightmare in My Closet* and *There's an Alligator Under My Bed*, both written by Mercer Mayer, deal with real fears of children and show them that they can be empowered to face and overcome these fears. In each of these books, a little boy stands up to the scary things that lurk in the darkness of his room and finds out they are not as terrifying as he thought.

How many of us have read a book in its entirety only to come to the end and think, "So what?" Instead of disappointment, books should hold your attention and excite you to turn each page and find out what happens next. They should leave you feeling happy, curious, or touched in some way. The ending should tie everything together and the story should make you want to read it over and over. When I'm selecting great books for my husband and me to read to Heather and her younger brother, Zack, I try to think like a child. *What would they like? What is at the heart and soul of a child? What will impact them emotionally?* Yet I admit that since most picture books are meant to be read aloud and shared by parent and child, I often select ones that would appeal on some level to both audiences. Good books can be whimsical and often a little silly. Many tickle us and make us feel happy. Doreen Cronin's *Click Clack Moo: Cows That Type* is a wonderful read-aloud because of its humorous plot that involves the cows demanding electric blankets from Farmer Brown. Children snicker and giggle and even laugh out loud at the antics of the characters and the illustrations in quality books. Preschoolers relish the obvious humor when they hear Audrey Wood's *Silly Sally*, a ridiculous story about Sally and her silly companions who create a topsy-turvy procession into town, "going backwards, upside down."

Universal Theme

Even picture books can contain universal themes that resonate with our preschoolers. In *The Empty Pot*, by Demi, a little Chinese boy named Ping works hard to become the successor to the throne. However, when he is the only one in the kingdom who is unable to grow a flower to present to the Emperor, he must bring his empty pot. It is soon revealed that all the flower seeds had been boiled and could not possibly have grown. Thus Ping is rewarded for his honesty in appearing with the "empty truth." This simple tale provides a beautiful story about the strength and courage in always doing your best.

Many other children's books present pertinent themes to our preschoolers involving change, growing up, friendship, and parental love. These quality books can serve to reassure children as they begin to assert their independence while still running back to Mom and Dad for confirmation that the world is a safe place. It is for this reason that I treasure sentimental stories that epitomize the love between a parent and child, and that calm and reassure. Books like Audrey Penn's *The Kissing Hand* remind preschoolers that the love of a parent is always present even if they are temporarily separated. In this heartwarming story, Chester Raccoon is nervous about his first day of school. Mom offers him a "wonderful secret." She kisses the center of his hand and tells him,

> ". . . whenever you feel lonely and need a little loving from home, just press your hand to your cheek and think, 'Mommy loves you. Mommy loves you.' And that very kiss will jump to your face and fill you with toasty warm thoughts."

Surprise or Twist in the Story

Some of my favorite books are those with a twist in the plot or a surprise ending. It is always fun to read the unexpected and revel in the cleverness from the author. I remember the first time I read Eve Bunting's *The Wednesday Surprise*, seemingly about a little girl who is being taught to read by her grandmother. In an interesting twist that is not clear until nearly the end of the story, it is the granddaughter who teaches her grandmother to read for a big birthday surprise. I could not help but smile and could not wait to read it again now that the unique plot had been revealed. Unpredictable stories keep children (and adults) interested and teach them to focus carefully on the written word because they may not realize what unanticipated places a story can take them.

Beginning the Search for Quality

Parents of preschoolers can begin their search for quality texts by utilizing the suggestions provided in this book. See page 289 for a Quality Literature booklist. I have also divided the subsequent chapters into specific areas of preschoolers' interests and those that will help them with literacy development. These include predictable texts, informational texts, books dealing with diversity, poetry, wordless books, and others. The titles that I recommend have many, if not all, of the elements of quality literature mentioned in this overview. These books have been read to countless children of preschool age and have received positive responses from children and parents alike. I think you will find that once you have read several of the suggested titles in this book, you will have a foundation for your own independent selection process. You will develop criteria based on what works best with your child. After all, parents usually know their child's interests, fears, challenges, and delights. As you read more and more quality books you will be empowered to distinguish the best literature.

Book Awards

Another wonderful starting point for your selection process is to refer to the most outstanding picture books published as determined by an outside professional committee. Parents may refer to the recommendations from various awards and medals given to authors and illustrators of children's literature. The Caldecott Medal, an honor awarded by the American Library Association each year for the most distinguished contribution in illustration, is the most prestigious picture book award given in the United States. The definition of an exceptional book as defined by the Caldecott committee may guide parents in their own picture book search:

A "picture book for children" as distinguished from other books with illustrations, is one that essentially provides the child with a visual experience. A picture book has a collective unity of story-line, theme, or concept, developed through the series of pictures of which the book is comprised.

The criteria for the Caldecott Medal is further defined as a children's book that displays respect for children's understanding, abilities, and appreciations. This should be kept in mind as you preview books for your child. Most local libraries have a list of all Caldecott Medal winners from the award's inception in 1938. Many of these same libraries keep all Caldecott winners in a special section to provide accessibility for parents and children. You may also visit the American Library Association website (www.ala.org/alsc) for a list of all the Caldecott award winners or see Appendix 3 on page 307 of this book.

There are many other noteworthy awards that can assist parents in selecting quality literature. The Coretta Scott King Award recognizes African-American authors and illustrators who have made an inspirational and educational contribution through their books. The award is given to books that promote understanding and appreciation of all cultures. It is designed to commemorate and honor the life and humanitarian works of Dr. Martin Luther King Jr. and Mrs. Coretta Scott King. The Laura Ingalls Wilder Award is presented to an author or an illustrator whose books have made, over a period of years, a significant contribution to children's literature. The Theodor Seuss Geisel Award is named in honor of Dr. Seuss and was first presented in 2006. The award is given annually to the author(s) and illustrator(s) of the most distinguished American book for beginning readers. There are numerous other awards for various categories of children's books. Also, consider checking the *New York Times Book Review* supplement in early November. A panel of experts reviews all the picture books published each year and creates a list of the best illustrated children's books of the year. Books that have received awards or recognition are a good place to begin your search for quality.

Additional Resources

The Internet offers numerous websites that categorize books by age level and area of interest. These lists can serve as a starting point for a parent's own selection process. Discussing books with other parents of preschool children, as well as preschool teachers and librarians, can provide ideas of what appeals to children. Librarians are usually great fans of children's literature and will often have lists of their favorites by age group. Also look for other books by authors that you and your child already know and love. If your son giggles and chimes in with *The Bear Wants More*, investigate other titles by Karma Wilson and Jane Chapman. If an author has an exceptional and creative writing style, check to see if he or she has written any additional books. Not only does this process help expose your children to quality texts, it helps familiarize them with the names of certain authors they love. In this way, preschoolers begin to develop a foundation for their own personal criteria of wonderful literature.

Selecting What Is Right for Your Family

Lastly, and perhaps most importantly, trust yourself. While looking toward recommendations and recognized awards and medal winners for resources of read-alouds, it is also beneficial to have a separate set of criteria to independently evaluate books. Although I am confident in the recommendations I have listed in this book, a title may not meet the current needs of your child at a particular time. You may want to read aloud something that discusses an issue that is pertinent to your family, focus on an area of interest for your child, revisit a familiar character, or specifically want something that is rhyming or silly, mellow, or the perfect way to say goodnight. Since new books are published every year and parents know their children better than any publisher, having independent criteria that distinguishes a quality book will be helpful.

Carol Lynch-Brown and Carl Tomlinson discuss the idea of quality in their book *The Essentials of Children's Literature:*

> Quality in writing is never easy to define, but it has to do with originality and importance of ideas, imaginative use of lan-

guage, and beauty of literary and artistic style that enable a work to remain fresh, interesting, and meaningful for years and years. These books have permanent value.[2]

I recommend that you take the Parent Reference Sheet for selecting quality literature on page 313 as well as the booklists I have included in this text on your next library or bookstore excursion. As you begin to read some of the titles and compare them to the quality criteria, consider what you and your child want from a good book. Then take some time to sit down, pull books from the shelves, leaf through them . . . and read. Explore. Dream. Savor. Delight in all that books have to offer. Then read some more.

CHAPTER 7

Tempt Them with Text and Illustrations That Complement Each Other

Llama llama red pajama
hollers loudly for his mama.
Baby Llama stomps and pouts.
Baby Llama jumps and shouts.

In Anna Dewdney's book *Llama, Llama Red Pajama*, the meaning of "llama drama" becomes quite clear when Baby Llama is afraid to go to sleep after his mother kisses him goodnight and leaves the room. When he calls for her and she does not come back immediately, he begins to "weep and wail," bringing Mama Llama frantically rushing up the stairs. This familiar experience for parents and children will have both audiences smiling and feeling reassured. The delightful rhyming verse begs children to participate in the reading. Dewdney uses natural language and precisely selects words that show the mounting fear and frustration of Baby Llama. However, it is the vivid illustrations that wonderfully complete the story. Detailed expressions on Baby Llama's face, with eyes wide open, capture his loneliness and then the panic he experiences as he waits, not so patiently, for his mother to come back upstairs. To show that he can wait no longer, we are provided an illustration of him screaming at the top of his lungs. A close-up of his face, mouth open so wide that we can see his tonsils, provides us a clear visual of his scream. When Mama Llama comes flying up the stairs and then sees that her baby is not in danger, she furrows her brows, puts her hands on her hips, and sternly, but lovingly, reminds him that she is never far away. It is the attention to detail of the deep dark paintings that clearly convey the scariness of the night for Baby Llama. The focus on expressive eyes, flailing arms, stomping legs, and a stuffed animal flying through the air shows us the llama drama that is taking place. The words, too, add significantly to the mounting excitement and then clearly tell the comforting ending. Together, illustrations and words create the story, one mirroring the other, both filling in blanks. The story is only truly complete with both the exceptional words and wonderful artwork, which dance a beautiful dance with each other. Words and artwork combine seamlessly to create this winning tale.

For any quality picture book, then, the two main ingredients are exquisite text and fabulous illustrations. They should work harmoniously to complement one another. The words should help paint a picture, and the artwork should fill in the blanks from the text. In the best books, the language is beautiful and rich and enchanting and delicious. Because of the obvious brevity inherent in picture books, the authors we love are those who select rare and distinctive words. When chosen with precision, these words have the power to make us laugh or bring us to tears. They must delight us enough to bring us back time and again. They should invite us and enchant us and shake us and warm us. The words should create a picture by themselves. We should be able to clearly visit the place from which they come. In the most memorable children's books, language is used to welcome, engage, and impact.

Additionally, young children who cannot yet read text should be able to invest themselves in the story and follow the plot through detailed illustrations. Since most of the books that parents read to preschoolers are picture books, it is important to make special note of the illustrations. In quality literature, the words in the book are illuminated through the art, sparking our imagination and completing the text. The children's books that capture our attention have art that enhances and complements the language. Careful selection of media, colors, and styles for the illustrations can enrich the text and help establish mood, theme, characters, and setting. Harsh or jagged lines in art suggest a certain mood. Soft and muted colors convey something different to the reader. Pencil drawings with shades of black, grey, and white can be used to highlight key features of the text.

When the words on the page are seamlessly combined with the artwork, a clear and complete experience for the reader is created. Some of the ideas to look for as you embark on your read-aloud selections include how literary elements such as mood, character development, setting, and theme are portrayed in a balanced way between words and illustrations. Each of these terms is further defined below through specific examples to help you build a clear understanding of them.

Mood

If the mood is tender, for example, the pictures should be soft and soothing, perhaps in subdued pastels or muted tones to help the reader feel peaceful. Beautiful full page paintings are often used in tender books. Watercolors provide a delicate quality, because they are usually void of harsh lines. There may be images of hand holding, hugs, and touching. The words themselves should be soft as well. Words like *love, warmth, snuggle, closeness,* and *tenderness* elicit comforting feelings to the reader.

If the mood is humorous, the words will often be lively or silly. They may rhyme to add to the bounciness and lighthearted feel of the book. The artist may complement the humor with bright, bold, vivid colors that make everyone smile. Intense shades of yellow, orange, and red brighten one's mood. Alternatively, the artist may choose impressionistic sketches or include pictures that exaggerate the features of animals and people to enhance the humor.

Character Development

In quality texts, the author offers details about the character's physical features, personality, and traits. Descriptive language (wicked, crotchety, grumpy, whiskery, wrinkled, flamboyant, jolly, sensitive) helps the reader understand the character. The artist complements the words with expressive portraits that often focus on the eyes and facial expressions. Smiles, smirks, raised eyebrows, tears, and heads turned downward provide insight into the character's emotions. Illustrations can also include details about the character's surroundings that support his or her personality.

Setting

Books about different periods of time, place, or culture should contain authentic words and dialogue. Words like *sarsaparilla, phonograph, blue-suede shoes, fried green tomatoes,* etc. conjure up very specific images in time and space. Pictures, too, should clearly show the setting. Illustrations of transportation, clothing, and architecture can help set the stage for a certain era. Combined, the reader has a mental (through words) and visual (through illustrations) image of what it looks like to be in the unfamiliar place.

Theme

Themes can be reinforced through what the author is saying as well as what the artist is showing us. Themes involving family closeness, for example, will be clearly written within the best books, but the illustrations will also reinforce this. Warm earth-tones may be used by artists showing the love of a family. Stories about friendship can be complemented with bright, vivid, happy colors. Authors will often use descriptive language that focuses on the humanness of all of us when they tell about loss or sadness. The illustrators of such texts may complete the story with stark scenes or a diluted color palette. The artwork may include detailed facial expressions that contribute to the somber tone.

Words and Artwork Dance Together

It is obvious that the main character from Cynthia Rylant's *The Old Woman Who Named Things* is eccentric based on the information provided in the text. The reader quickly learns that she named her car Betsy, her chair Fred, her sturdy bed Roxanne and her well-built old house Franklin. However, it is the whimsical illustrations that complete the picture for us. We see that the Old Woman has a swirling beehive of disheveled white hair, pointy cat's-eye glasses, mismatched clothes, and cowboy boots. She lives in a house atop a hill that is wrapped in a crooked and broken fence. Her car appears to be from the 1960s, with a grill on the front that grins from headlight to headlight. The "personalities" of her inanimate objects are revealed in Kathryn Brown's artwork. The character development of the quirky and unconventional Old Woman is echoed in both text and illustrations. This sweet and loving story about a renewed delight in life can only be told through the interdependence of words and watercolors.

The artist needs to reflect the author's intent and message. A playful mood may be enhanced by bold and vibrant acrylics. Collage or tissue paper illustrations may imply a lighthearted and friendly theme. Soft pastel chalks or watercolors may reflect a calm, dreamy, or perhaps even a sad tone. The key to a successful children's book is illustrations and text that support one another. In their textbook *The Pleasures of Children's Literature* (2003), Perry Nodelman and Mavis Reimer poignantly state the key role pictures play with the words of the story. "Viewers must consider not only the beauty of the pictures but also how they contribute to an unfolding knowledge of the story they're part of."[1]

The story of *Olivia* (2000), written and illustrated by Ian Falconer, is dependent on the illustrations to bring about much of its humor and fill in the blanks for the text. The endearing charcoal drawings are enhanced with bright red to spotlight Olivia and key objects on the page. At one point in the book, Olivia and her family head to the beach. The author uses only fourteen simple words to tell about how Olivia's mother showed her how to make sand castles. Accompanying this is an illustration of the mother pig forming a lump of sand. The next page shows Olivia sitting next to a prominent and towering replica of the Empire State Building. The text simply states, "She got pretty good." It is this satire that is only evident from the complementary artwork that gives the text its "laugh-out-loud" humor. Throughout the book, the brief text plays brilliantly off the artwork to create a complete story.

Expressive, winsome, dramatic, or soft and serene illustrations may invite a child to pick up a book and encourage her to want to find out more. Without an engaging and powerful story line, however, she will not want to continue with the text and surely will not revisit it. A good book has text rich in language. A quality book demonstrates a strong marriage between the illustrations and text that bring the reader back again and again to revisit the characters, relish the words, and discover the nuances in the story.

It is neither the words nor the images alone in Chris Van Allsburg's award-winning tale *The Polar Express* that tempts the reader to open the book time and again. Carefully chosen words—*hissing steam, squeaking metal, dark forests, barren desert of ice, thundered*—create the fantasy of a mysterious world where a little boy takes a train ride to meet Santa Claus. However, it is the majestic full-page illustrations that dominate the book. The deep and dark muted colors, the shadows, and the carefully placed luminescent highlights bring this dreamy and magical place to life. Mood is clearly conveyed through a combination of words and pictures.

Denise Fleming accomplishes the perfect interplay of text and artwork in her book *In the Small, Small Pond*. In the relatively brief text, numerous action verbs are used to describe the activities of animals that live in and around the pond. Words like *wiggle, jiggle, hover, shiver, lash*, and *lunge* evoke a feeling of continuous motion, which is also depicted in the handmade paper illustrations. Vibrant and bold colors add to the drama shown on each page. In order to enhance the overall tone of the book, even the placement of the words on the page is carefully calculated. Unlike the linear text found in most books, the words and the letters within them float, bounce, toss, and dance all over the page. By combining action verbs, brilliant colors, and careful word and letter placement, Fleming creates a mood of fun and frolic that seems to extend beyond the edges of the pages.

Warm and beautiful artwork perfectly mirrors the tone of the melodic text in Angela Medearis's nighttime lullaby, *Snug in Mama's Arms*. Soft, earth-tone paintings add to the quiet and comfort that is elicited as the reader hears about mothers and fathers everywhere gently tucking their children into bed. The words (*moon, clouds, soft, gently, snug, peaceful, dreams*) combine with serene depictions of nature and parents holding children, creating a sense of love and safety that everyone desires before they snuggle into bed.

In *My Big Dog*, by Janet Stevens and Susan Stevens Crummel, illustrated by Janet Stevens, the co-authors masterfully work together to meld words and pictures to clearly define the disposition of their main character, Merl the cat. The story is written from the feline's point of view, and readers immediately recognize his smug, superior attitude. He tells us that he is a very special cat and that everything inside *his* house belongs exclusively to him. It is *his* dish, *his* sofa, *his* chair, and *his* bed. That is, until a clumsy intruder invades his territory. Although it is clear that Violet, the dog, just wants to be friends, Merl becomes more and more irritated with her existence as the story progresses. After all, Merl is a cat and *it* is merely a dog. The authors' precision in word selection heightens the contrast between Merl's formerly peaceful and perfect life, full of naps and quiet, with the now loud and messy world shared with a dog. Although it is never overtly stated that Merl is intolerant, grumpy, and annoyed, it is nonetheless made abundantly clear through the carefully chosen words that describe the cat's thoughts.

The exceptional illustrations contribute greatly to the cleverly written story of Merl and Violet. Janet Stevens's layered artwork clearly depict the disgruntled expressions of the crotchety cat. Full page portraits of Merl, looking straight at the reader, are seen throughout the book. His uneven ears, furrowed brows, and squinting eyes, combined with a lifeless toy mouse dangling from his mouth, all contribute to the obvious irritation exhibited by Merl. Illustrations of the cat are contrasted with a two-page close-up of Violet, the Golden Retriever, warm and gentle brown eyes full of expression and happiness. She appears so fluffy and loveable, children will want to reach into the book and hug her.

Although the words themselves in *My Big Dog* create a heartwarming and funny tale that children and adults love, it is the illustrations that, literally, complete the picture for the reader. The co-authors have seamlessly merged the written material and detailed art to create a truly irresistible tale.

In the richest of texts, the listener can close her eyes, focus solely on the words, and visualize the characters, setting, and actions taking place. On the other hand, with the most captivating of illustrations, the reader sees subtle nuances that may not have otherwise been apparent were it not for the illustrator's contribution. In the best of children's books there is a seemingly effortless dance between words and art, and combined, the story is complete. As parents search for quality in the picture books they read aloud, they can focus on those that have achieved the delicate balance of beautiful language with beautiful artwork.

CHAPTER 8

Play with Predictable Texts

"Who will plant this grain of wheat?" cried the little red hen.
"Not I," said the duck.
"Not I," said the goose.
"Not I," said the pig.
"Not I," said the mouse.

When the main character in *The Little Red Hen* finds a grain of wheat and decides to plant it, she solicits the help of her animal friends. However, they are very lazy, leaving the little red hen to plant the seed, reap the wheat, take it to the mill to be ground into flour, and even bake the bread, all without help from anyone. In the end the other animals learn a valuable lesson about assisting with the chores when the little red hen is rewarded by eating the loaf of bread all by herself.

After Mike read a few pages from the story, Heather (age three) noticed that the hen asks her friends to help her, but each animal, in turn, replies, "Not I." She became excited that she knew what was coming next. When her father read another page and paused strategically prior to the response from the animal, Heather confidently stated, "Not I! said the ..." Mike pointed to the illustration and Heather finished the sentence by adding, "mouse." Mike reinforced her attention to the repetitive sentences found in the book by smiling and saying, "That's right. 'Not I, said the mouse.'"

Books where children can readily anticipate an upcoming phrase, sentence, or event are called *predictable texts*. Among other reasons, preschool children enjoy predictable books because they get to be like big boys and girls who are able to read. They chime in, and through numerous read-aloud opportunities, even "read" repetitive sentences like "Not I!" from *The Little Red Hen*, "Trip trap. Trip trap," from *The Three Billy Goats Gruff* and "not by the hair of my chinny chin chin," from *The Three Little Pigs*. Predictable texts contain patterns that enable listeners to anticipate the author's words. These patterns may be sequential, cumulative, or interlocking. They rely on recurring phrases or repetitive text, familiar sequence, rhymes, and other patterns to engage the child. Some involve a very close association between the illustrations and the text, thus enabling the child to gain meaning from the combination of the two. The author's inclusion of rhythm, rhyme, and repetition make the books easy to listen to and follow.

From the time Heather was a newborn, her grandmother would routinely sing to her the song *I Love You a Bushel and a Peck*, made famous in the 1950s musical *Guys and Dolls*. When her little brother, Zack, was born, Heather, in turn, would sing it to him. The song quickly became synonymous with special times with grandmother. It was so exciting when I was meandering through a bookstore (one of my favorite pastimes) and happened upon a book version of the same song illustrated by Rosemary Wells. Of course, I could not resist bringing it home. Thereafter, Grandmother, Heather, and I pored over the bright and engaging illustrations as we sang the song together. In this rendition, two ducks, one in overalls, the other in a pink skirt and headband, court each other while busily getting things done on the farm. In the end, they drive off in a red wind-up toy convertible. Because she was already familiar with the words of the song, Heather was able to look more closely at some of the letters and words from the book and associate them with what we were singing. The text was predictable and could, therefore, be "read" by Heather. Mike and I used this text as one way to help our daughter make the connection between written and spoken words, thus creating a bridge to her own independent reading in the future.

The Power of Predictable Texts

Predictable texts assist children with reading on their own by helping lay a foundation of some of the skills proficient readers use. Those of us who can read fluently will automatically use clues from the context and look at illustrations to help gain meaning. Active readers make predictions about the next words or events in the story partially based on the previous information provided in the text. Since predictable books use patterns, preschoolers can more readily decipher the "reading code" and know what is coming next. This creates early success for them, which can lead to enthusiasm for the reading process. Reading predictable texts aloud can help build confidence in children as they see that the act of reading is attainable and can even be playful and fun. Through repeated exposure to quality predictable books, children become familiar with the structure of the English language and begin to identify words and letters in print. Some children begin to recognize sight words (those words most commonly used in children's texts) as well as reinforce their knowledge of various letters of the alphabet. Since they see the same words over and over, they gradually understand that letters are grouped together to make words. They see that words are separated by empty spaces and come to understand that even these spaces have meaning.

Defining Quality in Predictable Texts

Parents should select quality predictable texts for their preschoolers as part of the read-aloud experience. These books should contain most or all of the criteria listed below. I have elaborated on each of these elements and provided concrete examples throughout this chapter to assist you in your search for the best literature.

- repetitive sentences or phrases
- interruption in the repetition at some point in the story
- rhyming
- sequential patterns
- cumulative patterns
- natural language
- the story has a clear beginning, middle and end
- the story can be retold
- books created from songs

As parents read quality predictable books aloud, they may invite children to become actively engaged with the text and eventually read all or part of it on their own. In Karma Wilson's *Bear Snores On*, rhyme, as well as repetition of the title phrase (the bear snores on), are used to assist the reader. I watch (and try to be unobtrusive) as my friend Christina encourages her son, Jackson, to help her read the text aloud. Christina reads aloud until she comes to the repetitive line, "But the . . ." When she pauses at this place in the book, she points to the letter *b* at the beginning of the word *bear*. Without hesitation, Jackson proudly "reads" the repetitive phrase ". . . bear snores on." Christina nods and then provides a quick summary of the plot of the story thus far. "That bear hasn't woken up yet with all the noise the animals are making!" Periodically summarizing the story helps Jackson see that reading is made up of more than just memorizing the words or looking at the letters. Reading involves understanding what is taking place in the story.

In her book *Becoming Literate: The Construction of Inner Control*, early reading expert Marie Clay advocates that the most helpful repetitive books vary the sentences somewhere in the text. Eric Carle skillfully interrupts the pattern midway through his book *The Very Lonely Firefly*, creating a much more interesting story. As the main character searches for firefly friends, he mistakenly is drawn to a lightbulb, candle, flashlight, lantern, and headlights.

> The firefly saw a light
> and flew toward it.
> But it was not another firefly.
> It was a candle
> flickering in the night.

The pattern is repeated several times ("The firefly saw a light and flew toward it. But it was not another firefly. It was a . . ."), with different light sources and descriptions. It is then temporarily interrupted as a fight breaks out between a dog and a cat, and children rush toward them. The pattern is later resumed until the firefly finds what he has been looking for and is no longer lonely.

When we read stories with patterns, our children can read along with us. By using books that deviate from the repetition at some point, we are helping our children learn early on that meaning is derived from a multitude of things. Among these are the cadence of language, clues gained from pictures, prior knowledge, and attention to letters and words. Later, when children become independent readers, they will recognize the necessity of relying on a variety of skills to assist them with decoding (sounding out the words) and comprehension (making sense of the words).

Distinguishing Read-Alouds from Emergent Reading Texts

There are numerous types of predictable books available to parents. When we are selecting those most appropriate to be read aloud to our preschool children, it is important to remember the goal of keeping natural language intact and selecting stories that are interesting and engaging, which helps reinforce the idea that reading is enjoyable. Some predictable books are better suited for older children who are embarking on independent reading. These books may include very simple sentences with repetitive sight words to help emergent readers become successful in their beginning attempts at the process of reading by themselves. However, such predictable books are not the best choices for reading aloud to our preschoolers. Consider the predictable text below, which has merit for emergent readers but is not a good read-aloud candidate.

> **The Dog Plays**
> The dog plays with the socks.
> The dog plays with the mitten.
> The dog plays with the blocks.
> The dog plays with the kitten.
> The dog plays with the boat.
> The dog plays with the bee.
> The dog plays with the goat.
> What happens next? The dog plays with me!

Accompanying each page of this type of predictable text there would be an illustration of the last word in the respective sentences (socks, mitten, blocks, etc.). This helps add to the predictability because close association between words and illustrations assists beginning readers with deciphering this part of the text. Additionally, each line in the story is nearly the same until the very end. Children could be easily supported through this part of the text with the help of a fluent reader. It is even common for emerging independent readers to "memorize" words, thus enabling recognition during repeated readings. The fact that sentences rhyme in the above text also helps with the readability. The subject of each sentence is a readily decodable word, *dog*. The text includes common sight words (*with, the*) and words that are very familiar to young children (*plays*), thus supporting the fluency of reading. All these elements help early emergent readers be successful and thus feel like part of the reading club, but at the same time, this text may not hold the interest of preschool listeners who are looking for a real story.

Children who are learning to read can use repetitive texts like the one above as part of their formal literacy program. Kindergarten, first, and second grade teachers may use texts similar to this one to assist their students in their early attempts at reading by themselves. Although there is a slight deviation from the pattern at the end of the text, nearly all of it could be read with minimal support from a parent or teacher. Emergent readers benefit from such books because they gain confidence in their own skills, practice decoding, learn to focus on illustrations as one tool for gaining meaning, and, through repeated readings, gain exposure to sight words.

Predictable texts such as *The Dog Plays* serve the very specific purpose of helping children transition into emergent readers. However, they do not meet the requirements for a quality read-aloud. Although parents of preschoolers may have some of the same goals in mind as we expose our children to predictable texts, our primary purpose is somewhat different. We want them to see that reading is both fun and, because of its predictability, attainable. Our focus is always on the ultimate goal of comprehending. We read to understand. We decode and learn sight words for the purpose of using these tools to help gain meaning from the written word. If there is no real story or connection to the child, it is highly unlikely that reading will seem enjoyable, and preschoolers may be reluctant to try to read on their own in the future. Their process may become stilted because of the boring, controlled language of this type of text. At the preschool stage of development, parents should carefully select predictable texts.

Let us once again examine *The Dog Plays*. The text is extremely basic and the language seems monotonous because it deviates from natural speech and is void of any substantive story structure. Ideally, the type of texts we read aloud should contain a clear beginning, middle, and end, as all real stories do. A good gauge for the predictable books we read aloud is to check and see if they can be summarized or retold. Additionally, parents should keep in mind the other goals discussed throughout this book, which also apply to predictable texts. Among others, they include exposure to the authentic, natural structure of the English language, building background knowledge, reinforcing phonemic awareness, and increasing vocabulary. The best predictable texts often accomplish many of these goals.

Contrast *The Dog Plays* with *The Magic Hat* by Mem Fox, a more appropriate predictable book to read aloud to our preschool children. When a magic hat mysteriously appears, it floats and flies in a whirl of confetti from one adult to another, changing each into a funny and entertaining animal for all the children in the park. This text contains many of the elements of quality predictable texts delineated earlier in this chapter. The language in the book is natural (instead of emphasizing sight words and basic sentence structure). The use of words like *warty, lofty, sparkling, nod, amused*, and *mischievous* are far from ordinary and add interest to the read-aloud. The storyline has a clear beginning, middle, and end and can easily be retold. It is fun and engaging, begging to be read time and again. The repetitive lines complemented by bouncy rhymes entice listeners to participate.

> Oh, the magic hat, the magic hat!
> It moved like this, it moved like that!

Children rely on the rhyme scheme teamed with the silly, bustling illustrations by Tricia Tusa to assist them in figuring out what animal the next person will turn into. A fruit stand seller shown juggling bananas is transformed into a baboon. When the hat lands atop a mother cradling a baby in her arms, she is changed into a kangaroo with a baby in her pouch.

Like other quality predictable texts best suited for read-alouds to preschoolers, there is interruption of the repetitive phrase to add to the interest of the language and the story itself. After the bright blue hat spins and twirls to several residents, a giant colorful wizard appears and stops the action.

> The toad, the baboon, the bear, and the 'roo,
> And of course the giraffe (Oh what a to-do!)
> Turned back into people, dazed and confused,
> Watched by a crowd that was highly amused!

The story ends with yet another magical twist as the wizard places the hat on his own head.

It is important for parents to note the overall quality of the book in addition to its predictability. Like all great stories, these texts need to be inviting for our preschoolers. *The Magic Hat* is a delightful book that houses many of the other criteria of great picture books that would appeal to child and parent. It is clever and imaginative and silly. The illustrations whimsically reflect the text and are full of motion and color, seemingly bouncing beyond the edges of the pages. Yes, children will likely chime in with the repetition and rhyme, but they will also enjoy the book simply because of its colorful artwork, rare words, and truly imaginative story.

Types of Predictable Texts for Reading Aloud

I have compiled a list of predictable books. It is separated into the five categories below to assist you in your quest for quality literature. It may be helpful to also refer to the booklist for phonemic awareness on page 273. Many books that reinforce phonemic awareness are considered predictable because of their rhythm, rhyme, and repetition of certain sounds. The more titles you preview and read to your child, the greater understanding you will gain of what constitutes a great predictable book. You will then be able to apply this knowledge with confidence each time you peruse the shelves at the library or bookstore.

In addition to repetition and rhyme and rhythm, sequential patterns, cumulative patterns, and books created from songs are also common predictable texts.

Repetition

Books with phrases or sentences that are repeated numerous times are predictable to children. They notice the repetition, anticipate it, and therefore find it almost irresistible not to chime in. Sentences like "Someone's been eating my porridge," from *Goldilocks and the Three Bears* or "Little pig, little pig, let me in," from *The Three Little Pigs*, help preschoolers "read" with their parents and gain confidence in this new process. Another type of repetitive text uses a question and answer format. In Sue Williams's book *I Went Walking*, readers are assisted in predicting the text because they get a glimpse of the back of the animal that will appear on the next page. After stating the refrain, "I went walking," the audience asks what she saw and a certain color animal is revealed. For example, a red cow, green duck, and a pink pig are all seen by the narrator. Thus, color names are reinforced as well.

Rhyme and Rhythm

Texts with rhyme and rhythm naturally engage children. Perhaps this is one of the reasons why Mother Goose is a favorite of so many generations.

> Handy-spandy, Jacky dandy,
> Loves plum cake and sugar candy.
> He bought some at the grocer's shop.
> And pleased away went hop, hop, hop.

The cadence and beat from such books help children attend to the words and keep their interest in the story. When a parent reads the following stanza from Anne Ginkel's *I've Got an Elephant*, children will logically fill in the word *me* because it makes sense and has a similar sound to *tea*, its rhyming counterpart.

Pretending they are royalty and putting on airs.
I've got eight elephants who prance down the stairs,
They gather round the table for a royal English tea,
Sipping from their teacups and having fun with _____.

It is unlikely that a preschooler would choose a word like *friends,*
Heather, or *giraffes* to finish the sentence. While these may fall within a
child's experiential background and may make sense, they do not fit
with the predictable rhyming scheme the author has laid out in the
book. From books with rhymes, children learn that texts often follow a
logical and predictable rhythm and pattern.

Sequential Patterns

Some predictable books use a familiar sequence such as the days of the
week, the numbers 1 to 10, or the letters of the alphabet. In Eric Carle's
book *The Very Hungry Caterpillar*, the numbers 1 to 5 are combined
with the days of the week as a caterpillar eats his way through different
foods. On the first Sunday he hatches from his egg and begins searching
for food. On Monday, he eats an apple, but still feels hungry. On Tuesday,
he eats two pears, but is still hungry. This continues throughout the
week until the poor caterpillar gets a stomachache. The next Sunday he
eats more sensibly, rests, and completes his metamorphosis, emerging
as a beautiful butterfly.

Cumulative Patterns

In cumulative texts, the storyline builds on the previous lines. After
each new event is introduced, all previous events are repeated. In Audrey Wood's *The Napping House*, various creatures find their way to sequentially pile atop one another and happily slumber. Rain is shown
falling outside the quaint two story napping house surrounded by a
white picket fence. The reader learns that inside the house there is a
cozy bed "where everyone is sleeping." Snoring Granny is subsequently
joined by a dreaming child, a dozing dog, a snoozing cat, and a slum-
bering mouse.

And on that bed
there is a granny,
a snoring granny
on a cozy bed
in a napping house,
where everyone is sleeping.
And on that granny
there is a child,
a dreaming child
on a snoring granny
on a cozy bed
in a napping house,
where everyone is sleeping.

But when a flea on top of the mouse decides to bite him, a hilarious chain of events ensues, waking each creature in turn. Because of its repetitive and cumulative lines, children are confident about what is coming next and gleefully participate.

Books Created from Songs

Picture books sometimes are created entirely around a single song or poem. These books offer a unique type of predictability for preschoolers. Since the words and tunes of songs like "Row Row Row Your Boat," "The Wheels on the Bus," and "Old MacDonald Had a Farm" are easy to learn, children are able to immediately read along and feel a sense of success. The song's natural rhythm, often accompanied by rhyme, enables children to participate. Therefore, the process of reading is associated with something pleasurable. Besides being fun, these predictable texts provide the opportunity for children to make the important connection between oral and written communication.

CHAPTER 9

Wander Over to Wordless Books

A picture is worth a thousand words.

Wordless books are those that are created without any text or with very little text. The illustrations are often particularly rich and detailed, providing the "reader" many clues to figuring out the story. Parents can read wordless books aloud and reinforce the literary elements of all good stories without being limited to the words of someone else. By telling the story to our children, we are showing them how plot, setting, and characters are all key elements of a quality book. We are teaching them in a supportive way that books are sequential and have a clear beginning, middle, and end. Since many wordless books have small vignettes on various pages, children need to follow these in sequence in order to make sense of the story. Parents can pay special attention to using sequence words like *first, next, then*, and *finally*. Once your child enters formalized schooling, the teachers will point out these types of words in books they read to the class and will also use these words as a way to help children learn to write stories. Therefore, it behooves parents to periodically include these in our wordless read-alouds.

Reading aloud wordless books also reinforces the concepts about how print works. We are demonstrating how print in the English language is read front-to-back and with left-to-right progression. Preschoolers can participate in the read-aloud experience by turning the pages, and even contributing to the text with their own words. They can add to the storyline, making the experience a cooperative activity where everyone is successful. After all, there are no right answers when it comes to one's imagination.

Regardless of a parent's own literacy level, or their primary language, all adults can readily read wordless books. More powerful, perhaps, is the idea of serving as a role model to our children about using one's imagination when telling a story. Although certain aspects of the plot are usually provided by the artist, the void of words leaves the story open to interpretation and presentation style of the reader. With each retelling, the story can be expanded or changed. Dialogue can be added. Background information can be included that perhaps even the artist did not anticipate. Parents can show children how stories are paced, how it changes the mood if we slow our speech or speed it up, if we whisper or if we shout. This is a great way to help our children learn to be wonderful storytellers themselves. We can provide models of typical story language including, "Once upon a time," and "They lived happily ever after." In doing so, we are laying the foundation of narrating a tale based on pictures or illustrations, an important skill for writing. All these things will help our children with future independent reading and writing endeavors.

Wordless books are the perfect genre for children who are just embarking on the world of reading, because they are not confined to what the author has written down. Preschoolers and emergent readers begin to recognize that it is important to look very closely at books in order to unfold a complicated plot or divulge a surprise on the next page. They get to practice the art of using language to tell a story. Ironically, wordless books promote language development because children experiment with finding the precise word or phrase to accurately portray the image presented. When parents read aloud these types of texts and focus on using language inventively, our children learn from our example and take their own risks with retelling the tale.

Many wordless books include a fantastical element in them, making them especially suited for young children whose imagination is ripe and ready to be cultivated. These types of books stretch the boundaries of the conventional, capitalizing on our child's creativity. Barbara Lehman captures the essence of childhood in *Rainstorm*, about a lonely boy who discovers a mysterious key. He searches the house to find the lock that it fits, and when he does, this leads him on an adventure down a ladder, through a long, twisted tunnel, and up, up, up a spiral staircase. He emerges on a sunny island, where he makes friends with a group of children and their dog. Both child and parent alike will revel in the idea of being able to escape to a secret destination full of sun and fun and friends. Lehman combines brightly colored full-page images, spreads, and pages of sequential panels to keep children coming back time and again to pore over the book.

In a clever twist on Goldilocks and the Three Bears, Brinton Turkle's *Deep in the Forest* stars a little bear who decides to investigate a house while its three human inhabitants have gone out. He tests porridge, chairs, and beds before being discovered by Goldilocks and her family. Of course, he is extremely frightened and runs back to the security of his own bear mother. The humor in this hilarious wordless book is clearly portrayed through delightful and expressive illustrations. Children of all ages will recognize the parallel plot to the traditional Goldilocks tale and will enjoy comparing the two. Since they are familiar with another story just like *Deep in the Forest*, many will have confidence in their ability to retell the story to you.

A delightful series of nearly wordless books for even the youngest of children involve the mischievous and loveable Rottweiler named Carl. A sampling of the titles from this collection by Alexandra Day include *Good Dog, Carl!*, *Carl's Birthday*, and *Carl's Afternoon in the Park*, among many others. Each is filled with child pleasing illustrations that perfectly capture Carl's expressions, helping all to see exactly what he is thinking and feeling. The beautiful artwork houses intricate details that children will love to examine carefully. The Carl books revolve around the close companionship of this gentle giant and his preschool friend, Madeleine, who seem to get into and out of trouble in the most interesting and humorous ways. Because the books spotlight the relationship between the canine and young girl, and adults are usually just supporting characters, children are naturally drawn to these stories about people just like them.

With each Carl book you read, your family will fall deeper in love with this charming pooch.

David Wiesner's *Sector 7* is a more sophisticated wordless book, but parents can simplify it in their "reading" or work to stretch the child's imagination, story sense, and language development by including the complex details evident in the pictures. Children (and parents) will need to look closely at each illustration to provide the oral twists and turns to this creative tale. On a field trip to the Empire State Building, a young boy makes friends with a jolly cloud. He is whisked away and brought to a secret location where clouds are given their daily weather assignments. As the clouds complain about how boring their shapes are, the artistic little boy creates new blueprints for each. However, when the New York skies become filled with fantastic fish and octopus shapes, the officials are furious and promptly send the boy back to his school group in a cloud taxi. The exciting story doesn't end there, though. Having tasted independence and creativity, the clouds will never again be the same old compliant shapes they once were. With each visit to *Sector 7*, all are guaranteed to see new and intricate details, making the story head down inventive and alternative paths. This is truly a spectacular adventure for children of all ages.

Another delightful book by David Wiesner is *Tuesday*. On this particular Tuesday, around eight in the evening, frogs from the local swamp are lifted into the air on lily pads. The adventure begins as the amphibians fly to a nearby suburb and wreak hilarious havoc on some unsuspecting humans, a bird, a dog, and a cat. At daybreak, life goes back to normal and the town is left puzzled by the stray lily pads scattered all about. However, the author keeps the reader's interest, perhaps for an upcoming tale, by providing us a final illustration which features a glimpse of pigs taking flight. This ending could serve as an interesting story starter (or even a picture starter) for you and your child. What will happen on the next Tuesday? Who will take flight or what other magical event will take place?

To support your initial search for wordless books, I have included a list beginning on page 303. Using the list and the information provided in this chapter, I hope that you will develop a sense of how to incorporate these types of texts into your read-aloud routine and have a magnificent word-filled adventure as you do so.

How to Read a Wordless Book

As I have pointed out through the examples in this chapter, some wordless books are very straightforward with an obvious plot and sequence to the story. Others are more sophisticated and may involve details about character, setting, and a complex plot with subplots as well. Do not dismiss a book as being easy to "read" just because it is wordless. As with all great books, I suggest parents read through (or, in the case of a wordless text, *look* through) the book prior to including it in the read-aloud routine. In this way, you will be more prepared to map out the story, plan the pacing of the retelling, and provide the right drama, suspense, or surprise for various parts in the book. You will also be able to have a feel for the intricacies of the illustrations and can anticipate when you should provide more time for your child to peruse certain pages. Without this key preview period, parents may be caught speechless in the midst of reading a wonderful wordless book.

CHAPTER 10

Delve into Diversity: Appreciating Individual Differences

Léeme y me verás crecer,
contándome todo
lo que puedas saber.
Porque en esta vida
necesito buena guianza,
déjame que empiece
 en tu regazo lleno de confianza . . .

In a simple and gentle rhyming verse, the author of *Vamos a Leer*, Judi Moreillon, celebrates families reading to their young loved ones. Parents, grandparents, and children from many different cultural backgrounds are shown sharing the fun, excitement, and beauty found in books. This book is also available in an English version, *Read to Me*. When our children sit upon our laps and we read to them or tell them stories, we are laying a strong foundation for them to learn and grow. The specific books that we select have the power to shape our children's beliefs, values, and perspectives on the world. Children's literature has the potential to teach our preschoolers what our society values and what we, as a family, value. For many of us, we hope that our children will see how truly special they are, unlike anyone else in the world. Yet at the same time, we want them to understand how everyone else is also unique and special. All children, all people, regardless of their backgrounds, color, language, gender, or religion, are equally important. We want our children to develop an appreciation of and respect for the diversity that exists in our own neighborhoods, schools, and throughout the world. We recognize that we can learn from one another and work together to make the world a peaceful and beautiful place. Literature has the power to celebrate our special qualities and affirm who we are. It can also inform us about the individual differences of others and help us appreciate them. Most importantly, literature can bring us together to celebrate the humanness that binds us as one people, one world.

It is important to look closely at texts that delve into diversity. We want to select a variety of books that reinforce our family's beliefs and culture. Yet we also want to be sensitive to how others view the world. We want to learn and grow through the perspectives and opinions of our peers, friends, and neighbors. A wonderful way to begin this journey is through the exploration of books that address our unique and individual differences.

Criteria for Selecting Multicultural Literature
Elements of Quality Literature
First and foremost, multicultural literature should include the same criteria of excellence that parents expect from any book we select to read to our children. We want our children to enjoy multicultural literature simply because it is wonderful literature. Therefore, all books, regardless of focus or story, should be quality. The book should be well-written, with carefully selected vocabulary and illustrations that capture the attention of the reader. Like all great literature, books dealing with diversity should tell an interesting story with characters that are well-developed and believable. Quality multicultural literature should include an ending that ties everything together and leaves the reader satisfied.

A multicultural book that meets the criteria for quality is *I Love My Hair*. Author Natasha Tarpley uses exceptional language to invite the reader into a young African-American girl's experience of having her hair combed out each night. The author creates vivid descriptions that add depth to the story.

> I love my hair because it is thick as a forest, soft as cotton candy, and curly as a vine winding upward, reaching the sky and climbing toward outer space.

The audience can feel Keyana's pain during the nightly ritual as she tries not to cry when Mama comes to especially tangled spots. We can also feel her delight as she is told about how beautiful and special her hair is. Through careful attention to exquisite word choice, the listener shares the joy of the little girl as she begins to celebrate the rhythm and music her hair makes when braided and beaded. "Tap! Tap! Clicky-clacky." The words by themselves create a distinct visual, enabling us to see her growing pride as she learns about her heritage and appreciates her own uniqueness.

In quality multicultural literature, the illustrations should be exquisite, captivating, and reflective of the mood, setting, and theme in the story. Minorities should be prominently and accurately portrayed. The graceful text from *I Love My Hair* is perfectly complemented by warm and vivid watercolor illustrations that showcase the mother-daughter bond and highlight the girl's love of her hair. Words and art are joined seamlessly to send a message that all people should cherish their ethnicity and the unique qualities that accompany it. The book provides us a view of an African-American experience, while also showing us the love between a mother and daughter that is universal. This quality read-aloud is worthy of a special place on everyone's bookshelf.

Universal Themes and Values

Parents should look for books that show universal values and themes so that all children can relate to the story. In Gary Soto's *Too Many Tamales*, which is also available in a Spanish version, we learn about Maria and her close, Hispanic family. We see cousins and aunts and uncles gathering for a Christmas celebration and learn about the special tradition of making tamales for the family to share. But we also identify with the universal theme of a little girl wanting to be grown up and sneaking her mother's diamond ring in an attempt to fulfill this dream.

> Maria returned to kneading the *masa*, her hands pumping up and down. On her thumb the ring disappeared, then reappeared in the sticky glob of dough.

The author and illustrator beautifully capture the festivity of a glittery holiday celebration with which nearly everyone can identify. The values of telling the truth and forgiveness are reinforced, providing the listener an opportunity to see themselves in the story, regardless of his or her own cultural background.

Characters

The characters in the story should be well-developed and multi-faceted. Quality literature should avoid stereotyping of any kind. Characters from various cultures should be presented as positive images that may have roles of leadership or other important skills. In *Amazing Grace*, by Mary Hoffman, the main character is strong and determined. Grace won't let her race or gender stand in the way of her goal of being Peter Pan in her class play. She is discouraged by her classmates because they feel that she does not fit the traditional look associated with this character. However, the love and support of her family remind her that she can do anything she imagines.

Cultural Details

The book should reflect accurate details of the culture and should counter any subtle or overt stereotypes that may exist. In *Abuela*, author Arthur Dorros takes the reader on a spectacular flight with a young girl and her first-generation immigrant grandmother. While feeding birds in the park, Rosalba imagines what it would be like to fly. She and her *abuela*, the Spanish word for grandma, embark on a wondrous adventure over New York. They soar above factories and trains, the Statue of Liberty, a harbor, an airport, and a local market. The author seamlessly integrates Spanish phrases into the simple English text, adding to the flavor and tone of the book. Vivid and detailed illustrations resemble folk art that reflects cultural details, perfectly complementing the tale.

> Today we are going to the park.
> "*El parque es lindo*," says Abuela.
> I know what she means.
> I think the park is beautiful too.

By artfully combining authentic Spanish phrases, exquisite illustrations, and a story about the close connection between Rosabla and her grandmother, the reader is provided many details that help inform us about a different culture.

Selecting Authentic Multicultural Literature

As we look closely at the bookshelves in libraries and bookstores in an effort to include a variety of multicultural literature in our read-aloud experience, it is important to select those that are considered quality and authentic. If the author and illustrator are members of the same culture as the characters within the story, there will usually be truth and authenticity to the text. However, people outside the minority group may also provide accuracy, depending on their intention in writing the book, cultural knowledge base, and their own sensitivity to the struggles and needs of the particular group. Is the author and illustrator team creating the book to help build understanding and/or empathy? Also, look carefully at books that have been translated from another language. When someone takes a wonderful book that was originally written in a language other than English and tries to rewrite the same story, it may well lose its full meaning. The language may become skewed, inauthentic, or less noteworthy. Often, there is no way to make a direct translation while still maintaining the beauty and substance of the culture.

When parents are trying to decide if a book is appropriate for their child and provides a better understanding of a particular cultural group, they should consider how the book makes them feel. What is the overall tone of the book? Are minority characters portrayed with respect? Is there some connection to the humanness of all people within the book so that every reader and listener can relate to the thoughts and feelings of the characters?

Multicultural literature can play a powerful role in reinforcing a child's identity and self-esteem. When preschoolers see people like themselves portrayed as problem-solvers, leaders, or heroes, they gain a sense of self-worth. When they read about characters that look as they do, use dialect or expressions like their family, or participate in familiar activities, they are drawn into books and feel "at home." When children listen to stories about people and cultures different from them, they question and wonder. This creates an avenue for discussions about others and ourselves. Children can begin to understand, appreciate, and celebrate differences. At the same time, children can see how people from all cultures are connected through our emotions, be they happiness, anger, love, or disappointment. They can see that all children have the need to be cared for and loved. They see that all children are just like they are in some ways, and all children are different from them in other ways.

A Window or a Mirror

Rudine Sims Bishop, a professor of children's literature, discusses how the best multicultural literature can serve as a *mirror* and *window* for the reader.[1] Quality multicultural books allow children to look closely at the characters and see a mirror or reflection of themselves, thus reinforcing their own culture. Books that are windows for us serve to give us more than a mere snapshot of another way of life. Instead, in the best multicultural books, the reader is able to look closely through the window and spend some time with people from a different culture. We are able to gain a multi-layered perspective on the people, the time, the culture. When I select a book to read to our children, I keep Bishop's terms in mind. I pick out a book and read through it, looking for the criteria cited throughout this chapter. I look for a wonderful, inviting story with illustrations that are exceptional in some way. I check carefully to make sure the book is void of all stereotypes. I am also deeply cognizant of how the book does or does not provide a window and/or mirror into diversity awareness.

When we look critically at children's literature, we must ask ourselves what underlying or even overt messages it is sending to our children. My friend Christine and her husband have three biracial children. Their youngest daughter, like so many little girls, became enamored with princesses and even wanted her room to be decorated in a princess theme. I was at a loss when my friend asked for a recommendation of a book about a princess of color. Although there are some titles available for older readers, I could not find a single book that was appropriate for her age and developmental level that showcased a princess from her culture. Instead, her daughter was only able to listen to books that were windows for her. There were no texts that offered her a mirror into her own princess fantasy. I cannot help but wonder what impact this may have on a young, impressionable little girl. Everywhere she looks, she sees Caucasian princesses. They are so often the ones portrayed as beautiful, the envy of all others, and the one the prince chooses to marry. Do we really want to send the message to our daughters and sons that being the "fairest of them all" equates to living happily ever after? Clearly there is a need for more multicultural books with role models of color. Regardless of cultural background, it is important for parents to read aloud books that showcase strong, beautiful, smart, and kind characters that provide both a mirror and a window for our own children.

Universal Themes Create Clear Understanding

I remember playing dress-up with my sisters when I was a little girl, trying on our mother's high heels, hats, scarves, and stockings, wanting so desperately to be all grown up. It seems that most young girls can relate to this universal feeling of wanting to be just like their own mother, dressed in her clothes, imagining being big one day. Pooja Makhijani, the author of *Mama's Saris*, has beautifully captured this worldwide sentiment and offers every girl a mirror into the fantasy of dressing up in her mother's outfits. Since this story is specifically about a Hindu mother and daughter, it also provides many of us a window into a different culture. The little girl who narrates the story wants to wear a sari just like her mother, but she is told that she must wait until she is older. It is the girl's seventh birthday and she yearns to be a grown-up. Her mother finally relents, and she is adorned in a beautiful blue sari and fancy bangles, with a glittery bindi placed between her eyebrows.

The author weaves authentic Hindi words (*chaniya choli, didi, Masi*) throughout the story, providing us a closer look into this culture. A glossary of these terms at the beginning of the book provides helpful background information for the reader. Through the story, we learn about the special occasions that are celebrated by East Indians and about the application of these for different generations in America. The Nanima (mother's mother) in the story wears a sari every day and even at night. The girl's mother dresses up in saris for birthdays, Diwali (Hindu New Year), weddings, and trips to the temple. The deep vibrant acrylic paintings by Elena Gomez reflect the patterns of the saris mentioned throughout the story and reflect the warm, close relationship of mother and daughter. Because this book provides us a view of the Hindu culture but also transcends cultural specifics by using a universal theme, it is a wonderful example of a quality multicultural book.

Emotional Impact of Exceptional Multicultural Books

When I look for a book that serves as a window or mirror, I am often pulled into the story. I am affected emotionally in some way. I am captured by the universal theme of love or forgiveness or closeness with family. However, if a book leaves me unaffected or uninvolved, it is often placed back on the shelf. I remember previewing a book about a child returning for a visit to her place of origin and bringing a friend. While the book offered many facts and authentic vocabulary usage for names of places, foods, and customs, it did not move me in any way. At the end of the story, the girl and her friend got back on the plane and left the island to return home. I literally felt like I, too, was just a visitor to this strange land. I had difficulty getting past the numerous lists of native fruits, vegetables, and animals. Because there were no intimate details about the thoughts or feelings of any of the characters, I felt no connections with them. The story did not hold my interest, make me question, or impact me.

Contrast the book discussed in the previous paragraph with Stephanie Stuve-Bodeen's *Elizabeti's Doll*. This sweet and touching story takes place in a Tanzanian village. A young girl longs for a doll after watching her mother care for her new baby brother. Elizabeti finally settles on a rock, the perfect size and shape to be her special baby. She names her Eva and, just like her mother, carries her in a kanga cloth, sings her lullabies, and feeds her (although Eva is too polite to burp). When Eva gets lost, no other rock can replace her. She is finally found, brushed off, hugged, and kissed. For many of us, this book serves as a window into another culture. We see lifestyle differences such as food being cooked over an open fire in a separate hut from where the family sleeps. We hear words like *kanga* and learn that babies are carried on their mother's backs in these brightly colored cloths. Children notice that Elizabeti brings water for her family to use in a large jug atop her head. Through this window we see that not all children have access to the same resources as we may. However, this gentle story also provides many of us a mirror to reflect upon our own lives. *Elizabeti's Doll* reminds each of us very clearly that regardless of where we live or how much money we may have, little girls around the world have wonderful imaginations and love deeply. Being both a window and a mirror, this book is distinguished as quality multicultural literature and beckons to be read by everyone.

Three Categories of Multicultural Literature

Multicultural literature can be placed into three main categories: Highlighting a Specific Cultural Group, Multiculturalism as Mainstream, and Different Cultures Displayed.

Celebrating Uniqueness—Highlighting a Specific Cultural Group

Books like *I Love My Hair* and *Mama's Saris* celebrate the uniqueness of the people from a specific culture. They provide clear, affirming mirrors for those who belong to the same group. They reflect and highlight the way we are different, thus helping our children appreciate their own individuality. They teach and inform. Books in this category offer us more than a glimpse into the traditions, language, food, and rituals of a certain group of people. They provide a deeper reflection of how each child is special because of her unique differences.

Multiculturalism as Mainstream

Multicultural books in this category often show minorities participating in activities and leading a lifestyle that is commensurate with mainstream America. However, there is no direct reference to any specific cultural group. Therefore, the reader gains a clearer perspective of the things we all have in common with others and, it is hoped, our children begin to recognize that we are more alike than we are different. Ezra Jack Keats's *Snowy Day*, for example, shows an African-American boy awakening to a snow covered city. He celebrates the magical experience of a world blanketed in white by making footprints and snow angels and attempting to save a snowball for another day. Many children of all ethnicities can relate to the exciting adventure of playing in the snow. *Snowy Day* crosses cultural boundaries because it focuses on the universal theme of seeing the world through the eyes of a child. Books like this show minorities as main characters who experience activities and emotions just like everyone.

Different Cultures Displayed

Some authors, illustrators, and even publishers strive to include elements of race in their books by showing children of all cultures and colors as a matter of course. It is a group of multicultural children who rescue a frightened bear in *Bear's Day Out* by Michael Rosen. At the end of Bill Martin Jr.'s popular book *Brown Bear, Brown Bear, What Do You See?*, children of many colors are prominently shown in a classroom. Aliki, the author of such books as *My Visit to the Zoo* and *Feelings*, often includes representation from many different ethnic groups in her nonfiction books. All these efforts help children see that we are surrounded by diversity.

Our Place in the Bigger World—Diversity All Around

Books like Ann Morris and Ken Heyman's *Houses and Homes* provide readers a view of different people and different cultures from around the world. Appealing full-color photographs give literal snapshots of people in homes made of stone, wood, mud, or straw. This eye-opening display of people from numerous countries invites discussions that compare and contrast homes as well as the lifestyles of others. *Bread, Bread,*

Bread, by the same writer and photographer team, unites the world through this common food. Simple text punctuates the pictures of people in different countries eating and sharing their bread of choice, be it pitas, tortillas, bagels, or baguettes. One of my favorites in this series is *Loving*, because a majority of the photographs are taken within the United States, clearly displaying the wide diversity that exists in this country. I have no doubt that you will be moved by this unique book, which highlights the close relationship between parent and child. Each of these titles includes an index with a miniature of the photograph, identification of the location in which it was taken, and a brief description. Several nonfiction books by Morris also have a map labeling the different places shown in the book. Consider these and many other books in the series to show your child the diversity and the beauty that connects all of us on this planet.

Connecting Us Through Religions and Values

Some books discuss the differences and similarities of religions from around the world. Do unto others as you would have them do unto you: in Ilene Cooper's *The Golden Rule*, a grandfather explains to his grandson the meaning of this simple phrase. He points out its universality and tells how many religions and cultures have their own variations, including Christianity, Judaism, Islam, and the Shawnee Tribe. Grandfather invites the child to imagine how he would like to be treated when he is entering a new situation, and then explains that this is the way to treat others. The boy wonders what kind of world it would be if everyone followed the golden rule and concludes that people would be nicer, kinder, and more loving. Although the rule is simple, it is not always easy to follow. Grandfather provides hope to the boy by explaining that "it begins with you." This thought-provoking book is gorgeously illustrated and serves as a reminder that each of us plays a part in making the world a better place.

Closing the Gender Gap

Books can also assist in dispelling stereotypes regarding gender and can serve as a way to add balance and equity to both sexes. Parents can make a conscious effort to select books that deviate from the traditional roles assigned to boys and girls or that provide room for discussion about the acceptance of individual choices. The heroine in Robert N. Munsch's *The Paper Bag Princess* is a feisty, intelligent, and courageous princess who is anything *but* a damsel-in-distress. Elizabeth is a beautiful princess with beautiful clothes and is planning to marry Prince Ronald. Quite unexpectedly, a ferocious dragon burns down her castle and everything in it, taking Ronald captive. Donning the only thing she can find left after the fire, a paper bag (of course, one can only laugh when thinking that a paper bag is the only thing that survived a huge fire), she sets out to rescue the prince. Elizabeth outwits the dragon and opens the door to his cave, only to have Ronald declare her a mess and reject her. She counters that he may look like a prince but does not have good manners. Needless to say, they do *not* get married and live happily ever after.

Parents can use *The Paper Bag Princess* as a way to point out the stereotypes associated with men as well. The book clearly shows that the prince is only interested in a woman's looks, implying that he is shallow. This opens up many possible discussion points for parents to begin talking with their children about how all people, regardless of gender, should not be lumped into any one category. Books that challenge the stereotypes of gender roles and behaviors can give pause to our children and help them think for themselves, a valuable skill for everyone.

Starting the Search

I have provided a list of multicultural books beginning on page 262. It is in no way exhaustive, but it will provide you a starting point for the conscious inclusion of books in your read-aloud routine that are centered around diversity. Another place to investigate is Bright Books, a publisher that specifically targets multicultural, bilingual, and foreign language books for children. The books span sixteen different languages. They carry books that "embrace children of all colors, nationalities, and abilities" in an effort to allow all children to see themselves in print.

Please keep in mind the ideas presented in this chapter to help guide you in your selection process. As you read through books, look for those that provide windows and mirrors into cultures. Select only those that speak to the greater human experience of all of us, those with universal themes of love, family, friendship, strength, empowerment, and overcoming hardship. Bring home those that avoid all stereotypes and seek to build understanding and empathy. Our goals should always be to inform our children and ourselves, open a door to discussion, celebrate our differences, affirm our similarities, and bring us together as one race, the human race. Peace to you!

CHAPTER 11

Pique a Passion for Poetry

Keep a Poem in Your Pocket
Keep a poem in your pocket
and a picture in your head
and you'll never feel lonely
at night when you're in bed.
The little poem will sing to you
the little picture bring to you
a dozen dreams to dance to you
at night when you're in bed.
So—
Keep a picture in your pocket
and a poem in your head
and you'll never feel lonely
at night when you're in bed.
— BEATRICE SCHENK DE REGNIERS

When parents include poetry in the read-aloud experience, they give preschoolers something special to hide deep in their pocket and take out whenever they need a little pick-me-up. They provide them a unique way to visualize the world. Poetry affords our children an infectious beat that can be accessed whenever and wherever they choose. Because of the pulse and rhythm of great poems, children quickly memorize portions of them and then sing them to themselves. The power of poetry is far-reaching. So give your child a poem to keep in his pocket or to share with a friend.

Most children are introduced to poetry and verse through Mother Goose. They begin to delight in the silliness of the English language as they meet eccentric and fanciful characters. But poems of all types offer us much more than fun rhymes that twist and tickle the tongue. Reading poetry aloud to our preschoolers can advance their emergent literacy. The rhyming and repetition inherent in many poems teaches and reinforces phonemic awareness, a key skill to future reading, writing, and spelling success. Poetry helps children bridge into independent reading as they "pretend" to read their favorite verses on their own. It is through this practice that preschoolers gain confidence in reading and even begin to identify letters, words, and punctuation marks.

Poetry is such a special form of writing, different from any other. Using a few carefully chosen words and placing them strategically on a page, a poet can tell an entire story. The poem can make us laugh, think about something in a new way, or move us to tears. The allure of poetry lies in its ability to share beauty, wonder, emotion, and the heart of all that is human.

Children are naturally drawn to the melodic rhythm in poetry and nursery rhymes. Since poetry is written for the purpose of being read aloud, it is no surprise that preschool children love to listen to its lyrical sounds as they roll off a parent's tongue and seem to dance in midair. These sounds make clear the message of the poet and permeate the listener. Some purr quietly, creating a calm and reassuring feeling, as in this excerpt from a Mother Goose rhyme:

Come hither, sweet robin
And be not afraid,
I would not hurt even a feather
Come hither, sweet robin
And pick up some bread
To feed you this very cold weather.

Other poems seem to pop off the page in excitement. Still others rumble, twinkle, splash, or bang, creating a mood of drama, suspense, playfulness, or serenity. Poems can drape us and warm us. They have the power to comfort or frighten us. Poetry is unlike any form of writing because of its ability to evoke strong emotion with just a few words.

Children delight in how poets play with language, both in words and in careful pauses and timing, creating an emotional impact of humor or a more serious feeling that stays with the listener. Poetry makes children giggle. It makes them nod in agreement, question how another saw it, or see a new perspective of something old. They love to chant it and hear it over and over again. Preschoolers are drawn into the rhythm, rhyme, and clever use of words that can create a story unlike any they hear in narrative or expository texts. Nothing need make sense in poetry. There are seemingly no hard and fast rules. Grammar, punctuation, and parts of speech take on new forms and are used in innovative and exciting ways. All of these aspects of poetry appeal to the imaginative world of a young child.

Adults, on the other hand, can sometimes be intimidated by poetry. Many equate it with an abstract form of language or a puzzle that must first be broken apart, mixed up, carefully deciphered, and then put back together in an exacting manner. Some have memories of feeling left out in school, being unable to grasp the poet's deep message. Most of us have been forced to memorize lengthy poems and then been tested on this skill. We have inspected too closely the syllables and meter. Laboring over the same poem for days or even weeks has driven us to associate poetry with boredom and frustration. I ask parents who fall into this category to abandon their previous notions of poetry and look at it from a fresh perspective. In doing so, you will open up a whole new world of literature for both you and your children.

Poetry needn't be dull, lifeless, and anemic. Read poetry for the sheer pleasure of it. Instead of trying to "figure it out," read it because it sounds pretty or silly or fun. Experience the poem as it was meant to be heard. Languor over the language, savoring the alliteration, metaphors, and imagery. Or, when the poem invites you to, move, tap, shake, and dance the words in front of your child. They will no doubt do the same with great enthusiasm. Repeat the lines with emphasis. Laugh out loud and then read it again, but forget about analyzing it. Each time you read it, you and your child will deepen the experience with it, and that is analysis enough. Give poetry a second chance.

Picking Perfect Poetry to Share

I like to purchase books that have great collections of poetry. In Caroline Kennedy's anthology of poetry for children, *A Family of Poems*, for example, the selections range from silly poems to more serious ones. The table of contents is separated into seven categories, including About Me, That's So Silly, Adventure, and Bedtime. All of these focus on topics that children love. A sampling of the poets from this collection are Emily Dickinson, Robert Frost, William Blake, Carl Sandburg, Langston Hughes, and e. e. cummings. Poetry books that combine the traditional with the silly give parents and children something that can be read over time. *A Family of Poems* is a special treasure because of the gorgeous paintings by Jon Muth that accompany the poems. They center around the child and are expressive, playful, dynamic, soft, sweet, comforting, and thought-provoking, a perfect extension to the poems themselves. The illustrations add beauty to the text, helping children associate this genre of writing with something magnificent.

We can grow into great poetry collections. Some of the poems may become our "old favorites" and others are there to be read when the mood strikes us or when something new occurs that invites us to read something different. The benefits of well-selected collections of poetry are that they provide parents an easy way to introduce some of the more classic poems to our children. We can read a poem that makes our child laugh and then one that evokes a different emotional response. Poems are usually so brief that we can easily fit in several during one read-aloud session, or periodically add a poem before or after a great fiction or nonfiction text. In this way, our children are able to hear, compare, and contrast many different genres of writing. They see how authors use different formats depending upon the message they are trying to relate to the audience.

When selecting the best poetry to share with your loved ones, look for poems that resonate with the experiences of young children and all that makes up their world. The poems should be focused on the themes and issues important to them like fun and play, sweets and treats, animals, and adventures to secret places. The experiences of children are those that include baby brothers and sisters, the world seeming unfair, and wanting desperately to be all grown up. As with all writing, choose poems that use exceptional language and include sensory images and literary elements to create a unique visual for the listener.

Appropriate Content to Preschoolers' Experiences

A closer look at poetry reveals collections and anthologies especially catered to the interests of young children. Subjects include animals, friends, fun, play, brothers, sisters, mommies, daddies, and childhood experiences. Children enjoy poems like *Junk* by Eve Merriam. All the broken household items get thrown out with a clank and a clunk, but it is the twist at the end that will have listeners giggling as the author captures the fleeting secret fantasy of many children. If there is nothing left to throw out, perhaps they could give away the child's "little baby brother."

Young children still think the whole world revolves around them (It doesn't?) so they love to hear poems that capture all that is childlike. I look for poems that tell about their playful adventures, both real and imaginary. Children love make-believe and going on wild—but perfectly safe—trips to enchanted forests and islands and faraway lands where they get to be in charge and they decide all the rules. Nearly every child likes to laugh, so I am always searching for great poetry that tickles the funny bone. Poems like "Come Out to Play" encourage breaking all the rules and focus on having fun, just what childhood should be.

> Girls and boys, come out to play,
> The moon doth shine as bright as day;
> Leave your supper, and leave your sleep,
> And come with your playfellows into the street.
> Come with a whoop, come with a call,
> Come with a good will or not at all.

Up the ladder and down the wall,
A half-penny roll will serve us all.
You find milk, and I'll find flour,
 And we'll have a pudding in half an hour.

—MOTHER GOOSE

Fresh Approach to the Ordinary

Children love looking at their world in a different way. It is for this reason that they fantasize about befriending animals that talk, love to hear about grownups making mistakes, and think all kinds of messes are fun. There are many poems that highlight the ordinary. A ride in the car, a trip to the grocery store, or having absolutely nothing to do on a rainy day take on a new personality when they are presented in poetic form. Consider the sweet poem "Cat Kisses" by Bobbi Katz. She has beautifully captured the charm of cat behavior for kitty lovers everywhere. You can't help but smile, for the scenario presented will resonate with anyone who has ever made a feline friend.

Sandpaper kisses
on a cheek or a chin—
that is the way
for a day to begin!
Sandpaper kisses—
a cuddle, a purr.
I have an alarm clock
that's covered with fur.

Luscious Language

Great poetry appeals to our senses. We can almost hear, touch, taste, and smell what the author is describing. Poets select words carefully and use precision to place them on the page. These words invite us to enter the poem, leaving our current world behind. We can *hear* the seagulls calling from afar. We *feel* the warm sand as it crunches beneath our feet and wriggles between our toes. We *smell* the salt in the air as the breeze blows against our face, spreading our hair wildly over our eyes. We *hear* the rhythmic crashing of the waves, bearing down hard and then quickly retreating. The ocean beckons us. We are there. Our experience is real. The best poets help us escape to another place through the strong use of sensory images. They capture the mood and tone of the event by surrounding the reader with clear sights, sounds, and smells.

The best poets incorporate metaphors, similes, and powerful personification into their writing to create unique images that resonate with the listener. Similes and metaphors provide the reader a comparison of two entirely different things, and personification gives humanlike qualities to inanimate objects. These comparisons offer a different approach to the ordinary and help us more clearly envision what the author is describing. Poets can use words inventively by capitalizing on the strength of these and other literary elements. By stating, "The thunder loudly clapped her angry hands, threatening the swift approach," the author helps the reader envision a terrible storm without simply stating this. The storm has human parts (hands) and human feelings (anger). Its hands clap loudly, helping the reader associate the thunder with an angry person. When I read this line, I envision an ominous sky, and because of the anger I feel afraid. The author has creatively personified the storm so that we may access our own vision of storms and associate an emotion, fear, with it. Consider some of the comparisons below and how different the poems would be if the author had simply told us, instead of a using a powerful literary element to "show us" something.

Metaphor (an implied comparison)

> Her eyes were sapphires, sparkling from across the room.
> The toddler was a clown, falling on purpose to make us smile.

Simile (an explicit comparison of two dissimilar things using like or as)

> Her cheeks were as pale as the faded roses she held.
> The sea seemed as still and lifeless as the sand on which it broke.

Personification (inanimate objects possess humanlike qualities)

> Gusts of wind stoked the fire.
> Snow swirled and danced against the leaded glass, beckoning
> to come in.

Plunging into Poetry: Beginning the Search

I suggest that parents first introduce children to poetry through nursery rhymes. But do not stop there. Add to a child's listening repertoire by periodically including some of the more serious, thoughtful, and classic poems by other well-known poets. I believe that whatever poem we read to our child, it should appeal to them in some way. We do not want to repeat the pattern, experienced by so many of us, of listening to poetry that felt outside our realm of comprehension, that was too heady, or boring, or monotonous, or tiring. However, do not judge a poem by the skewed impressions that some have of classic poets. Just because a poem is written by a famous poet does not mean that it will be beyond the reach of our child. Many great poets beautifully capture the essence of childhood in their writing and therefore connect with our little ones. "The Swing," by Robert Louis Stevenson, appeals to a child because it explores the joy of flying high, being free, having fun, and seeing beyond what is right in front of us. Other poets write about silly topics, making listeners from every age group laugh out loud. One of Heather's favorites is "The People Upstairs" by Ogden Nash. Heather has nearly memorized every line, recounting all the ridiculously bothersome things the people upstairs do to their neighbors below. Their living room doubles as a bowling alley. Every time they take a shower it causes the narrator's ceiling to leak, and the people upstairs even go to the bathroom on roller skates. Needless to say, the narrator would rather that the people upstairs live below him. Even though we do not live downstairs from anyone, the author has portrayed this annoying experience in such an exaggerated way that Heather can easily find humor in it. Another one of our favorites by Ogden Nash is "The Octopus," a very short and funny poem that almost serves as a tongue twister. Poems like these help our children hear how authors can play with sounds and manipulate language in a way that makes us smile.

Consider picking up poetry books from the library or the bookstore that reflect a certain theme or holiday. When we read poems about the seasons or something that is taking place in our child's life, we help celebrate this event. We spotlight it and make it more meaningful to him.

Parents may question where to begin the process of selecting perfect poetry to read to our young ones. A great starting point is the National Council of Teachers of English (NCTE) who, every three years, give an award to a poet whose poetry has contributed significantly to the lives of children. Table 3 lists the recipients since its inception in 1977. (For the first six years, the award was given annually.) This can serve as a starting point for parents. You may choose to seek collections from these poets or look for some of their poetry in themed books. The best place to begin is by simply considering what you and your child like to do. Poems about picnics, soccer, dance, and riding bikes give children a different spin on these ordinary events. Children love to hear poems that reflect what matters most to them.

Table 3. NCTE Excellence in Poetry for Children Award Winners

1977 - David McCord	1988 - Arnold Adoff
1978 - Aileen Fisher	1991 - Valerie Worth
1979 - Karla Kuskin	1994 - Barbara Juster Esbens
1980 - Myra Cohn Livingston	1997 - Eloise Greenfield
1981 - Eve Merriam	2000 - X. J. Kennedy
1982 - John Ciardi	2003 - Mary Ann Hoberman
1985 - Lillian Moore	2006 - Nikki Grimes

In the poetry booklist beginning on page 278 you will find titles that appeal to young children. Perhaps many of them will resonate with your own child as well and will reflect the big world around her that beckons to be explored. I hope that poetry will find a place in your read-aloud routine and a place in your child's heart.

How to Read Poetry Aloud

Because poetry often is not written to conform to the traditional placement of words on a page, it should be read in a unique way. In order to appreciate the subtleties of poetry, parents need to make a special effort to read poetry differently from how we read other genres of writing. The rhythm and beat should guide your pacing. Many adults tend to pause at the end of the line whether the poet has punctuated it or not. This can make all poems have the singsong quality of nursery rhymes. In order to read the poem correctly, pay close attention to the punctuation provided by the author. Pause or briefly stop only when it is indicated that you do so, as with a comma or period in any form of writing. Be conscious of using a natural voice that doesn't overemphasize certain words. Instead, let the words themselves and careful pacing—as indicated by the author—establish the mood, theme, or impact. If it is read correctly, the poem will no doubt evoke an emotional response that is authentic and deep. Otherwise, a forced reading can leave the listener feeling confused or uninvolved. The reader must stay true to the message of the poem by relying on all manner of clues presented to her by the author. So read a poem to your child. Read it with enthusiasm and delight and wonder and surprise. Help your child bury it deep in her pocket so she will never be lonely again.

CHAPTER 12

Capture Their Attention with Concept Books

One, two, Buckle my shoe.
Three, four, Knock at the door.
Five, six, Pick up sticks.
Seven, eight, Lay them straight.
Nine, ten, A good fat hen.

—TRADITIONAL NURSERY RHYME

Concept books help teach and reinforce key concepts to our emergent readers through repeated examples of a particular element. Common concepts presented in such books include:

- Letters of the alphabet
- Counting numbers (usually 1 through 10)
- Colors
- Shapes
- Opposites (up/down, hot/cold, in/out)

Since books serve as invitations into learning about the world, concept books offer a natural and enjoyable way to help our children learn key literacy and life skills. They help teach and reinforce high frequency terms which are considered part of academic language. Colors, numbers, different shapes, and words denoting opposites are used throughout our daily lives and are essential building blocks for future learning. These concepts will be heavily stressed in formal education. Teachers may ask a child to sit on a certain color square on the rug. They may assign children to groups based on shapes. "You are in the red triangle group today." They will frequently provide instructions that require understanding of direction words and opposites. "Place your backpack *below* your desk. Come to the *front* of the room. Leave your sweaters at the *back* of the classroom. Recess has *ended,* and it is time for everyone to come *inside*." Children entering school are expected to have a working knowledge of many essential concepts that books can teach in a unique and inviting way.

By reinforcing the letters and their respective sounds, many alphabet books, for example, help prepare our children for reading and writing. Without a working knowledge of the alphabet, children cannot embark on independent literacy learning. Numbers, also, are used universally for so many aspects of our lives (page numbers in books, quantities of ingredients for recipes, prices of toys and food, number of cookies we are allowed after dinner). It is imperative that our children understand numbers and learn to count. Wonderful counting books provide access to this skill with brightly colored illustrations, rhyming schemes, or clever stories about numbers.

Learning to classify things is a higher-order skill that must be acquired by our children to assist them with day-to-day activities and help reinforce the idea that the brain is a pattern-seeking device. Children need to understand and be able to categorize by attributes. We sort utensils by their various functions and shapes. All sweaters are placed in a certain drawer for easy access on a cold day. We ask our children to put the trucks in a certain box or building blocks in a particular area of the play room. Sorting or categorizing is a foundational skill to many other aspects of learning throughout our lives.

The ability to categorize helps reduce the complexity of our environment. Our brain looks for ways to place new learning into groupings. Without this skill, learning can be extremely overwhelming. If we have not acquired the ability to sort and organize by attributes, each new item needs to be learned separately. If a child is given a box of buttons and asked to sort them into groups, he may decide to put all the red buttons into one pile, the green buttons into another pile, and the blue buttons into a third pile. Children (and all learners) need to be able to look at the large pile of buttons and see that all the red ones have something in common and therefore "belong" together.

In chapter 2, "Build Background Knowledge," I discussed the idea that the brain is like a file cabinet. We have many different files that help bring order and sense to our world. The more items we can put in one file, the better the brain is at organizing information. When a child sees a red button, the brain says (figuratively speaking), "I have a whole file of red items. I also have a sub-file, as it were, of red *buttons*." This new information already has a special place in this file and it can be grouped there. Contrast this with a child who does not have the ability to sort and quickly recognize things based on color, shape, or size. Each new item he encounters requires a separate folder. The amount of folders in the brain becomes overwhelming because a new folder must be created for each and every new learning. The brain says, "Oh, that is a red button, and that is another red button, and that is still another separate red button." The brain has not "learned" to quickly identify all the red buttons as being part of one category.

A more sophisticated learner has such a strong sense of concepts and sorting by attributes that he can find more than one file folder into which an item will fit. For example, buttons may be sorted by color, but they may also be sorted by size, shape, or the number of holes in them. When a learner is able to look at a group and see alternative ways to categorize them, he is assisting the brain in learning. How? The brain now has more than one way to group the items and therefore has more than one attribute file folder. Higher-level thinking and learning involves being able to look at something from many different aspects. Any new buttons that a child encounters can be placed in all three folders—the general button folder, the color folder, and the number of holes folder. Thus, the child adds information to each of these separate folders, making them thicker with knowledge. Later, when the child sees a yellow button with four holes, the brain will say, "I already have many examples in my button folder of what constitutes a button. I will check this new item against the others in my file of information. Yes, this yellow button fits in that folder. I also have numerous examples in my four-button-hole folder to help me decide if the button fits this category. After comparing it with the examples in my existing folder, I can see very clearly that it does, indeed, fit in this folder as well. Now I have even more examples from which to draw upon in the future."

Application to the Classroom and the World

The knowledge of colors, numbers, shapes, opposites, and other specific concepts is used every day to differentiate, define, direct, and clarify. It is essential that our children have a strong working knowledge of these concepts. Teachers give countless directions that require children to use these skills. "Put your name on the *left*hand side of the paper. Raise your *right* hand. Everyone needs a *red* pencil for making corrections. The *first* row may leave. If your last name begins with *A* through *F* you are to line up here. Let's get together and form a large *circle*. Turn to page *seven* in your books. Lunches are stored *beneath* your desks. Draw an *oval* for the face of your self-portrait. Turn *off* the light before you leave the classroom."

The ability to categorize can help with reading, spelling, and writing as well. If our brain is used to identifying patterns, we can transfer this knowledge to other aspects of learning. We can begin to see patterns in words. All words containing a particular vowel-consonant-vowel pattern, such as *-ote*, can be placed in a file folder for this category. Then every time we see another word with these same letters (for example, *quote, vote, denote*), our brain quickly accesses this folder and is able to see if it follows the same general rule. If it does, it becomes part of that same folder and is therefore easier to read, write, and apply to future words. When we understand the concept of numbers, we can begin to categorize them by multiples of two or five, a helpful skill for other areas of math. As we organize learning into categories, we see science and history terms in groups that make sense. All learning becomes more clear, manageable, and meaningful.

These key skills are foundational for life beyond the classroom as well. Teachers stress concepts in school so that children may have an understanding of them for future learning and independent life as an adult. When we think about all the times throughout the day that adults rely on concepts to communicate and function within our society, it brings home the importance of these skills. In order to follow directions from a map or even a GPS system, we must know the difference between left and right. The importance of knowing top from bottom becomes quite evident when we are opening a delivery box with fine crystal in it. Colors are used to distinguish choices and label things. The knowledge of shapes is used in many professions, including architects, contractors, seamstresses, and engineers. An understanding of numbers assists us with telling time, money management, reading the speed limit, and calling our friend on the phone.

Count on Books to Teach Concepts

It is for all these reasons that we want our children to be able to identify colors, shapes, numbers, and the concept of opposites. In addition to talking to our children about each of these and providing hands-on experiences to teach them, parents can turn to books as a way to help children understand and memorize various concepts. Many of us spend time naming the colors of the crayons as we draw with our child, or point out the shapes of tires, stop signs, or the door to a bedroom. These are all valuable strategies for teaching concepts. However, books can serve as a more comprehensive, rather than random way to bring concepts into our child's life. The value of books is far-reaching. Concept books provide a tangible way for children to see numerous examples of a given concept presented in one venue. Children see all the shapes or colors or numbers 1 through 10 and are able to compare and contrast them, reinforcing the concept. Books serve as a detailed overview of a given concept, making them the perfect learning tool.

Support Sound and Letter Recognition

Reading aloud can help children learn the letters of the alphabet and their corresponding sounds, which are key components of future reading and writing success. Researchers have suggested that careful selection of alphabet books can help acquaint children with printed letters and their sounds. Specifically to introduce the concept of the alphabet and then reinforce it, I choose books that are not too cluttered with pictures, words, or information. I want the connection between the letter and the object associated with it to be very obvious.

When selecting alphabet books for the purpose of teaching and reinforcing sound and letter development, parents should focus on those that have simple representations of the upper- and lowercase letters and have a clearly identifiable object connected with each letter. If the letters are drawn too artistically, children may have difficulty recognizing them in other texts. The illustrations and words that accompany each letter should be familiar to a preschooler and not too abstract. Children should be able to readily identify an *alligator, apple*, or *ant* for letter *A*. I like alphabet books that are beautifully illustrated with bold colors that grab and hold a child's attention. They should be inviting and perhaps even involve humor to keep the child engaged. If the book includes words, be sure they are not too complicated.

Dar Hosta's *I Love the Alphabet* is a beautiful book that reinforces letters and sounds but also serves as an excellent example of alliterative, playful, and exceptional language. Each upper- and lowercase letter is prominently displayed in bright color and is accompanied by a clever rhyme. The inviting cut paper collages that show a multitude of animals romping through the alphabet are full of life and simply gorgeous. A delightful little ladybug is strategically placed on every page spread. Can you find it? *I Love the Alphabet* is a wonderful resource to teach the letters to preschoolers and will certainly beckon them back time and again.

My husband Mike and I also read aloud stories whose main characters are the letters themselves. Bill Martin Jr. and John Archambault's *Chicka Chicka Boom Boom* follows the lowercase alphabet as they race each other up a coconut tree. The reader watches as Lois Ehlert's wonderfully illustrated coconut tree tilts over with the added weight of each of the letters. *Oh, no!* There's a big crash as all the letters fall to the ground. Luckily, the uppercase "mamas and papas" are there to help mend the letters after their big fall. Not only does this book clearly label and illustrate each of the lowercase letters, it offers a lively rhyming text that holds the attention of preschoolers and their parents too. Children see that the alphabet is comprised of useful and fun letters.

The Alphabet Tree, by Leo Lionni, is a favorite book of mine because a story format is used to introduce the idea of letters coming together to make meaning. The reader is reminded that language is complex and multi-layered. It is a great way to show children that words are formed by combining letters together, and how words can be carefully placed in a certain order to create sentences. In this parable, the letters are tossed and torn in a windstorm, only to realize that they gain strength by banding together, strategically forming words and sentences. In the end, the letters and words recognize their united power and decide to create a "really important" message about peace.

Knowing the Numbers

I like to introduce the concept of numbers with nursery rhymes like "One, Two, Buckle My Shoe," cited at the beginning of this chapter. The catchy rhythm makes them enjoyable to listen to and easy to memorize. Since so many parents begin reading Mother Goose to their children from birth, these sing-song verses are a natural springboard into more specific texts that highlight numbers and counting. Familiar and lesser-known Mother Goose rhymes involving numbers are showcased in *Mother Goose Numbers on the Loose* by Leo and Diane Dillon. Vibrant illustrations extend the playful tone and mischievous action of the numbers as they dance, skip, laugh, and even hide, through the rhymes.

Quality books about numbers and counting should have beautiful illustrations that clearly label the quantity of a certain object on a page or provide several examples of the respective number for children to count with a parent or on their own. In *The Baker's Dozen: A Counting Book*, author-illustrator Dan Andreason distinctly shows a direct correlation between the number presented and the number of yummy desserts displayed. A short rhyming verse accompanies each, adding to the playful tempo of the book. The round and cheery baker begins early in the morning to meticulously make one éclair. He bakes through the numbers, finally whipping up twelve yummy cupcakes, just in time to open the door and welcome thirteen (a baker's dozen) eager customers. Retro-style oil paintings add to the robust feel of the book and surely will make all children hungry for a tasty treat. (Don't worry. It's okay to have just one.)

Share Books about Shapes

Shapes can be taught and reinforced through books that cover this concept in creative and informative ways. In *Brown Rabbit's Shape Book*, Alan Baker cleverly integrates learning into a short, simple story. A soft little brown rabbit that is "rabbit-shaped" opens a square gift box and discovers five balloons inside. The helium-filled toys delight him when they form various shapes, including rectangle, oval, circle, square, and more. The illustrations are bright and inviting and will keep children turning the pages to guess what shape comes next.

Attract Children to Books About Opposites

Up and down, short and tall, right and left, as well as many other pairs of opposites can be reinforced through quality picture books that focus on this concept. Parents can begin the selection process with Tana Hoban's *Exactly the Opposite*. Using a striking collection of photographs of people, animals, and objects, opposites are showcased in this wordless book. The book is especially unique because each of the picture pairs cleverly invites open-ended discussion among viewers. Looking at the cover, for example, one may see shoes that are tied and untied, but they are also neat and messy, new and old, big and little. This is a wonderful concept book that will entertain both child and parent.

Capitalize on Great Books About Colors

Three white mice head out on a colorful romp in Ellen Stoll Walsh's *Mouse Paint*. They begin atop a white sheet of paper that cleverly camouflages them from the local feline. Once they discover three jars of paint—one red, one yellow, one blue—the adventure begins. Dipping toes and tails into more than one jar creates exciting new color combinations. Cut paper collage illustrations add to the whimsy of this book, which serves as a great reinforcement of colors.

Using rhyming couplets that center around different colors, we are provided a peek into the Chinese-American culture in *Red is a Dragon*, by Roseanne Thong. Deep and rich illustrations are reflective of the intricate patterns in Chinese paintings and fabrics. We see red dragons, melons, and lychees, orange crabs, yellow incense sticks and taxis, pink peonies, and white dumplings. The book has a rhythmic beat and is a visual delight. It ends with an invitation to notice all the colors that surround us.

Books Are Beautiful Ways to Teach Concepts

I hope that you can clearly see the value of selecting wonderful books that can teach and reinforce various concepts. Refer to page 257 for a list of these types of books to read to your child. The book you bring home should provide numerous examples of a given concept and each should be easily recognizable and understood by your child. Additionally, as with any other book you choose to read to your child, select ones that are inviting, colorful, and fun. Pictures of objects they know and can relate to will entice them to look closely and learn. Complement their knowledge from books with outside resources and information, such as tangible objects to see and hold as well as frequent interactions with you and others. The totality of these experiences will help to build a strong foundation of learning in your preschooler.

CHAPTER 13

Challenge Them with Chapter Books

When I get a little money I buy books, and if any is left
I buy food and clothes.

—DESIDERIUS ERASMUS

Some young children are developmentally ready to listen to chapter books in addition to picture books. These offer a variety of benefits to our preschoolers. Since many chapter books are written for a slightly older audience, they may contain more complex vocabulary and sentence structure. This can help extend our child's word choice for both verbal and written communication, as well as develop background knowledge on many new words. Chapter books, by design, are usually much longer than picture books, so the author has the added benefit of being able to more thoroughly develop the main characters as well as supporting characters and extend the plot to include sub-plots and many interesting side events and issues. When parents read aloud these stories to their children, they are giving them more fuel to envision the characters and the main events in the story. They see more ways to approach stories and come in contact with a greater variety of writing styles.

Chapter books can help extend the attention span of children because they are required to carry over information from one read-aloud session to another. Since the story is not all neatly tied up within one sitting, children must remember facts about characters, setting, and plot from previous readings. They need to make connections to prior experiences with the book and weave these together to form a cohesive story.

Selecting the Right Chapter Books for Your Child

There are many different types of chapter books available to read aloud to our young children. I think it is important to distinguish great read-alouds from those that are more appropriate for independent reading. Some chapter books are specifically intended to assist emergent readers in their early attempts at reading on their own. Although these may be great candidates for this specific purpose, they may not be the best books to read aloud to our child. If a child is ready to attempt reading on their own, look for books that are specifically written for this purpose and support this process. Books for emergent readers often make use of repetitive sight words and controlled vocabulary, helping our children see and recognize these elements with automaticity. This helps them become fluent readers. See chapter 23, "Building Bridges to Independent Reading," for more information on appropriate book choices for children emerging into reading.

The chapter books we select to read aloud to our children should include all the same criteria that we use for any book with this intended purpose. They should have an interesting, informative, and creative storyline. A wide range of exceptional vocabulary should be included and used naturally within the context of the story. Authentic and interesting language and dialogue should add to the text, bringing more depth of character development. Humor, a plot twist, or some other element of surprise may be included to make the story even more interesting to the listener.

Lois Lowry's *Gooney Bird Greene* is a wonderful example of a chapter book appropriate for reading aloud to our children. The main character in this story arrives at her second-grade classroom in pajamas and a pair of cowboy boots. She requests a seat smack in the middle of the room. The eccentric new student mesmerizes the class with her fantastic stories that she insists are "absolutely true." These stories include a flying carpet, driving from China to her new home, receiving diamond earrings from a prince in a palace, and directing a symphony orchestra. Through creative wordplay, the classmates and teacher find out that the stories really are true. Gooney does a wonderful job at spinning a fantastic tale, while helping the class understand the key features of any good story. A delightful tale in its own right, this book also gives sound advice for all aspiring writers. Through firsthand modeling from Gooney Bird, we learn that stories should start with a clever title that captures the listener's attention, and they should have a clear beginning, middle, and end. The main character should be interesting and should be right smack in the middle of everything. The word *suddenly* creates suspense and should be strategically placed into good storytelling (and writing). Gooney Bird takes the class with her on numerous adventures through her captivating stories.

This book helps parents introduce young children to longer, more complex texts. Because of the silliness of the stories within, children will eagerly listen to find out what Gooney Bird will tell about next. The book's reading level is middle second grade, so it should be within the range of many children's listening comprehension level. The chapters are short enough that each one (or more, depending on your child's attention span) can be covered in a single read-aloud session. Delightful illustrations are sprinkled throughout the text to support interest and understanding of what is taking place. Lowry uses descriptive passages (another tool for good storytelling) to bring depth to the characters in the story so that listeners will remember them and relate to them. Comprehension of the text is also supported through the use of different-sized typefaces for the action taking place in the classroom and the stories that Gooney Bird tells. A parent can further help distinguish the two different events by changing his or her voice when the typeface changes or overtly pointing out when Gooney is telling one of her tales. This short but thoroughly entertaining book provides children an opportunity to increase their attention span and conquer an authentic chapter book.

Another choice for a longer book is *Socks* (1973), by Beverly Cleary. This humorous story is written from a cat's point of view. Socks is loved and pampered by his owners until a new baby joins the family and then he gets into all sorts of trouble. As the baby grows up, Socks becomes friends with him and finds a new place in the family. This book is a good fit for children bridging into chapter books. The reading level is about third grade, so it is within the listening comprehension level of many younger children. The typeface is large enough to follow if a listener desires to do so and the chapters are the perfect length for completing one per session. The book contains humor that will appeal to many children who may have a sibling with whom they are competing. Illustrations help transition preschoolers from the picture books they are accustomed to and add to the silliness of the story. *Socks* may just be the perfect chapter book to begin your new literature adventure.

There are numerous other potential choices to read aloud to your child. Consider *Charlotte's Web* and *Mr. Popper's Penguins*. Some younger children greatly enjoy *Stuart Little* or *The Cricket in Times Square*. However, other preschoolers may find all of these too lengthy or have difficulty comprehending the more sophisticated vocabulary and detailed plots. As with any book we read aloud to our child, be sure he is enjoying it. We always want this time to be special, inviting, and pleasurable. Read these or other chapter books only if everyone is having a wonderful time and loving every luscious word.

Popcorn, a Movie, and a Good Book

So many great books have been made into movies, and viewing these can serve as a way to extend the wonderful experience of the book or see how someone else interpreted the characters and storyline, comparing their view and our view. I always recommend that classroom teachers either read the book aloud first or have students read it on their own prior to viewing the film version. In this way, students are not swayed by someone else's perspective of the events as they hear the story. Teachers who have their class experience the book first can help students learn their own comprehension strategies, create visuals for the reading, and predict based solely on what they have already read and their own prior knowledge. These are all important strategies that can be applied to other reading as well. However, if they have seen the movie, the visuals have already been established for them and there is no need to attempt predictions because all the information has previously been provided. I am sure that many of us have had the common experience of reading a book and then seeing the movie, only to be disappointed that the film version neglected many intricacies. For students in the classroom, the ideal situation is to read the book first, form their own viewpoints, and then see how someone else has done the same.

Younger children who have not yet entered formalized schooling, on the other hand, can sometimes greatly benefit from seeing the movie first and then following it up with hearing the book read aloud to them. The movie can serve as a motivator to hearing the words presented in print form. Without this, some children become overwhelmed at the prospect of hearing a chapter book. They fear it will be too long and complicated, and, of course, boring. However, if viewing the movie is a pleasant experience, tackling the book may seem less daunting. Another powerful reason to show the movie version first to our preschoolers is because they may need the visual scaffolding to help them comprehend the text. Since children at this stage of development may have just begun to learn the strategy of visualizing from text, previously seeing the film version may provide this for them. I suggest that parents take into account the child's current attention span and his or her cognitive ability to understand and visualize stories as they are read aloud. In this way, you can determine better if seeing the movie first will help or hinder your child's comprehension of the text.

Heather had seen various segments of the original movie *Willy Wonka and the Chocolate Factory* based on the book by Roald Dahl. She loved the Oompa-Loompas and the personalized silly songs they belted out for each child who misbehaved and left the factory. The fantasy elements of the story and the humor presented were strong motivators to hearing the book read aloud. Throughout our nightly readings, we used the movie as a springboard to help us analyze the book. We more closely looked at the details to discover the differences and similarities presented in each version. For example, we noticed right away that the book included Charlie's mother and father, whereas the movie showed only his mother. We also discussed why the producer may have chosen to take out the father in the story. Since Heather liked the songs in the movie so much, she was initially disappointed to find that the book did not contain these same lines. However, once she accepted this fact, she grew to appreciate each of the poetic versions given by the Oompa-Loompas. One scene in the movie had frightened her, but she was pleased to find out there were no such scary parts in the book. We caught differences in the scenes in which Charlie finds the dollar and noted the changes in the ending. Once we had completed the book, we talked about how both the movie and the book had their strengths and what we liked best about them. Although in my very biased opinion (no surprise) the book was much better than the movie, Heather concluded that she enjoyed each in its own right.

Please note that if parents elect to have their child see parts or all of a movie, it is important that they preview the movie first. Also, carefully check the rating of the movie to help you decide if it is appropriate for your child. Unfortunately, we cannot always assume that because a book contains content that we find acceptable, the movie will follow suit. As I have pointed out earlier in this chapter, the film version may portray a different perspective than exactly what the author had intended. Consider, also, that the producer for the movie may have a different audience or goal in mind in creating the movie. If you are not sure, I suggest erring on the side of caution and skipping the movie entirely.

How to Read Aloud a Chapter Book

Since we are expecting our children to increase their attention span by reading chapter books to them, we need to provide support for this process. One way to accomplish this is to summarize the previous events in the story just prior to reading each day. "When we stopped reading yesterday, we had found out that Gooney Bird's cat, named Catman, had been consumed by a cow. Luckily, she finally explained that the cat had been consumed by *love* for the cow, not eaten by the cow. Thank goodness Gooney Bird clarified that important point. Remember we thought that was very funny? She is quite a good story teller. Now she's going to tell *us* how to get our own stories. I can't wait. Let's read and find out."

Many chapter books intended for a younger audience include a few illustrations. However, this artwork is not necessarily used to help support the meaning of the text (as it is with many picture books). The focus of the illustrations is often simply to help motivate the reader and bridge them from picture books into chapter books. I vividly remember the first time one of my elementary school teachers gave our class a book to read that had no illustrations whatsoever. I thumbed through the entire book searching for the artwork, only to feel overwhelmed by the prospect of reading a book without any "fun" in it. Chapter books drizzled with illustrations help children feel more confident as they make the next step into even more complex texts. Parents can support the process of understanding meaning by helping their child create his or her own visuals, or "mental artwork," to accompany the storyline. Periodically throughout a chapter book, we can stop and summarize or specifically discuss what we *see* taking place in the story. If there are some particularly descriptive passages, this is the perfect venue to pause and help your child create a clear picture of the text. When the author purposely uses color words, adjectives, and adverbs to describe something in the book, parents should emphasize this and may even choose to reread the particular passage. Consider, also, sharing your own visuals and making personal connections to the book as a way to model this for your child. "I can picture the green and red checkered tablecloth the author is describing because we used to have a similar cover for our table. It was green and pink. Do you remember it? We used to bring it with us to the park to put on the picnic bench."

Although I always recommend that parents thoroughly preview any book prior to reading it aloud, it is especially important to do this with chapter books. Because chapter books can often be intended for an older audience, they may contain some vocabulary, content, or themes that a parent may consider too mature for their child at this age. I admit to substituting words in the midst of reading aloud when I come across ones that I do not think are the best choices for younger children. A friend of mine is a fourth grade teacher who experienced firsthand the necessity to carefully consider the audience when reading aloud a book. She had read an award-winning chapter book to her students with great success. All the children enjoyed the book and many even purchased their own copies. Since her child, who was in first grade at the time, loved many picture books about the same topic (castles and dragons), she decided to read this book aloud to her. However, after just one evening of reading, she realized that although her daughter was old enough to understand the book, she was not yet mature enough to tackle the content. The little girl was awakened in the middle of the night from a terrible nightmare that she directly attributed to the book. This was a strong reminder to my friend that there are many factors to take into account when previewing a book to be read to a child. Know and understand the child's cognitive level as well as her maturation and developmental level. With these in mind, parents can more confidently select the right book to read to their child.

Celebrate the Completion of a Chapter Book

It is fun for youngsters to specially celebrate the accomplishment of completing a chapter book. I know that when we finished reading *Charlie and the Chocolate Factory*, Heather and I did the most delicious, and obvious, thing we could do. We went to the local market, picked out our favorite candy bars, went home, and ate them all up with some cold milk. Yum! When we had read *Charlotte's Web* in its entirety, we planned a special mother-daughter movie date to see the film version, complete with lots of buttery popcorn. The celebration needn't be something outlandish. Ask your child to help the two of you decide on a special way to commemorate this monumental accomplishment and tie it into the theme, characters, or setting of the book.

Choose Chapter Books When Children Are Ready

Some younger children are not interested in listening to chapter books read aloud. They may not be ready to follow story lines from one day to the next or just may prefer the picture book format. Please do not force your child to sit through read-alouds of chapter books unless he or she is a cooperative and enthusiastic listener. The quality picture books listed throughout this book are certainly beneficial to your child's development and are excellent resources for preliteracy skills. Consider periodically including a longer read-aloud, but only if it is well received. You may refer to the chapter books booklist that begins on page 255 to get you started. However, try not to have expectations that are outside the realm of interest or ability of your child. Let him learn and grow in an inviting and supportive setting with books he loves to hear again and again. Let him lead you to the book choices that are the best for him. Challenge children with chapter books, but only when they are ready.

CHAPTER 14

Invite Children into Informational Text

Frogs and toads and
salamanders
lay eggs,
and when they hatch
they're tadpoles
who grow legs
and climb a lily pad—
just like their mom and dad.
They don't have
claws or
scaly skins.
They are called
amphibians.

When children hear Ruth Heller's *Chickens Aren't the Only Ones*, they quickly learn that hummingbirds, sharks, spiders, snails, and many other animals lay eggs. The author cleverly uses prose and rhyme complemented by beautiful illustrations to discuss oviparous animals and their unique way of laying eggs. What a wonderful way to approach science, expand vocabulary (for example, oviparous, amphibians, extinct, mammals), and invite preschoolers into the world of nonfiction! Not all children develop their love of reading through stories. At just over three years of age, Heather pored over *Emergency!*, a book by Gail Gibbons about the various modes of rescue transportation and the people who keep us safe. She had always been simultaneously afraid of and captivated by emergency vehicles. The sirens startled her, and yet she was caught up in the excitement of where they were headed and how the police, firefighters, and paramedics were going to help someone. The book helped answer many of the questions Heather had regarding these important people in our lives.

Heather also excitedly anticipated her monthly issue of *Your Big Backyard*, a magazine published by the National Wildlife Federation, in which she learned about puffins, seahorses, exotic birds, polar bears, and other incredible animals from around the world. Upon its arrival, she would look through the entire magazine and then decide which pages she wanted us to read to her first. On subsequent readings, we would turn to the table of contents and read through it so that Heather could select what she wanted to hear. Then, we would read a page, a section, or a caption here or there. By doing so, Mike and I were modeling some of the differences between informational (nonfiction) and narrative (fiction) texts. Unlike fiction, many nonfiction texts can include a table of contents to help direct the reader. Not only is the text written in an entirely different format, it is also approached differently by the reader. When we read nonfiction, we do not necessarily read each page in order. Instead, we pick and choose according to our current needs and interests.

Selecting Quality Informational Texts

Parents are encouraged to read aloud informational texts, magazines, and journals that are written especially for preschool-age children. When selecting nonfiction that is appropriate for your child, consider these five qualities:

1. Authenticity—The facts are accurate and complete. Photographs are used to add to the authenticity.
2. Format—The format makes sense and is easy to follow. The amount of text is balanced by the illustrations so that it does not seem overwhelming. Illustrations, photographs, diagrams,

and maps clearly connect to the text to help explain what is being read. Captions are used to clarify the information presented.

3. Objective and Balanced—The information is free of bias. The text provides room for multiple perspectives.

4. Design—The book is visually appealing to the audience. The design invites the reader to look more closely at the text. The layout enhances the reader's ability to understand and use the information.

5. Style—The language in the text is descriptive and lively, capturing the child's attention. Colorful words and humor may be used to make the material less intimidating. There may be a hint of conversational tone to help the reader understand the material more easily.[1]

Children Enjoy Informational Books

As part of their study on the use of nonfiction trade books in the primary grades (kindergarten through third), Rosemary Palmer and Roger Stewart gave thirty-one children each a stack of ten books (six nonfiction and four fiction). When asked to look through their individual piles of books and select two they would like to read, more than half of the books they chose (63 percent) were nonfiction.[2] Preschoolers, too, love nonfiction because it addresses the real world, waiting to be discovered through their eyes. A quest for knowledge about dinosaurs, airplanes, ladybugs, firefighters, or a sports hero can lure a child into reading. As suggested by Roy Doiron, nonfiction texts can be very enjoyable to children who naturally seek facts and are curious about their world.[3] They are captivated by caterpillars, seashells, rocks, trains, and the squawk of an unfamiliar bird. Through reading nonfiction, also known as expository texts, to our children, we fuel their excitement and ignite their natural curiosity by leading them into a whole new world of information and fun.

Preparing Preschoolers for Reading Informational Texts

Expository texts abound in our daily adult lives as we seek answers to questions and quench our thirst for knowledge. As independent readers, we follow step-by-step directions from recipe cards to ensure that our cake is baked perfectly. We read maps and road signs to find out where we are now and where we are going. The newspaper offers us information about the weather, our favorite sports team, and the latest headline news. We scour it to locate who, what, when, where, and sometimes how and why. We read textbooks, sift through journals and magazines, and search the Internet to investigate which school is the best for our child, which breed of dog will be most compatible with our parrot, and what are the latest diet trends. Instruction manuals, tables, graphs, and maps are used daily to inform, direct, and explain. Informational texts of all types assist us with our endeavors.

In order to prepare our children for the world of print, it is imperative that we expose them to informational texts. It is not enough to limit our read-alouds to stories. Although narrative texts have far-reaching benefits to the future literacy of our children, they can also be limited. Parents can support their children's future literacy success by demonstrating the power of both fiction and nonfiction.

Comparing Reading Strategies for Expository Text and Narrative Text

It is important to note that narrative and expository texts are written with different purposes and therefore are read in different ways. Readers utilize strategies unique to the type of text they are attempting. Narrative texts, or stories, tend to focus on specific elements of literature that are quite different from expository texts. Plot, setting, characters, point of view, and theme are noteworthy narrative text structures. Stories are often intended to invoke an emotional response, to echo a universal theme, or to touch the human spirit in some way. We read them sequentially from beginning to end. Strategies that good readers implement during narrative texts include predicting, creating visual images, inferring, and summarizing.

Nonfiction texts are specifically written to instruct or provide information. They rarely use unnecessary words or flowery language. Informational texts are written in specific organizational formats that focus on the general categories of description, sequence, comparison, cause and effect, and problem-solution. A person who is reading an expository text starts with an entirely different premise than someone who is reading narrative. Instead of reading for the beauty of the story, the language, or simply to escape, informational readers seek answers to specific questions or to add to their general knowledge.

Nonfiction texts are organized around specific topics and main ideas and have distinguishing characteristics and features. A table of contents, headings, index, glossary, and appendix, as well as diagrams, tables, graphs, and maps often separate nonfiction from fiction. Important terms are emphasized with bold print, varied fonts, or italics. There is even a unique type of written "language" associated with expository text. Words and phrases such as *in conclusion, for example, if . . . then, in contrast*, and *finally* signal importance to the reader. Generic nouns and timeless verbs separate nonfiction from narrative (that is, "Snakes eat rats," instead of "That snake is eating a rat.") When we read aloud nonfiction, our children become familiar with the language of informational texts and are better prepared for future independent reading in school.

In addition to recognizing specific text structures, the reader uses a unique set of strategies to comprehend nonfiction. Proficient readers of nonfiction often highlight, skim, scan, access the text through the index, and use headings to help narrow down their search for information. They know to focus closely on the photographs and detailed diagrams to promote comprehension. Children are often surprised to see that readers of nonfiction can read the pages out of order and do not necessarily read every word.

The Importance of Including Nonfiction During Read-Aloud Time

Narrative and expository texts are indeed presented and read quite differently, which poses a problem for many children. In fact, some scholars—for example, Chall, Jacobs, Baldwin, and Duke—attribute the so-called fourth-grade slump to the fact that children do not know how to readily transfer the skills associated with reading narrative texts over to those needed for expository texts. Historically, kindergarten through third-grade teachers have placed heavy emphasis on teaching the basic components of the reading process, focusing on narrative. This is logical, since many young children can more easily relate to narratives, which have a clear beginning, middle, and end. The fantasy world of fairy tales and many other types of picture books invite children into reading.

Typically, however, the school curriculum changes abruptly in fourth grade and beyond. No longer are children learning how to read. They are now required to apply their skills in reading to learn a variety of content area material including history, science, and math. Fourth grade marks the *reading to learn* stage. Without explicit exposure and instruction in how expository texts differ from narrative texts, many children feel confused and overwhelmed, and thus begin to fall behind in school. Parents of preschoolers can do their part in helping their children have future school and life literacy success by including factual texts with their other read alouds.

Exploring How Fluent Readers Approach Informational Text

In order to help you better understand the unique strategies associated with expository text, take a moment to reflect on your own reading process for this genre. This will provide you valuable insight into how readers implement strategies specific to informational text. As a fluent reader, you instinctively know how to navigate through text without overt thought.

Consider how you read the newspaper. You probably peruse the front page, looking at the headlines. Your attention is drawn to the large photograph in the center and the accompanying story. You notice the top story of the day, which you decide to read. You do not focus on every word as you might with narrative text. Instead, your brain looks for memorable information, the who, what, when, and where of the story. You then survey the remaining headlines, deciding which sound interesting. One of them may intrigue you or may prompt a question from you. You read the accompanying story to answer your self-generated question. If the story is continued on another section or page in the newspaper, you may locate that page and continue reading, or you may be satisfied with the amount of information you have already gathered and skip the remainder of the story. Next, you may look at the index, which is often located on the first page. You quickly find the section that interests you, be it Calendar, Sports, Comics, or Obituaries. Skipping the others, you locate that section, read through the headlines, and find one that intrigues you, and the process starts all over again. After prioritizing the various sections, those not high on your list get read only if there is enough time. Proficient nonfiction readers use strategies such as survey, glance, skip around, and scan to comprehend and find pertinent information.

Contrast this with reading a novel, where we read every chapter in the book sequentially. We go beyond looking at chapter headings and attend to nearly every word to ensure the comprehension of subtleties within the plot, setting, and characters. Narrative and informational texts are written for entirely different purposes and are therefore read in entirely different ways. In order to afford our children thorough opportunities for literacy success in life, parents need to include both types of texts in their read-alouds. We can support our children's learning by exposing them to informational text and modeling the way nonfiction is read.

Preschoolers' Curiosity Leads to Exploring Expository Text

Questions like "Why do cats have whiskers?" may be easily answered by parents with a few simple words. On the other hand, parents can view such inquiries as opportunities to research and explore nonfiction texts and discover numerous facts about felines. Asking how chocolate is made is an open invitation to find books about candy-making to read to your child. "What do roly-polies eat?" becomes the impetus for an Internet search or a trip to the library. We can read the weather section of the newspaper to reassure our son or daughter that it will not rain on their birthday party. Our child's natural curiosity can be turned into a nonthreatening lesson about what real readers do to gather information. None of us knows all the answers, but lifelong learners know where to find the answers.

Every parent of a preschooler has experienced their child's seemingly endless questions about plants, animals, machines, and the world around them. The following are some of the questions that Heather and her preschool friends asked over a three-week period.

- Do earthworms have ears?
- How do babies get in your stomach?
- Are there knights today?
- Can we get a bulldozer?
- Do all animals have babies?
- It doesn't rain a lot in the summer. Why?
- What's a *pod*? Miss Marie told me whales live in a *pod*.
- How many spots does a ladybug have?
- How come this rock's sparkly?
- Are those rain clouds? How come it's not raining?
- Do we live near a volcano?
- Do mice lay eggs?
- How come firefighters don't get all burnt?
- What are whiskers on kitties for?
- Are dinosaurs real?
- What's the group called for all those flies on the pond?
- Are there good spiders and bad spiders?
- Is that a Black Widow?
- Do other animals have pouches like kangaroos?
- Which ones were the mean dinosaurs?
- What kind of rock is that?
- Do caterpillars bite? Are they nice?
- What's a dungeon?
- Are there birds out at night?

Each of these questions invites further exploration in nonfiction texts. In an attempt to answer some of these questions and model what real learners often do, I investigated numerous nonfiction sources and found a series of excellent books that capitalize on the inquisitive minds of preschoolers. The *I Wonder Why* series by Kingfisher caters directly to a younger audience, but also includes enough information to entice listeners and readers to revisit them for many years. Titles include the following:

I Wonder Why . . .

> *. . . I Blink and Other Questions About My Body*
> *. . . Stars Twinkle and Other Questions About Space*
> *. . . Trees Have Leaves and Other Questions About Plants*
> *. . . Triceratops Had Horns and Other Questions About Dinosaurs*
> *. . . The Wind Blows and Other Questions About Our Planet*

(A more extensive list of titles in the series is contained in the non-fiction booklist on page 270.)

Each book in the series offers a wealth of information in an easy to understand question-and-answer format. You may even be pleasantly surprised to learn a few new facts after reading these books aloud to your children. The books include realistic illustrations as well as engaging cartoons, which add amusement and help engage the reader. The *I Wonder Why* series is especially noteworthy because the books replicate many textbook formats and help clarify for our children the different format and features of expository texts. There are large headings in the form of questions for each section of the book. The pages are numbered for easy reference, and there is a table of contents and an index. Additional fun facts are provided in short captions in a smaller typeface, helping our preschoolers learn that information is not always sequential in non-fiction texts. Therefore, they need to look closely at everything on the page to gain full meaning.

Butterflies Help Expository Reading Bloom

When Heather received a butterfly hatching garden for her fourth birthday, she quickly declared it her favorite gift. She watched the caterpillars every day and anxiously awaited the next stage of development during their metamorphosis into butterflies. She grew impatient and wondered why the process was taking longer than she had hoped. Mike and I used this creative present as an opportunity to obtain some informational texts about butterflies, such as *Monarch Butterfly,* by Gail Gibbons. In this beautifully illustrated book, the author artfully combines extensive information about the metamorphic process from egg to butterfly within a succinctly written and well-organized format perfect for preschool children. The first two pages of the book introduce the title page:

A monarch butterfly settles on the leaf of a milkweed plant. She gently presses a tiny egg onto one of its leaves. The egg is the beginning of another ...

MONARCH BUTTERFLY.

The stages of development are described, as well as the body parts, diet, and migratory patterns of the monarch butterfly. The bright illustrations fill three-fourths of each page, and many include labels to help clarify the text. A detailed chart listing the parts of the butterfly and a map of North America showing migratory instincts serve to bridge our children into future nonfiction reading, which often includes maps, charts, tables, and graphs.

In fact, Gibbons is one of my favorite authors for introducing very young children to the world of nonfiction. Her books span such topics as firefighting (*Fire! Fire!*), spiders (*Spider*), home building (*How a House Is Built*), sports (*My Soccer Book*), tropical rain forests (*Nature's Green Umbrella*), and government agencies (*The Post Office Book: Mail and How It Moves*). While some of her books are more appropriate for older children, most are easily accessible to preschoolers. Gibbons is notorious for using brightly colored illustrations and concise text to cover general information in a manner that young children can understand. She includes inset captions, labels, and diagrams that help define terms and elaborate on the basic text. As parents read aloud quality informational texts like those written by Gail Gibbons, they can model the process of "reading" beyond the words. Parents can teach children to look closely at photographs, diagrams, and maps. They can demonstrate how good readers reference labels on pictures and pay special attention to bold or italic print to help understand the information being presented.

Mike and I enhanced Heather's knowledge of butterflies through a variety of resources. We read aloud Judy Allen's *Are You a Butterfly?* This book includes numerous facts about the butterfly. It is presented in a conversational tone—one of the quality criteria I delineated at the beginning of this chapter—which is readily understood by preschoolers. The reader is invited to imagine what it is like to be a butterfly. Allen puts the reader in the role of becoming the butterfly. You will eat and grow, climb out of your skin several times, glue yourself to someplace safe, and make your chrysalis. The large, up-close and intricate pictures help the reader see tiny details of the changing process. Such illustrations echo those often found in nonfiction texts and serve as support for the comprehension process. Because of the book's balance between facts and readability, *Are You a Butterfly?* helps transition preschoolers from narrative stories to nonfiction texts. Our young children begin to recognize that different types of books have different purposes. In addition to imaginative tales, books can provide facts about a wide range of interesting topics and whet a child's appetite to want to learn more. Allen has written a series of books utilizing the same clever approach to learning about various insects. Titles in the series include *Are You a Ladybug? Are You a Snail?* and *Are You a Spider?*

Each of the butterfly books we read to Heather provided answers to her questions and also helped familiarize her with a different genre of text. Mike and I could have chosen to *explain* what we knew about the butterfly cycle, or we could have investigated on our own and then *shared* our findings with her through our conversations. Instead, we decided to model the natural process that many of us embark upon when we are curious about something. We turned to books. We read to her, discussed the newfound knowledge, and then supported it with the real experiment that was taking place in our own home. The information we found in the books created prior knowledge to help Heather better understand what she was witnessing in the butterfly garden. The caterpillars grew larger each day until they molted, attached to the top of the cup, formed a chrysalis, and then became beautiful butterflies and were set free! The information and diagrams we read helped solidify what we saw in the butterfly garden and vice versa. As Heather witnessed the process of metamorphosis, the information we had read to her made sense and was reinforced.

Adding Informational Text

By adding nonfiction to our read-aloud routine, Mike and I eased Heather into a different genre. We did this in a natural way so that Heather would not be intimidated by the unique format or writing style of informational texts. Our goal was to show her the differences among types of texts and also to model what real readers do. Sometimes readers turn to stories to satisfy their craving for humor, drama, suspense, or escape. On other occasions, readers have a different goal: They need an answer, or they wonder about something, or they need assistance. It is at these times that readers turn to expository texts. Please refer to the nonfiction booklist that begins on page 270 to start you and your child down "the expository road to reading." You are helping your children build an understanding of the process proficient readers use, as well as laying the groundwork for later academic success, by remembering to periodically include nonfiction during "story time."

Part C

How to Read Aloud and Excellent Extension Activities

CHAPTER 15

Read Right: An Overview of How to Read Aloud

A book is a garden carried in the pocket.
—CHINESE PROVERB

Although most of the books we read to our preschoolers are merely "children's" books that seem easy to read aloud, it is important that parents make a concerted effort to fully prepare for this experience. Reading books with a certain pace, intonation, and expression can make a significant difference in how the text is perceived by our child. Therefore, I have provided you several key elements for a successful interaction between your child, you, and a great book.

Select a Sensational Book

Be mindful of your child's current social, emotional, and intellectual level as you select the best book to read aloud. Although we want to stretch our child's vocabulary and knowledge base, we do not want the material to be too far beyond his ability to understand the content of the book. Always take into account the developmental level of your child, and even his current mood and disposition. When your child is tired, grumpy, or frustrated with something that may have occurred during the day, he may turn to you to calm him down and reassure him through a great book. If he is in a silly mood, he may want a humorous book to continue the levity. Therefore, try to keep in mind the purpose you are establishing with your read-aloud selection. Do you want to set a warm and comforting tone right before bed? Do you want to expose your child to new information about a particular topic? Do you want the book to serve as an example to your child of how to deal with a certain issue? Perhaps you want to create a balance between serious material and light books. Consider all of these as you carefully select the best books for this unique time with your child.

Read the Story to Yourself Beforehand

Never try to read aloud a book that you have not previously read before. This may seem unnecessary for picture books, but it can make quite a difference regarding the impact on the listener. Even simple texts have a certain rhythm and pacing that is required for a thorough enjoyment of the story. The reader should have a sense of the page turns, intonation, and expression to truly bring the book to life. Some books offer a surprise at a certain point, thus the reader needs to anticipate this and adjust the pace accordingly. I have seen the same book read by two people and have had a completely different reaction to each. The preparation done by the reader can make a world of difference in how memorable, fun, or interesting a text is to the listener.

Beginning

In addition to reading aloud the title of the book, always pay respect to the author and illustrator. This shows your child that being a writer or illustrator is a noteworthy accomplishment. It also helps your child begin to recognize certain authors and artists and begin to create a list of his favorites. In this way, he builds his own personal criteria for quality in literature. Help make this process overt by creating connections to previous books that you may have read aloud by the same person.

Slooow Down!

Probably the most common error that adults make when reading aloud is to do so too quickly. Because we are fluent readers, it is easy for us to read rapidly and figure out what is taking place. However, rushing through the story makes it difficult for a child to collect his thoughts, wonder, question, and understand. Read at a leisurely pace, and pause to give your child time to think about what you are reading. This way they can begin to imagine the people, places, and events in the story. Many illustrators of children's books include details in their art that require extended periods of time to appreciate. Some even include little surprises like Denise Fleming does in her book *Mama Cat Has Three Kittens*. A small mouse is hidden on nearly every page spread. Can you find it?

Read to Reflect the Mood of the Story

When reading to your child, speak with inflection that conveys meaning. Read with enthusiasm, and try to use an animated and lively style that demonstrates your own enjoyment and comprehension of the story. Be dramatic and create character voices to hold your child's attention. Conversely, slow down and speak softly when the story warrants it. Pace yourself to add excitement and create anticipation. The read-aloud experience should be reflective of what is taking place in the book. It is through this modeling that children will begin to recognize the power of the written word. Parent expression will help the listener to better follow and comprehend the story.

Take Cues from the Words and Illustrations

Pay special attention to the text and illustrations to provide you assistance on the best way to read. If the author puts words in bold print, they are undoubtedly giving the reader a hint to emphasize this part. If the author has used all capital letters, they are telling the reader to shout the text. Consider how some authors have chosen to carefully place words that appear to be floating on the page or dancing off of it. These beg to be read cheerily, replicating the playful tone set by the author. Do not hesitate to use a deep voice and shout "Fee, Fi, Fo, Fum!" when the giant enters the scene. If a mouse is talking, use your squeaky voice. If the author tells us that the characters are whispering so as to not frighten away the owl, as in Jane Yolen's *Owl Moon*, the reader should say these words more softly. The tone of the reading needs to reflect what is taking place in the book.

When I read *Snug in Mama's Arms* to Heather before bed, I use the words and illustrations to help determine the tone of the book. I slow the tempo of my words, pause before turning the pages, and almost whisper the soothing rhymes in the melodic text. I stop for a moment so Heather and I can almost feel the rich, earth-tone paintings that help evoke a quiet mood. Goodnight, Heather!

Pause Periodically

In order to make the read-aloud particularly effective, select key times to involve your child. Parents can strategically pause in the midst of a predictable or rhyming text to invite the listener to become an active participant in the reading. By stating a repetitive phrase or filling in an obvious rhyme, preschoolers get to chime in and feel like real readers. Parents can also periodically pause to model a Think-Aloud. (See chapter 20 for more information about Think-Alouds.) Consider stopping during or after the reading to engage the listener by asking a question, checking for comprehension, making a connection to previous readings or events in the child's life, predicting what will take place, or summarizing the story. Since all of these are things that good readers do, parents are scaffolding their child to independent reading success.

The Finale—How to End the Book

Parents should stretch out the last line and read it very slowly. This provides a special emphasis and tells the child that the story is wrapping up and coming to an end. Carefully pace each word, reading them separately, deliberately slowing the rate of speech. There is no need to announce, "The end." If you read the story correctly, this will be obvious. Read the last line, pause, take a slow breath, and then close the book. Sit quietly for the briefest of moments. Let the audience (you included) reflect one last time on the story. Soak in the words, the message, the art, the beauty.

Read Aloud Throughout the Day

In addition to your special daily read-aloud times before bed, early in the morning, and before or after nap, let your children see you reading aloud for authentic purposes. Periodically read aloud an article in the newspaper, recipes, signs on the road to Grandma's house, directions to the amusement park, labels on toys, warnings on medication, and instructions on how to put together a bicycle. Some of you may find yourself automatically reading out loud when trying to concentrate and better understand complicated directions. (See how you are modeling reading aloud as a strategy that helps readers focus and understand information better?!)

It is important for our children to hear text from a wide range of genres. The rhythm and cadence of fairy tales differs greatly from a comic strip or news article. Poetry, manuals, and magazines all sound different because each has a different purpose. The more we expose our children to a variety of text, the better prepared they are to comprehend a wide range of reading in the future. Marie Clay summarizes this well by stating, "A diet of texts with one style of writing . . . will not lead to sufficiently flexible reading strategies for the variety of texts a reader will encounter."[1] By giving our children opportunities to hear the nuances found in predictable text, game rules, movie reviews, and sports journals, we are demonstrating that different texts read differently. Later, when they are reading on their own and make an error, they can stop and ask themselves, "Does that sound right? Does that make sense?" They will have heard the cadence of numerous types of texts and will be better able to understand them. Again, by exposing our children to read-alouds from different genres, we are establishing a foundation for future independent reading and writing success.

CHAPTER 16

Create Comprehension by Asking Questions about the Text

To read without reflecting is like eating without digesting.
—EDMUND BURKE

Since understanding the text is at the heart of the reading experience, parents may wish to periodically ask questions to help preschoolers make sense of the print. By asking questions when reading aloud, parents are inviting their children to become active participants in the reading process instead of passive listeners. It is important to give children opportunities to tell you what they recognize, what they know, and what they are curious about when reading to them. Use extended pauses that give them time to consider the question and their answer. The questioning process assists children in accessing their prior knowledge and helps them better comprehend what is taking place in the story.

Consider posing a question before, during, or after the reading that will prompt your child to think, express herself, or relate the story to his own experience. Some educators have classified questions in their classroom into two main categories, *dry questions* and *juicy questions*. Parents can use these terms to help them remember to include both types of questions as part of the read-aloud experience with their preschoolers. Dry questions are literal questions requiring a rote answer from the child. They are also sometimes referred to as "right there" questions because there is usually just one correct answer, which can be readily located "right there" in the text. Dry questions are valuable because they help children listen carefully to the story and focus on facts and details. Below are some examples of dry questions:

> What color is the house in the story?
> Who is the story mainly about?
> How many pigs are in the story?
> What does the Little Red Hen bake at the end of the story?
> What is Little Red Riding Hood carrying in her basket?

Although most dry questions require only one word or a short phrase to reply, parents can restate their children's answers in a complete sentence and even provide additional information about the story to enhance their understanding of it. For example, when the child responds, "Blue," to the first question, the parent could respond, "Yes, the house in the book was painted blue. I also remember that it had many different rooms, but the family liked to gather in grandpa's room for story time." When we respond in this way we are modeling good sentence structure as well as providing extra details from the book. Parents may be able to better understand this approach by relating it to the interactions we had with our children during their early attempts at acquiring language. When our child said, "ba-ba," for bottle, we responded, "Oh, you want your bottle. Here is your bottle." We validated their utterances and rephrased them in an articulate manner to model appropriate speech and expand their vocabulary. Parents can use a similar technique when their children respond to questions regarding books. We can restate their response and, in a natural context, extend their knowledge of the story.

It is also important to ask open-ended, or juicy, questions that lead your child into thinking about how and why events take place in stories. These questions invite reactions that promote a variety of responses and encourage your child to reach beyond literal comprehension. Asking a child to state what Little Red Riding Hood was carrying in her basket requires one "right" answer. Asking a juicy question like, "What feelings might Little Red Riding Hood be experiencing throughout different parts of the story?" helps your child learn to analyze, apply, or synthesize information while fostering a creative thought process. Help your preschooler make connections from the current story to personal and family experiences, as well as notice similarities between characters, settings, and emotions from previously read stories. Parents can periodically end the story and then discuss what happened, why it happened, or which feelings the story might have elicited. Examples of juicy questions include:

- Do you think you would want to be one of the Three Little Pigs? Why?
- When have you felt afraid like Hansel and Gretel in the forest? What happened?
- Do you think Jack (from Jack and the Beanstalk) was smart? Why?
- Why do you think the cat, dog, and mouse refuse to help the Little Red Hen?
- Do you think it would be fun to live in a shoe like the Little Old Lady?

Building Understanding with Bloom's Taxonomy

Many teachers use *Bloom's Taxonomy*, a system of categorizing levels of questions, to assist them in asking a range of questions of their students. In this way, teachers balance the questioning process with low-level, or literal, questions, and higher order, more complex questions. In 1956, Dr. Benjamin Bloom headed a group of educational psychologists who developed a theoretical ranking of the levels of thinking that people use. They identified six levels of learning ranked in order from the lowest, Knowledge, to the highest, Evaluation. These are listed in Table 4 on the next page.

Table 4. Bloom's Taxonomy of the Cognitive Learning Domain

Category	Definition
Knowledge	recognize, remember, recall information
Comprehension	understand, describe in one's own words, interpret, retell facts
Application	problem solving, relationships, examples
Analysis	classify, compare and contrast, provide evidence, identify motives
Synthesis	combine ideas to form a new whole, create something new from information provided, organize thoughts and information from the content
Evaluation	make value decisions about issues, develop opinions, prioritize by value, create criteria to assess something, personal reflection

I have used the framework of Bloom's Taxonomy to create examples of leveled questions for parents to use as a reference. In Table 5, each level is labeled with a corresponding question that comes from a story. There is also a brief summary to help parents see how the question fits within the scope of that particular story. Reviewing these may guide you in developing your own questions as you read aloud with your children.

A Cautionary Tale

Notice that I have purposely only included one question per story. One of my main goals in doing so is to help parents better understand the different types of questions that can be asked to promote creative and analytical thinking. It is not to force our children to view the read-aloud

Table 5. Story Questions Based on Bloom's Taxonomy

Bloom's Taxonomy Level	Book Title and Synopsis	Question
Knowledge	*Little Red Riding Hood*	Who is the story mainly about? (Who are the main characters in the story?)
Comprehension	*The Alphabet Tree.* In this parable, the letters of the alphabet are tossed and torn in a windstorm, only to realize that they gain strength by banding together, first strategically forming words and then sentences.	Why do the letters come together and form words?
Application	*The Kissing Hand.* On Chester Raccoon's first night of school, he admits to his mother that he is scared and would much rather remain in the warmth and coziness of his own home. Mrs. Raccoon reassures him with a time-honored secret called the Kissing Hand.	Other than a Kissing Hand, how could you show someone like mommy, daddy, or your baby brother that you love them?
Analysis	*The Rainbow Fish.* Rainbow Fish is undoubtedly the most beautiful fish in the sea, covered with green, blue, purple and sparkling silver iridescent scales. The other fish admire his beauty and ask him to share his most prized possession, the scales. Rainbow Fish refuses to do so.	Why do you think the rainbow fish was unhappy?

table 5 continued on next page

Table 5 continued

Bloom's Taxonomy Level	Book Title and Synopsis	Question
Synthesis	***Cloudy with a Chance of Meatballs.*** There's no need for grocery stores in the town of Chewandswallow, where it rains soup and snows mashed potatoes. Eating is a breeze until the weather suddenly changes for the worse.	What would happen if it rained food in our neighborhood?
Evaluation	***Goldilocks and the Three Bears***	Do you think this could be a true story? Why or why not?

experience as a time to be quizzed and held accountable by their parents. Periodically ask a question here or a question there. It is perfectly acceptable if your child does not know the "right" answer or does not even want to answer at that moment. Benjamin Bloom advocated asking questions where there was not necessarily only one right answer. On the contrary, answers were subjectively based on a multitude of things, including one's own background experiences and mood while reading the book. By simply asking the question, our children will begin thinking and will eventually learn to approach texts from a more thoughtful stance. The next time you read that same story, they may have an answer. Regardless, try not to judge their answers. Rather, allow them to take ownership of them. Validate them and inquire further, but keep in mind that their answers are a glimpse into their thought process. The answers can serve as valuable information into your child's development of reading, listening, and comprehension skills.

Although we want to invite our children into the thoughtful process of interacting with text in an effort to better understand it, we do not want to suffocate the story or their enjoyment of it. I caution parents not to turn read-aloud time into test time. Please, please, please do not quiz your children during your read-aloud time together. If there does not seem like a natural place to pause, or if the book does not prompt your child to ask questions on their own, simply spend the time reading. Reading should be, first and foremost, enjoyed. Unnecessarily interrupting the story, the message, and the natural cadence and flow of the book can be unnerving for both your child and you.

In the midst of writing this book, I was approached by Nancy, the mother of a preschooler and a third-grade child, about how to prepare her daughters to better comprehend texts. She was aware of a series of books specifically published for school use that had a list of questions at the end of each story. When it seemed that she was unable to obtain the series, she asked where she could get similar stories with built-in questions. She strongly suggested that I write workbooks for parents that gave specific examples of the "right" kind of questions to ask at the end of a short story. I cringed at the thought of this and attempted to explain my philosophy about how children learn best in a natural context (like during read-aloud or other authentic interactions with parents and siblings) when they are developmentally ready. I reinforced the idea that as parents we have the power to instill the love of reading and the love of learning in our children. I was certain that workbooks were not the answer. Authentic texts that could be read, explored, and questioned naturally were the answer. After all, we are ultimately preparing our children to read fluently, proficiently, and actively for their future as adults. When adults read, we do not finish the chapter or the book and immediately take a quiz. If we have questions, we seek the answers. We reread for clarification. We turn to outside sources to assist with our query. We discuss the books we read with others whose opinions may differ from ours, thus providing us a new perspective to help answer our questions. But we do *not* fill out a worksheet and have it graded.

While I agree that we want children to think critically and understand texts deeply, I believe that we need only look for places to pause in the books we read aloud. Listen carefully to our children's questions in the midst of the text and help them unearth the answers. Guide them by asking rote questions as well as some of the higher level questions from Bloom's Taxonomy, but do so sparingly. Let these young children experience books as they were meant to be read. With enthusiasm. With joy. With inquisitiveness. With humor. With awe. Be mindful that it does not matter how capable our children may be at reading or how much they are ultimately able to read independently. If they view reading as a chore, as a test, as a way to make them accountable, they may choose to never pick up a book. Reading may be attainable, but may not be pleasurable.

I recognized that some of Nancy's anxiousness stemmed from the mandatory standardized tests that loomed in her daughters' future. As part of these tests given to our children at the end of each school year, students read short stories and answer basic as well as more analytical questions. Results from the standardized tests can often impact our children's classroom placement. Will they be in the gifted class? Will they receive the adequate help they need to succeed? Will they be with academically successful children who can serve as role models? Will they be unnecessarily labeled and not challenged to their full potential? I understand these fears, but I also believe strongly that "teaching to the test" or quizzing our children every time they pick up a book is not the best way to foster higher-level thinking and lifelong learning. Our goal as parents of preschoolers is to prepare children to be responsible, productive members of society who are self-sufficient, who care about others, and who give back to our world. Most of us hope that they will think for themselves, think critically, think sensibly, think deeply. Just think. Since parents have the awesome responsibility and beautiful opportunity to foster the love of reading and critical thinking, we need only take advantage of it. The best learning occurs naturally, stemming from real questions and a desire to seek the answers. Learning takes place when there is a problem that needs solving. Learning blossoms when we work with others to listen, consider, and form opinions. It is through authentic interactions with text that the most memorable learning can take place. So, we ask questions. We seek answers. Yet we must be careful not to demandingly quiz our children, strangling the love of reading and learning and growing. Without the intrinsic motivation to read and learn, very little of either will take place.

CHAPTER 17

Build Coping Skills with Bibliotherapy

Books are the quietest and most content of friends;
they are the most accessible and wisest of counselors,
and the most patient of teachers.

—CHARLES W. ELIOT

In her poem "Some Things Don't Make Any Sense at All," Judith Viorst writes from the perspective of a child whose mom just had another baby. The poet poignantly addresses the child's confusion and dismay when a new sibling joins the family. After all, his mom had always said that he was perfect. Children often feel they will be displaced by a new brother or sister, and they wonder if their parents' love will still be the same for them. Just like adults, preschoolers can sometimes have difficulty dealing with changes in their lives. The arrival of a baby, moving to a new home, adjusting to preschool, or having their first sleepover at grandma's house, can create anxiety that requires special attention. Parents can utilize books as one means to discuss these real-life experiences with children and help them cope with these changes. Books can serve as springboards to meaningful conversations about issues that are currently affecting your children. In addition to selecting books based on their interests, parents can be sensitive to the challenges and fears of children and look for quality literature with these themes.

Bibliotherapy refers to the idea that books are used to help someone problem solve and cope with changes and struggles in life. Parents can utilize books to show their preschooler how someone else has dealt with a similar situation. We can talk to our child about how the characters in the story felt and how it is similar to or different from the way she is feeling. We can invite our children to express their feelings and share their excitement or anxiety. Books can assist in this process by providing children with an outlet of self-awareness as well as a possible solution.

When our daughter was not quite four I became pregnant again. In addition to numerous discussions with Heather about her new sibling, we also utilized stories as a way of helping her prepare for the inevitable changes that would take place in all of our lives. We turned to books as one means for exploring the topic of a new brother or sister. Mike and I read aloud books like Audrey Penn's *A Pocket Full of Kisses*, about a reassuring raccoon mother who reminds her son Chester that she has more than enough love for both him and his little brother.

> "When somebody loves you, their kisses are like the sun's rays—always there and always shining. No matter how many Kissing Hands I give you and Ronny, I will never, *ever* run out."

Mike and I would tell Heather that we were like the raccoons. Nothing could lessen our love for her. After all, she would always be our little baby girl.

One of my other favorite books to help foster discussion about the changes taking place in our family was Madeleine L'Engle's *The Other Dog*. The author takes a unique approach to the topic of a new baby in a household. The story is written from the point of view of Touché, a poodle who is quite confused as to why her master and mistress need another dog. After all, Touché has all the qualities that any family would need from a pet. She is patient, useful, helpful, and perfect. This new Jo-dog doesn't even have a tail. She hardly has any hair and they have to put *clothes* on her. "So why another dog?" As Jo gets bigger and more active, Touché grows protective of her and realizes how much this new "dog" depends on her. In the end, she is rather fond of "Jo-girl" and concludes that every home should have at least two dogs. We used this humorous story as a way to talk about how there was room in our family for *two* special children. We stressed how much the new baby (just like Jo in the story) would no doubt be most interested in everything Heather had to do and say. He would look up to her and love her because she was so wonderful.

When Hurricane Katrina wreaked havoc on much of the Gulf Coast in the fall of 2005, some of the psychology faculty at the university I am affiliated with organized a bibliotherapy drive. They collected funds to purchase copies of *The Blue Day Book for Kids: A Lesson in Cheering Yourself Up,* by Bradley Trevor Greive. Black and white photographs of various animals are included, with expressive faces that demonstrate a range of emotions. The adorable, silly, clever poses serve to open up a dialogue about one's own feelings and ways of dealing with them. This therapeutic book was specially selected because of its accessibility to children of all ages and literacy levels. It was hoped that it could serve as a springboard to discussions about feelings regarding the devastation that had taken place. In addition to much needed supplies, food, shelter, and monetary donations, the psychology faculty recognized the need to address the emotional toll that such a tragedy could have on children. They turned to books as a way to deal with this.

Trained therapists have long known about the power of literature as one way to help children examine and deal with issues and problems in their lives. Bibliotherapy utilizes books and storytelling as a means of helping children cope with life. It has been used as a vehicle to assist children in looking at how someone else of their same age level handled a similar situation. It can also be valuable because it allows the child to momentarily distance himself from the issue so he can approach it from a different perspective, the perspective of the character in the book. Preschoolers begin to identify with the characters in stories and connect the world of books to their own lives. Through reading and discussion, children can gain deeper insights into issues and discover new problem-solving techniques. Children feel a sense of comfort knowing they are not alone. Bibliotherapy topics include everything from adoption, divorce, and moving to a new house to the death of a pet and dealing with various disabilities and conditions.

Although most parents are not qualified to provide therapy, we can still offer our children support and potential solutions through books. We can use stories as a way to begin a conversation. We can ask our children, "What would you do in this situation?" Getting our children to start thinking about others' perspectives helps them learn to be independent thinkers. Books can help build awareness of differences and lay the foundation for creating empathy with the challenges of others.

Criteria for Selecting Books for Bibliotherapy

When making a book selection for dealing with an issue in your child's life, be sure that the book is sensitive and objective. We want all children to feel comfortable about what is taking place in their lives and even see a mirror of themselves in the books we read to them. The book should avoid all stereotypes concerning people with special needs and should have a positive and hopeful ending. I think the best books to use for Bibliotherapy answer children's questions and even provide invitations for discussion. Books that offer one or more solutions to an issue prove helpful to a child. Some books will include information for parents to guide and support their child. If this information is offered by a reputable person (a trained therapist or medical doctor, for example) it can be extremely valuable.

Sally Goes to the Vet meets many of the criteria listed above and is therefore an excellent example of how a book can be used to help preschoolers cope with their fears. Author Stephen Huneck presents the story from Sally the black Labrador's point of view, as she is rushed to the vet after she falls over a tree stump while chasing her feline friend. Upon returning home, she snuggles with Bingo the cat and tells him about her x-rays, the medicine she is required to take, and the shot she received. To help deal with the injection, she recalls, the vet suggested she think a happy thought. (What a great strategy for anyone dealing with an unpleasant situation!) So Sally closed her eyes and visualized a strawberry ice cream cone. This tender story peppered with humor provides children one way to cope when they are frightened. It can help reassure preschoolers about their pet's visit to the vet and perhaps even their own trip to the doctor. The book is well-written and includes bright illustrations, making it very inviting for children. The vet shows sensitivity to Sally regarding the pain she may be feeling, and the book even offers a solution to an issue. Since it covers the various personnel and procedures involved with a visit to the vet, many questions that children may have about this situation are answered. *Sally Goes to the Vet* is a wonderful example of how a picture book can double as Bibliotherapy.

Books like *Cat Heaven* and *Dog Heaven*, both written and illustrated by Cynthia Rylant, tenderly deal with the emotional topic of the death of a pet. Rhyming text, complemented by primitive, childlike art, provide a beautiful visual of what is it like for our favorite feline or canine once they reach heaven. God doesn't give dogs wings because he knows that what they love best is running. Instead He gives them fields and fields and fields. Dog heaven has angel children, biscuits shaped like cats, fluffy cloud beds, and lots of petting hands. When cats cross Rainbow Bridge into Cat Heaven, God is there to attend to their every need. There are lots of toys, angel laps in which to cuddle, full bowls of food, butterflies and crickets to chase, and pastures for frolicking. These sweet and sensitive books offer hope, comfort, and even some gentle humor to anyone mourning a pet. They provide the perfect discussion starter for dealing with this difficult issue. Children (of all ages) can use the books as one more way to deal with loss and begin the healing process.

Books for Understanding

Books can serve as vehicles for helping children, their siblings, and childhood friends understand and deal with disabilities. I think it is very important to read books about people with special needs to *all* children. In this way, it is hoped that we are building a sense of awareness and acceptance in our society. Parents and caregivers have an opportunity to discuss Down syndrome when they read Stephanie Stuve-Bodeen's *We'll Paint the Octopus Red*. This beautiful little book explores the emotions that a family experiences when they discover that their new baby has Down syndrome. Although initially unhappy about the prospect of having a baby in the house, six-year-old Emma begins to imagine a million things she can do with Isaac. When her father comes home from the hospital sad because the baby is born with Down syndrome, Emma worries that everything she imagined cannot come true. After careful thought, though, she and her father see that Isaac will be able to do all the things on the list. They just may take him more time or require more patience from them. This wonderful book provides positive messages of acceptance and helping others. It includes an appendix with questions and answers for children that tells about what Down syndrome is, why some babies are born with it, and some things to expect from a baby who has it.

In *Susan Laughs*, Jean Willis uses a show and tell format with simple rhyming phrases to describe all the *abilities* of a little red-headed girl. She can laugh, swim, paint, dance, swing, and throw "just like me, just like you." She experiences a range of emotions including joy, fear, and anger. It is not until the very end of the book that it is revealed that Susan is in a wheelchair. Darling pencil and crayon drawings make the book whimsical and accessible to young children. I have been intrigued by the reactions of children and adults when they have seen this book. Oftentimes, adults are surprised by the unexpected twist at the end. Many children, on the other hand, simply smile, not taken aback in the least, confirming that Susan really is just like everyone else. *Susan Laughs* helps us see wheelchair-bound individuals in a very different light. We can begin discussing with our children what others are *able* to do, not what they *cannot* do. This may help build empathy, but more importantly, it may build understanding of the humanness in all of us.

Books that Target Specific Issues

One place to begin the search for books that target a specific issue is through Magination Press. These books are published by the American Psychological Association specifically for children and their caregivers and cover many of the challenges children face. Most Magination Press books have been written by mental health professionals or those who work closely with children. Topics include the everyday struggles of childhood, including coping with changes involved with moving or entering school for the first time. They also cover more serious issues such as divorce, autism, trauma, terminal illness, and death, as well as living with family members who may have experienced health issues or disabilities. The authors and illustrators of Magination Press cater their format and wording specifically for the children's audience. The books are not preachy, but instead offer practical coping strategies and solutions. Parents can even use the books as a way to model role-playing of common situations and the feelings that accompany these. Many of the characters are animals or young children, helping the listener relate to the story. Although some of the selections are more appropriate for an older audience, there is no shortage of books suited to the preschooler. Consider titles such as *Big Ernie's New Home: A Story for Children Who Are Moving*, *When Lizzy Was Afraid of Trying New Things*, or *Tibby Tried It*, a story about a bird who is unable to fly. Each can be read aloud and used as a means to deal with the anxieties common to preschoolers.

Admittedly, I feel that the strongest aspect of the books published by Magination Press is the Note to Parents at the back of many of them, which clearly provides guidance for helping children. For example, at the back of *Mookey the Monkey Gets Over Being Teased*, the author (who is also a psychologist) discusses the effects of being teased, provides coping strategies for children, and offers support for parents (and teachers) for working with children who are being teased or bullied. This expanded information especially for parents helps them use the books in the most effective manner possible. Parents may even choose to purchase some of these books for the main purpose of gathering information for themselves.

Everyday Books Build Awareness and Empathy

In addition to reading books that specifically address issues in the lives of our children or those that discuss the challenges of others, there are numerous opportunities to discuss feelings and build awareness and empathy through books we read every day. Books like *Unknown* can spark discussions about one's own emotions, as well as empathizing with the feelings of others. In the story, the little dog in the last cage is routinely overlooked by the humans who visit the animal shelter. She is too shy to bark and cowers in the back, unnoticed, scared, and shivering.

But when a fire breaks out in the middle of the night, it is Unknown who gets help, saving all the animals. Because of her newfound notoriety, she and several others from the shelter are adopted. While this makes Unknown happy, the story ends with her suggesting the tables be turned. Perhaps all the humans should be put in cages and the dogs could walk along with their "noses in the air" and choose the owners they wanted. This thought-provoking ending leaves the reader with many possible discussion points. Parents can dialogue with their children about what it is like to feel small and insignificant at times. Since most of us have felt sad, afraid, or lonely before, this book provides an opportunity for families to discuss ways to deal with one's emotions and better understand the emotions of others.

Books that discuss emotions can be valuable tools to help children understand their feelings during times of change in their lives. In *Today I Feel Silly and Other Moods That Make My Day*, author Jamie Lee Curtis makes it easy to begin talking about the variety of emotions we all experience. She uses singsong rhymes to cover thirteen different moods, from silly, joyful, and excited, to confused, angry, and grumpy. *Today I Feel Silly* is a resource that parents and children can use to to explore their range of emotions together, helping preschoolers understand that all humans have moods. A picture of a girl's face with cutouts for the eyes and mouth is included at the end of the book. Children can spin the wheel behind the face to change eye and mouth expressions to show various moods. On the corresponding page is written, "How do YOU feel today?" Parents can also use the wheel to discuss issues in the child's life and how each makes him feel. Children can learn to understand their own emotions and to be mindful of the moods of their friends and family.

Parents do not necessarily have to purchase special books to discuss issues with their child. Consider how my friend Catherine capitalizes on the feelings of the littlest bear from *Goldilocks and the Three Bears* to help her daughter better understand the feelings of one of her friends. The interactions between Catherine and Mickaela (four years old) are recorded in the gray box). Mickaela is familiar with the story as it has been read to her several times before. On this reading, however, Catherine pauses at the part where the bears return home from their walk in the woods and discover that somebody has been sitting in their chairs. The Baby Bear looks at his chair and sees that it is broken.

Interactions During the Reading of
Goldilocks and the Three Bears

Catherine: Look at the Baby Bear. What do you think he is feeling?

Mickaela: Ummm . . . I don't know. Sad?

Catherine: He's probably sad. Can you imagine what it would be like to come home from a walk with mommy and daddy and find that your special chair has been broken?

Mickaela: I have that special rocking chair that Grandma gave me. In my room. That was hers when she was little.

Catherine: Uh huh. That's the rocking chair that Grandma's mommy had when she was a little girl. It's your great-grandma's. Great-Grandma gave it to Grandma and she gave it to me. Then I gave it to you. Maybe someday you can give it to one of your children. It's very special isn't it?

Mickaela nods.

Catherine: So you think the bear is sad. How would you feel if your special chair was broken and you didn't even know how it happened? You came home and you saw it broken. Oh my goodness.

Mickaela: Sad. Maybe a little mad.

Catherine: So you'd be sad and maybe a little mad, too. Remember when we were at Talia's house last weekend. Remember her tiara got broken. How do you think *she* felt?

Mickaela: I don't know. Not happy . . . sad. Probably.

Catherine: I bet she *was* sad. Do you think there's anything we could do to help her feel better? We don't want our friends to be sad. What could we do?

Mickaela: We could get her another one.

Catherine: Yes, we could get her another one. What else? Any other ideas?

Mickaela: I could let her play with mine. I have a pretty one. And she could play with it. She could come over and play with it. When can she come over, Mommy?

Catherine: If she played with yours or got a new one, how do you think she might feel?

Mickaela: Ummmm . . . she'd feel better. Ummm. . . . I guess she'd be happy.

Catherine: Happy if she could play with yours. You had good ideas. We'll keep thinking. Let's read and see what else happens to the bears. I wonder what the Mama Bear and Papa Bear are feeling too.

Refer to page 250 for a list of books that you and your child may find helpful for various situations in his or her life. Also, when considering books to use for bibliotherapy, you may wish to talk to a librarian or the children's literature resource personnel at the bookstore about the issues that your child is encountering. Ask if they can recommend an age-appropriate book that focuses on the same topic. Always preview the book yourself to determine if it might be beneficial for your preschooler. I am a strong believer that parents often know their child best. Trust your judgment as you make the final decisions about which books would invite positive discussions between you and your child.

CHAPTER 18

Make the Most of Reading Aloud with Multiple Intelligences

We shouldn't teach great books; we should teach a love of reading.

—B.F. SKINNER

When do you get to travel the world to make an apple pie? When the market is closed of course! In Marjorie Priceman's book *How to Make an Apple Pie and See the World*, an adventurous little baker sets off on a whimsical journey around the world, visiting exotic and exciting places, to collect the finest ingredients for her apple pie. She gathers eggs from France, cinnamon from Sri Lanka, sugar from Jamaica, and apples from Vermont. Back home, she quickly whips up the pie and invites friends from all over the globe to share. After the conclusion of this delightful book there is even a recipe for making your very own apple pie. What a wonderful way to connect cooking with a delicious book!

By combining cooking, art, or drama with the read-aloud experience, parents are helping preschoolers enjoy the book more, but are also assisting them with building layers of comprehension. When we give our children additional opportunities to explore the text, we are providing them various avenues for comprehending it. Research tells us that children (and all people) have different kinds of minds and learn in different ways. Some children learn primarily through linguistic intelligence, which includes reading and writing. Others rely largely on a spatial approach (seeing, artistic) or through quantitative means. Still others need to manipulate objects to learn best or perhaps gain the most information when they interact with other individuals. Based on this notion that each of us learns differently, Dr. Howard Gardner, professor of education at Harvard University, developed the theory of multiple intelligences in 1983. He suggested that the traditional notion of intelligence, based on I.Q. testing alone, was far too limited. The theory was first laid out in his book, *Frames of Mind*, and it has since been refined in subsequent texts and articles. Dr. Gardner originally proposed seven different intelligences (he has since proposed more) to account for the broader range of human potential. He considered each of these alternative pathways to learning. According to Gardner, these intelligences are invoked and combined to carry out a variety of tasks. Gardner states that we each have a unique way of thinking and learning, and he suggests that educators and parents should take this into account when working with children. Additionally, he states that children have a better chance of understanding material if it is presented in multiple formats. The first eight multiple intelligences as labeled by Gardner are presented below.

Table 6. Multiple Intelligences by Dr. Howard Gardner

Intelligence	Explanation
Linguistic	Words
Logical-mathematical	Numbers or logic
Spatial	Pictures
Bodily-Kinesthetic	A physical experience
Musical	Music, rhythm
Interpersonal	A social experience
Intrapersonal	Self-reflection
Naturalist	Experience in the natural world

Many teachers are proponents of Gardner's theory of multiple intelligences and try hard to give their students varied and layered experiences with subject matter to assist with understanding. Parents can also implement this idea of looking at children's individual learning styles by adding an art project, game, activity, or a cooking experiment related to the reading at hand. Although many of us learn by reading something, most also benefit from additional interactions with text to help promote deeper understanding. If parents periodically extend the read-aloud experience with an engaging activity, they are giving preschoolers opportunities to learn more than they may learn from just the reading alone.

To help you relate to the theory of multiple intelligences, think about the first time you used a digital camera. You may have read the directions carefully. Or, perhaps, someone may have explained how to take pictures with the camera, how to put them on your computer, and even how to manipulate and print the images. Or you may have only felt comfortable taking the camera in your hands, experimenting with different settings, moving the cursor to a variety of spots on the computer screen, and actually printing pictures yourself before gaining a true grasp of how to fully use the camera. The point is that some of us learn best through reading (the directions to the camera), others through listening (someone explaining to us), and still others through our own manipulation (practicing with the camera). Thus it is often true with all learners. In order to gain depth of knowledge, it is helpful to recognize how one learns best and then to be given multiple opportunities to learn the material in a variety of ways.

Exploring your own multiple intelligences can build self-awareness, which can then be used to help you begin to identify the unique way your child learns. His or her primary learning strength may be quite different from yours. Knowing and understanding this can help you approach new material with your son or daughter in the specific way that suits him or her best. Although each of us may have one preferred mode of learning, research suggests that we can gain depth of knowledge about a given topic if we are exposed to the same material in multiple ways. Thus, parents can help strengthen their child's comprehension of text by extending the read-aloud experience through multiple intelligences.

A Glimpse at Multiple Intelligences in the Classroom

To assist you further in understanding the application and value of Gardner's theory, let us apply it to the classroom experience. Consider how an exemplary preschool teacher might plan a unit on snails, taking into account the multiple intelligences that exist in her students. She may read aloud several factual books about snails, as well as a variety of stories that include snails as characters, thus piquing the interest of the students and helping them access their prior knowledge. The teacher may also have numerous snail books available in the classroom library for children to peruse, attend to the pictures, notice key words, or pretend read. All these interactions cater to children who learn well from a linguistic intelligence stance. To help students gain a better grasp of what snails look like, how they live, and what their ecological purpose is, the teacher may bring in snails for children to observe over a period of time (naturalist). Perhaps the class will keep a journal of the snails during their visit to the classroom. Additionally, each child may write a reflection piece about what it would feel like to be a snail (intrapersonal, linguistic). Children might draw and paint pictures of snails or make one out of clay (spatial, bodily-kinesthetic).

Garden songs and poems might be sung and chanted to reinforce the snail theme and excite the students who learn best through rhythm and music (musical). The class may compare the weights of different snails by putting them on scales and talking about measurement in grams and ounces (logic-mathematical). Students might be asked to bring in different types of leaves and other foods to see what snails like best to eat. A visit to a local garden might turn into a hunt to locate snails (naturalist). Children may add more math to the unit by counting all the snails they can find in their own garden or a garden at school (logical-mathematical, naturalist). They may organize snail races, tracing the trails left behind within a specified amount of time, and then measuring each to see which snail went the farthest (interpersonal, logical-mathematical). Videos may be viewed on the life of snails in an effort to access the visual learners in the classroom (spatial). Children may take turns acting out a snail crawling on its wet foot, eating a nice juicy leaf, or moving as quickly as possible to escape the grasp of a hungry bird (bodily-kinesthetic). Perhaps the class will even "cook up" some delicious snail morsels made from cinnamon rolls (bodily-kinesthetic, spatial).

By the end of the unit, all children will have been provided numerous ways to learn about snails. Since each preschooler will be able to truly explore snails from many different facets, they'll have more depth and breadth of knowledge than they could have gained through only hearing about them from read-alouds. This approach to teaching motivates the children in the classroom, and it also gives them opportunities to learn from their strongest modalities.

Parents Putting It into Practice

Of course, it is not necessary for parents to create such in-depth units of study for their children, but you may want to look for ways to extend the read-aloud experience and focus on your child's area or areas of learning strength. Consider periodically using a quality book as a springboard for an art project, cooking lesson, or a time for the two of you to enjoy a special treat. After you have read a book to your child, invite her to join you in acting out the sequence of events in the story. If you are reading a nonfiction book about something in nature, take a walk around your garden, the neighborhood, or a local park and see if you can confirm the facts presented in the text.

In the following sections, I suggest ways to help your child delve deeper into the story, understand more completely, extend the learning, reflect more thoughtfully, and perhaps most importantly, have a wonderful time along the way. By singing, painting, acting out favorite parts, or eating your way through books, preschoolers do more than listen to read-alouds, they share a special experience with their parents.

Cook to Create Scrumptious Reading (Logical-Mathematical, Spatial, Interpersonal)

Throughout this book I have provided a variety of ways to extend the read-aloud experience. In addition to exploring great literature, predicting, asking questions, and clarifying new vocabulary, parents can help deepen children's understanding of text in a unique and special way. I am a firm believer that "If you feed them, they will *learn*." There are numerous "recipes" to making the read-aloud experience fun and informative. By cooking up some yummy dishes that reflect the themes or details provided in books, parents help their children see reading as a pleasurable experience, and also help children comprehend text better. Cooking with books provides parents and children time to discuss the events in the story and how the particular food or drink may have played a key role in the plot. This gives children additional time to reflect on the literature and deepen their understanding of what was taking place or of the facts presented. By enjoying a special drink, snack, or dessert before, during or after a quality book, preschoolers readily associate reading with yum!

Even if you are intimidated by the prospect of following a recipe, there are still many creative ways to connect food or drink with a good book. Thank goodness for the local bakery, prepackaged goodies at the grocery store, or mixes where the only requirement is to "just add water" and then pop it in the oven. I also do not always find it necessary to literally cook something related to our book. When I am reading with Heather, I try to look for times to enjoy something simple like a glass of lemonade or a piece of fruit. After one of our readings of How to Make an Apple Pie and See the World, I felt hungry and asked Heather if she would like to split an apple with me. I cut the apple into several slices and we sat down at the kitchen table, munching away and talking about our favorite part of the book. When we eat something scrumptious together related to a great book, both of us remember fondly the total experience. Reading aloud becomes an even more special time to be together. If I felt it necessary, the interaction after a book could also potentially provide me time to clarify misunderstandings from the text or informally check to see if Heather had questions about what was read. Although I am not suggesting that parents quiz their children while eating, I am saying that we can learn a great deal about our children and their literacy level just by taking the time to listen. I find that sharing a delicious snack is a wonderful venue to do just that.

In Table 7 I have provided some ideas for you to begin your culinary journey through books. It is hoped that these will help spark your own "tasty" connections between reading and cooking in the kitchen. I now invite you to pick up an appetizing book and get ready to eat, drink, and read merry!

Table 7. Cooking Up Some Great Books

Title and Author	Brief Synopsis	Ways to Eat, Drink, and Read Merry!
How to Make an Apple Pie and See the World by Marjorie Priceman	When the market is closed, a young baker must travel around the world to get the finest ingredients to make an apple pie.	Make an apple pie (the recipe is at the back of the book) or simply slice some apples and sprinkle with cinnamon.
The Baker's Dozen: A Counting Book by Dan Andreason	A jolly baker whips up a tasty treat for each number, 1 through 12.	Share a tasty dessert of your choice. Find inspiration directly from the book and consider an éclair, strudel, or cupcake.
Too Many Tamales by Gary Soto	When Maria sneakily slips her mother's diamond ring on while kneading the masa for tamales, trouble begins. After losing the ring, she and her cousins decide they must eat all the tamales in order to find it.	Get the family together and make some tamales (or order some from the store) and have a family feast.
Cloudy with a Chance of Meatballs by Judi Barrett	After a pancake is accidentally flipped too high and lands on Henry, his Grandpa tells a tall tale all about food. In the town of Chewandswallow all the meals rain down from the sky. That is, until the weather takes a turn for the worse.	Make pancakes for breakfast and then read the book as everyone eats.

table 7 continued on next page

Table 7 continued

Title and Author	Brief Synopsis	Ways to Eat, Drink, and Read Merry!
The Apple Cake by Nienke van Hichtum	An elderly woman wants to make an apple cake but she only has plums. Through a series of exchanges, she winds up helping many people along her journey.	The book includes a recipe for Granny's Apple Cake on the back cover.
The Runaway Latkes by Leslie Kimmelman	Three crisp and brown potato latkes escape the frying pan and head out on a mischievous adventure.	The book includes a recipe for Latkes. Yum!
Little Pea by Amy Krouse Rosenthal	In an ironic twist to the dinner battle most parents endure with their children, Little Pea is forced to eat candy for each meal. He chokes it down and is rewarded with his favorite dessert . . . spinach.	Eat something healthy, of course!
Miss Spider's Tea Party by David Kirk	After Miss Spider helps a rain-soaked moth, the good word spreads of her kindness. Finally, the insects are no longer afraid to come for tea and be her friend.	Brew some tea. Invite friends if you would like and have a tea party. (Consider placing some plastic spiders around the table to add to the theme and the fun.)
The Gingerbread Baby by Jan Brett	When Matti opens the oven too soon, out jumps a gingerbread baby. A rollicking chase ensues as townspeople and animals try desperately to catch it.	Bake and decorate a gingerbread baby. Unlike the book version, it's O.K. to catch and eat this one. (Jan Brett even has a recipe on her website.)
Growing Vegetable Soup by Lois Ehlert	Deep, intense colors are used to illustrate the entire process of growing and nurturing your own vegetable soup, from seed to cooking pot.	A tasty and easy vegetable soup recipe is included on the end flap.

table 7 continued on next page

Title and Author	Brief Synopsis	Ways to Eat, Drink, and Read Merry!
If You Give a Pig a Pancake by Laura Numeroff	If you give a pig a pancake it will lead the two of you into some exciting and hilarious adventures.	Enjoy some pancakes and see what fun it may lead to. . . .
Thunder Cake by Patricia Polacco	Grandma has the perfect "recipe" to allay her granddaughter's fears of a thunderstorm.	The book includes a recipe for Thunder Cake. (To create the perfect mood, wait for a rainy day to read the book and bake this special cake.)
The Popcorn Book by Tomie de Paola	Numerous scientific and historical facts are presented in a fun and inviting format.	Enjoy some popcorn together. (Two different recipes are provided.)
The Tale of Peter Rabbit by Beatrix Potter	Mischievous Peter Rabbit doesn't listen to his mother and gets into all sorts of trouble in Mr. McGregor's garden.	Share chamomile tea and berries. You do not have to have a stomachache like Peter to find these soothing and satisfying.
The Ugly Vegetables by Grace Lin	The Chinese-American girl is very disappointed that she and her mother are growing "ugly vegetables." However, when they harvest the crops and make an aromatic soup, all the neighbors come to join them.	Make vegetable soup and invite the neighbors over to share. (The book includes the recipe.)

Add Art for Awesome Book Exploration (Spatial Intelligence)

Drawing, painting, coloring, and making crafts revolving around the characters, plot, or themes in books makes reading more memorable. When preschoolers are given opportunities to react creatively to stories, they develop a deeper understanding of the text. Most importantly, children are reminded of the close connection between reading and fun. Perhaps you, yourself, might even sit down and participate in the project with your child, or work side by side as you create your own work of art. Think of what a powerful experience this could be as your child sees your unique impression of the story. To assist you with ways to begin the artistic process, I have provided you ideas related to several books. These can be found in Table 8. None require extensive planning or a great deal of expense. It is also important for you to keep in mind that it does not have to be a lengthy or overwhelming process. A simple drawing that you later post on the refrigerator can be a reminder about the book and the wonderful time you and your child spent together. Also, remember that all of the extensions listed in this chapter are only valuable if your child is an enthusiastic participant. We do not want to turn the positive association our child has with the read-aloud experience into a dreaded "work assignment." Read, explore, and create together. And don't forget to have fun!

Table 8. The Art of Books

Title and Author	Book Information	Art Activity
Rainbow Fish by Marcus Pfister	When Rainbow Fish agrees to give away his shiny iridescent scales to the other fish, he learns the meaning of sharing and friendship.	Help your child color firmly with crayons to create an underwater ocean scene of fish, octopi, seaweed, etc. Then wash over the art with light blue watercolors to simulate an underwater oasis. Add a few colored sequins or a bit of glitter to replicate the scales that Rainbow Fish gave away to his newfound friends.
Elizabeti's Doll by Stephanie Stuve-Bodeen	A young Tanzanian girl creates her own doll from a rock, the perfect size and shape to be her baby.	Make a doll instead of purchasing one at the store. This can be as simple as finding a special rock and painting a face on it, making a sock doll, or creating something more sophisticated that involves sewing help from Mom or Dad.

table 8 continued on next page

Title and Author	Book Information	Art Activity
Fancy Nancy by Jane O'Connor	Nancy likes everything to be fancy, including her family. She provides them lessons on how to speak and live a fancy lifestyle.	Transform something from plain to fancy with sequins, beads, feathers, and more. Look around the house to find an ordinary object such as sunglasses, shoes, a picture frame, toy, or an old box.
Swimmy by Leo Lionni	A little black fish devises a plan to camouflage himself and his friends to protect them from their natural enemies.	Cut out a small black fish and have your child incorporate it within a scene his or her choice so that it is somehow camouflaged.
Red Is a Dragon by Roseanne Thong	Using rhyming couplets that center around different colors, we are provided a peek into the Chinese-American culture. We see red dragons, melons, and lychees, as well as orange crabs, yellow incense sticks and taxis, pink peonies, and white dumplings.	Let your child select a certain color and then have them create a collage. Help them look through old magazines, clip, and paste pictures that revolve around the specific color.
Changes, Changes by Pat Hutchins	Two wooden dolls are perfectly content to live in their house made of various shapes. That is, until it catches fire. They rearrange the shapes to create a fire engine, but then there is so much water they must design a boat.	Cut out geometric shapes in a variety of colors. Children can try to replicate the designs from the book, form abstract art, or create something new from various shapes.
Mouse Paint by Ellen Stoll Walsh	Three white mice discover jars of paint and a colorful adventure begins. Dipping toes and tails into more than one jar creates exciting new color combinations.	Provide paints or play dough for your child and let them experiment with color. Encourage mixing colors to see what magical new ones are created.

Since parents and families are so busy, consider open-ended art projects that require minimal planning. I often find these to be the most creative because our child is in charge of his or her own artistic process. The product or outcome has not been predetermined by you or anyone else. This truly becomes the child's work of art, her vision, her creation. In order to allow for open-ended exploration by Heather, I keep a box filled with old buttons, colored puff-balls, popsicle sticks, pipe cleaners, shells, pebbles, sequins, and other miscellaneous items. She also has a writing drawer that holds crayons, markers, paints, and different forms of paper. Sometimes after reading a book together, Heather and I will sit at the table and discuss the story or text. I invite her to look through the boxes and create a work of art representative of the beginning, the end, a character with which she identifies, or her favorite part of the story. I am often amazed at what she imagines and creates.

Dive into Drama to Bring Books Alive (Bodily-Kinesthetic, Intrapersonal, Interpersonal)

When children are given opportunities to be physically engaged with a story, books come alive. Drama ignites one's imagination. It helps preschoolers relate the characters in stories to themselves so they can more easily understand the thoughts, feelings, and actions of those characters. Children can use silly voices to reenact the tale, or even dress up with whimsical hats, scarves, coats, or shoes borrowed from Mom or Dad. If your child is feeling shy, invite him or her to hold a stuffed animal and provide the voice of one of the characters in a story. Impromptu "skits" can be developed just by having individual family members read the dialogue for different characters.

Table 9 provides you ways to help your child find his or her inner actor. Some of the suggested activities serve to get one's whole body moving, twirling, wiggling, and giggling. Others invite your child to play a certain part within the story. Since so many children are kinesthetic learners who benefit from becoming actively engaged with the text, think of innovative ways to allow your child to hop, skip, slither, or make gestures and funny noises with selected books. Surely these ideas will awaken everyone who participates in the read-aloud experience, sending out a casting call for all actors and actresses. A star is born!

Table 9. Adding Drama to the Best Books

Title and Author	Book Synopsis	Action
We're Going on a Bear Hunt by Michael Rosen	A family heads on an adventurous bear hunt only to find numerous obstacles in their way. They have no choice but to bravely and noisily go through each one.	Hide a teddy bear and then go on your own family hunt. Go "swishy swashy" through the carpet, "splash splosh" through the imaginary river until you enter the "narrow, gloomy cave" (behind the couch). Try to act out the story in the correct order to reinforce the idea of sequencing events.
The Very Lazy Ladybug by Isobel Finn	Ladybug has never learned to fly. When she wants to find a new place to rest, she hitches a ride on various animals, but none is a peaceful endeavor.	Pretend you are the ladybug hitching a ride on various animals. Hop, roar, swish, and snooze just like the animals in the story.
Giraffes Can't Dance by Giles Andreae	All the animals in the jungle make fun of Gerald because he can't dance. However, when a cricket helps him find the beat of his own music he surprises everyone.	Help your child find their own rhythm and then dance together.
Two Bad Ants by Chris Van Allsburg	When the troop of ants discovers sugar crystals to bring back to the queen, two greedy ants decide to stay behind and have their fill. They fall asleep in the sugar bowl, but are dramatically awakened when a large scoop pours them into a hot cup of coffee. The mishaps continue from there.	Select a scene from the book to act out and then have fun as your child and you become "two bad ants."
Are You a Butterfly? by Judy Allen	Listeners are invited to imagine what it is like to be a butterfly and enter each of the stages of this impressive creature.	Act out the stages of a butterfly, from egg to caterpillar to chrysalis and finally to the beautiful insect that spreads its wings and flies away.

Knowing About Nature (Naturalist Intelligence)

According to Gardner, those who learn through the naturalist intelligence have an affinity with the outside world. They see patterns and make connections to elements in nature. The preschool stage of development seems almost synonymous with exploration. Young children discover new things each and every day. They wander and watch in backyards, parks, and neighborhoods, hoping to unearth an insect, flower, pebble, or the unknown. Children at this age love to dig in and find out more. The world outside holds vast treasures and answers to questions yet to be asked. Curiosity overtakes any thought of squeamishness. They pick up roly-polies by the dozens, noting the variations in size and color. They run to Mom and Dad to share their new discoveries. Trees and rocks are meant to be climbed, puddles are meant to be splashed in, and sticks, leaves, and seashells beg to be brought home and collected. For so many preschoolers, the outdoors is a giant museum and science lab and adventure. It is through active engagement with this world that so much is learned and where curiosity to know more is sparked.

It's no wonder then that young children gravitate toward nonfiction books about animals, plants, and everything in nature. They are fascinated when we read aloud books about dinosaurs, fossils, honey bees, and polar bears. It seems only natural to connect books with the world outside. Parents can do this by listening and watching closely as our children become excited over the discovery of a bird's nest, the turtles on the nature walk, or the fluttering butterfly that almost lands on their finger. Then we can find books that revolve around these same themes, capitalizing on their interest and extending the learning.

When Heather and I were inspired to create a fairy garden in our backyard, we spent several weeks planning and prepping. We took a trip to the nursery to locate the perfect container, purchase potting soil, and investigate the difference between plants that would do well in the sun and those that prefer the shade. During these weeks, we also borrowed and read as many books as we could find about fairies. This heightened our excitement for the project as well as provided us important "facts" about a fairy's preferred habitat, food choices, and perfect resting place. By reading stories about fairies, we were able to connect our earthy project with the enchanted world of these imaginary creatures. The garden seemed to have more purpose and was definitely more fun. What we "learned" from these books directly impacted how we created our garden. We read that fairies love lots of soft moss to rest upon as well as different forms of foliage to hide in and snuggle beneath, so we made a point of including those. The books enlightened us to the fact that fairies enjoy a cup of nectar in the early morning, so Heather selected a small iron table and chairs to provide the perfect spot for sipping tea. We tended our miniature garden, watching daily as caterpillars came to visit and the miniature flowers seemed anxious to bloom in their new surroundings. Heather was in charge of watering and seeing if any of the furniture had been moved by one of the fairies in the middle of the night. This creative project drew us closer to nature and closer to one another. By reading so many books about these magical creatures, we felt confident that our little garden was a dream spot for any little fairies who happened by.

Families can capitalize on the interests their children have in nature by finding books that expand their knowledge of these topics. Or parents can choose to begin a project with a great book and then extend the read-aloud experience by connecting it to something in nature. After reading Kathy Henderson's *And the Good Brown Earth*, Heather, Zack, and I were inspired to grow some of our own vegetables. This became a project that developed over time, but it was always associated with this sweet book. It depicts the special relationship between Joe and Gram, who are good friends but like to do things quite differently. When they head down to the vegetable patch in the fall, the two begin a yearlong adventure of tending a garden. With the good brown earth playing its key role in this process, grandmother and grandson each grow their own vegetables in their own way ... perfect!

In Table 10 I have provided ideas for you and your child to begin the journey, both real and imaginary, into the backyard, the wild jungle, or perhaps even the African plains. Feel free to curl up together on a blanket outside basking in the warm sun, read an adventurous book, and uncover something new. Gather your trowel, your butterfly net, and your magnifying glass and let's dig deep into the soil, discovering all Mother Earth has to offer.

Table 10. "Naturally" Connecting Books

Title and Author	Brief Synopsis	Nature Connection
A Ladybug's Life by John Himmelman	The life cycle of the ladybug is recorded and a glossary of terms included for some additional information. Beautiful illustrations complement the text.	Ladybug hatching kits can be purchased. It is fascinating to watch the stages of the ladybug and then reap the bonus benefit of releasing them to eat the aphids on your rose bushes. What a wonderful lesson in helping the environment by not using any harmful pesticides.
Peek! A Thai Hide-and-Seek by Minfong Ho	Highlighting a cultural twist on the familiar childhood game, father and daughter play "Jut-Ay." The little girl cleverly hides throughout a lush jungle in Thailand.	Play hide and seek in your own backyard or neighborhood, or play peek-a-boo in the house.
Red Leaf, Yellow Leaf by Lois Ehlert	We learn about the life of a maple tree, from tiny seed, to young seedling, to full-grown tree with beautiful autumn leaves in shades of red, yellow, gold, and orange. An appendix provides detailed information about trees and leaves.	Take a leaf walk, collecting beautiful leaves of all colors and sizes. You may also choose to make a bird treat out of a piece of bread, egg white, and bird seed. The directions for this creative project are on the back flap of the book.
Stranger in the Woods by Carl Sams and Jean Stoick	The forest animals are in a frenzy after a winter snowstorm when they find out that there is a stranger in the woods. Once they discover that the snowman poses no danger, they help themselves to some tasty treats. His carrot nose, nuts for eyes, and hat brim filled with seeds are soon gobbled up.	Build a snowman in the woods. Be sure to add lots of edible parts for all the animals to nibble upon when you are gone.

table 10 continued on next page

Title and Author	Brief Synopsis	Nature Connection
If I Were a Tree by Dar Hosta	Listeners are treated to a melodic tribute to different types of trees throughout the four seasons. Information about trees and photosynthesis is provided at the end.	1. Make your own paper from recycled materials. You can find recipes on the Internet. 2. See how many different types of trees you can find. Discuss what distinguishes each—leaves, bark, flowers, fruit, etc. Can your child name any of the trees?
Butterfly House by Eve Bunting	A young girl saves a tiny black caterpillar from a jay who was about to make it his lunch. With her grandfather, she creates a beautiful home for the soon-to-be butterfly, decorated with flowers and a painted blue sky.	The book includes detailed instructions on how to raise your own butterfly.
Leaf Man by Lois Ehlert	A narrator tells us about the Leaf Man, who used to live nearby but blew away in the wind. The narrator imagines all the different places it could have gone. Collage art of various leaves form animals and objects on each page, making the book a visual delight. Readers are invited to head outside in search for their own Leaf Man.	Collect leaves and then create a collage on colored construction paper just like one in the book or make your own innovative project.
Mavis & Her Marvelous Mooncakes By Dar Hosta	Did you know that the moon is a cake made by a striped orange cat? For fourteen days and nights, Miss Mavis Sugar makes more and more shining slices of mooncake. Then she spends the next fourteen days and nights eating it all up with her friends, one slice at a time.	Watch the moon with your child for one month. Keep track on a calendar of what you see by drawing a picture of the size of the "mooncake." Watch it as it gets bigger, bigger, bigger, and then is slowly "eaten."

table 10 continued on next page

How to Read Aloud and Excellent Extension Activities 179

Table 10 continued

Title and Author	Brief Synopsis	Nature Connection
Secret Place by Eve Bunting	Amidst a bustling, concrete-riddled, pollution-filled city, a boy discovers a secret treasure. A small patch of wilderness is home to sparrows, mallards, an egret, ducklings, and even a nocturnal coyote and possum with babies.	Help your child be a nature detective. Wherever you go, keep a watchful eye for nature in the most unsuspecting places.

Investigate the Internet for Connections with Reading

Many children's authors have their own websites that include biographical information, a list of books they have written, appearance dates and locations, as well as frequently asked questions. Some have even provided activities to correspond with certain book titles. Denise Fleming (www.denisefleming.com), author of such treasures as *In the Small, Small Pond*, *The Everything Book*, and *The Cow Who Clucked*, includes coloring pages, mazes, and creative art activities for various books. Detailed instructions guide parent and child into making a paper plate version of Boris, the cat who naps throughout most of the book *Mama Cat Has Three Kittens*. Fleming provides closeup photographs of all the letters of the alphabet from *Alphabet Under Construction* so that you and your child can replicate these at home. Consider working together to create the letters in your child's name and hanging them in her room. The website also includes various art activities, such as paper hats, sock snowmen, tree I.D. tags, papermaking directions, and scrumptious snacks. All are directly related to her books and serve as extensions that will make the read-aloud experience more memorable.

Another wonderful author website is provided by Jan Brett (www.janbrett.com), best known for her detailed, beautiful artwork with ornate borders and intricate vignettes in such books as *The Three Snow Bears*, *The Gingerbread Baby*, *The Mitten*, and *Town Mouse, Country Mouse*. Brett offers an expansive activities page, with links to fun and innovative ideas listed in alphabetical order that include coloring, cooking, and crafts, as well as puppets, paper dolls, and placemats. Step-by-step instructions tell parents how to work with their child to build their own bird feeder (to accompany *The Umbrella*), bake Annie's Corn Cakes (from *Annie and the Wild Animals*), and create a hedgehog sock puppet (*Hedgie's Surprise*). The recipe for a gingerbread baby, from the book with the same title comes complete with a warning to heed during baking. "Do not peek!" Although there are many materials that are more appropriate for teacher use in a classroom setting (flash cards for sight words, patterns for alphabets, and school hall passes), there is no shortage of great ideas for parents. You can almost get lost (happily) in the extensive list of wonderful activities to do with your preschooler.

Another excellent website is that of Kevin Henkes (www.kevin-henkes.com), author of so many loveable characters including Lilly (*Lilly's Purple Plastic Purse*), Chester (*Chester's Way*), Wemberly (*Wemberly Worried*) and Chrysanthemum (*Chrysanthemum*). Several coloring pages, stick puppets, and yummy recipes directly related to characters and events in Henkes's stories are easily accessed through the Internet. You and your child will love to make Wemberly's Don't-Cry-Over-Spilled-Punch as well as Chester and Wilson's Never-Better Peanut Butter Cookies. Do not hesitate to try all the delicious ideas presented.

Not all authors include extension activities for their books. However, by using a search engine, I have found many related websites where teachers or others have created innovative projects for different texts. I have found the recipe for Dr. Seuss's famous Green Eggs and Ham, as well as art projects for making critters out of egg cartons. If you decide to use one of these wonderful ideas, be sure to email the creator and thank them! Search the Internet for your favorite author or simply type in the title of a specific book. There are many fabulous extensions created by school districts, teachers, and parents that are perfect for use with preschoolers.

CHAPTER 19

Create Connections Between
Reading and Writing

(Linguistic, Intrapersonal, Interpersonal)

I like dinosaurs.
I think about them all the time.
I read about them
I talk about them.
Oh, how I wish the dinosaurs
could come back!

Using a repetitive opening phrase on nearly every page of the book *If the Dinosaurs Came Back*, author Bernard Most describes all the ways dinosaurs could be of great help if they were to return. Dinosaurs could scare away robbers, help firefighters put out fires, take swimmers for rides at the beach, or just be great pets for people who love dinosaurs. When you read this fanciful tale to your preschooler it will surely spark imaginative responses as to what could happen if the dinosaurs came back. The bright purple, red, and yellow dinosaurs in the book are painted prominently atop a black and white backdrop, drawing all eyes to their silly endeavors. The dinosaurs work harmoniously to assist with daily chores and make life easier and more fun for the smiling people all around. Children will giggle through each page, delighting in the idea that perhaps it really would be advantageous to have a dinosaur as a friend.

After reading this book to numerous preschoolers over a period of time and seeing their obvious excitement about the tale, I began asking each what special service a dinosaur could offer to our world today. Many of the preschoolers jumped at the chance to think of creative ways for dinosaurs to help. Here are some of their responses to my question, "If the dinosaurs came back, what could they do for you? They could ..."

... make a swimming pool with their giant claw prints and I could go swimming.

... rescue cats trapped up in trees.

... take me to my grandma's house.

... crush old buildings with their tails.

... scare away my bad dreams.

I wrote each child's answer on a separate sheet of paper, carefully repeating each word aloud as I did so. I then invited the child to read with me the text that we had just created together. Afterward, I provided colored pencils, crayons, and markers for the preschoolers to produce an accompanying illustration to their writing. We talked about their sentence and their drawing while they spent time adding details and color. Once the picture was completed to their satisfaction, I held up the illustrated page and read aloud their sentence, then I asked them if they would like to do the same.

When we transcribe what our children say or the stories they tell us, we are showing them the close relationship between spoken and written word. Since we write down the child's own language, we are also making it clear that we value them and the importance of their voice. They, too, can be authors whose work can be written on paper and read by others and themselves. This concept is a powerful way to help our children connect the communication processes of reading and writing.

The Language Experience Approach

The Language Experience Approach (LEA) is a strategy that parents can use to demonstrate to preschoolers that print conveys meaning. It also serves to support vocabulary growth as well as reading and writing development. The LEA shows children that anything they say can be written, and anything that can be written can be read or spoken. Thus, when our children have something to say, we can validate them and write it down. Since what is written is the direct language of the preschooler, they can more aptly "read" it on their own.

The procedure for LEA follows a specific series of steps.

1. **Provide an experience**—Create an experience that will spark interest, capture a child's imagination, or that has special meaning to the child. The read-aloud experience is the perfect venue for this. Since parents are already selecting quality books that have interest and value to their child, these can easily be extended into a writing activity. Consider how your child learns best. This will help you determine whether to use LEA when you introduce a new book to your child or if you would rather have numerous experiences with the book over time before deciding to write from it.

2. **Discuss the Experience**—By talking about the book together, we can model exquisite language as well as help our children organize their ideas. Additionally, when discussions of text take place, our child is given time to process the information or the story and make his or her own connections to it. Great teachers recognize the importance of providing time for reflection whenever they want their students to prepare to write. The best writing teachers often provide a common and powerful experience to bridge the students into the writing process. Then they have the class discuss the experience to give students time to put their thoughts together and to gain ideas from one another. Most of us, even as adults, find the blank page very intimidating. When someone asked Ernest Hemingway what frightened him the most, he replied, "A blank sheet of paper." Therefore, it is important to give our children prewriting time. This is the time to think, look back through the illustrations in the book, and discuss some additional ideas with their parents if needed. Children can also take this opportunity to ask clarifying questions or gain

additional information or insight into the book. It is from these prewriting activities that our children will have the strong foundation to dive into the writing process.

3. **Record What Your Child Says**—Parents should then write down what the child dictates. The child may choose to create a sentence that summarizes the story, tell a favorite part, or share something unique that the book inspired. The purpose is to empower the child to become an author whose words are so important they are permanently written down. Careful attention should be made to preserve the child's natural language whenever possible. In this way, the child has familiarity with the text and can read it easily. Purists of LEA state that the parent or teacher must record the child's words exactly as they are stated. You know your child best, and I trust that you can make the decision whether to strictly adhere to this or not. Do what you feel is the most beneficial for your child at his age and literacy readiness level. I admit that I have a slightly different philosophy that deviates from this view. Since children at the preschool stage of development are still making approximations and experimenting with standard grammar, I will sometimes rephrase the statement a child makes to me, just as I do with Heather or Zack when they are speaking. If a child tells me, "The dinosaurs could help *cutted* down the trees," I may restate this correctly and then meticulously record the child's sentence. "Oh. The dinosaurs could help *cut* down the trees." In this way, I am reinforcing proper use of language and the way words are put together. If you elect to use this variation of LEA, be sure to do so in a non-threatening and nonjudgmental way. It should glide out of one's mouth naturally, making it clear to the child that you understood what he was trying to say but just adjusted it slightly to conform to standard English.

4. **Read the Text**—First read the text to your child, pointing to each word as you do so. Parents may elect to do this several times, reinforcing the text. Then, invite him to read the text with you. He may choose to point to each word as well. It is sometimes valuable to take this opportunity to make overt the connection between oral

and written language. "Look what you said. Here it is written down. And now we can read it. Wow. You are just like the author from the book. He thought of something and then wrote it down. Now we are reading it. You, too, thought of something important and now everyone who wants to read it will be able to do so."

5. **Illustrate the Text**—Although this is not an essential step in LEA, children sometimes enjoy extending the writing activity by adding their own artistic element to it. This helps reinforce the words they have written by providing them time to think extensively about their text in order to recreate it in picture form. It also helps them feel like a real author and illustrator. Connecting writing, reading, and art makes the entire process more meaningful and pleasurable.

6. **Make a Book**—Consider keeping some of your child's dictation sentences and binding them into a book. This becomes a text that can be revisited and reread any time your child desires. I keep several of these in our home library right next to other books by "real authors." I also like to bring bound books in the car on long trips. Children can usually read these independently and delight in the accomplishment of creating their very own book.

7. **Extend the Activity**—Periodically, you may wish to record one sentence that your child dictates to you on a large sheet of paper. Practice rereading the text together as you point to each word. Read the text several times. Then, cut the words apart, creating a puzzle. Work with your child to place the words back together in the correct sequence. Depending on the developmental readiness of your child, or even his enthusiasm level for the activity on that particular day, you may wish to point out punctuation or specific vocabulary words. For example, as you work side by side and place the words back into their correct order, you may note, "Oh. I see the word *If* has a capital letter. That helps me know that we placed it in the right spot at the beginning of the sentence. I know that all sentences begin with a capital letter." Or you may choose to take a moment to reinforce your child's strong use of vocabulary. "Wow! There's the word *enormous*. You said the dinosaur was enormous. What a great descriptive word. I am so impressed with your word choice."

Benefits of the Language Experience Approach

The Language Experience Approach brings together speaking, writing, reading, and sometimes art. It provides meaningful texts for our children to read, either with our support or on their own. Children have a vested interest in the text because they have created it themselves, using their own ideas and their own words. Thus, the reading material is predictable, laying a foundation for understanding that all written language has some predictable element to it.

Since parents are modeling writing directly in front of children, they are able to demonstrate the concepts of how print works, which are key skills to independent reading and writing success. Our children see us writing from left to right, leaving spaces in between each spoken word, using capitals for the beginning of sentences and proper nouns. Children begin to notice that *how* they say something can be transcribed as well. The English language has special symbols that signal to the reader how the text should be read. Preschoolers see us placing periods at the ends of statements, question marks when they are inquisitive, or exclamation points when they say something with enthusiasm. Emergent readers and writers begin to recognize certain letters of the alphabet and even common sight words as they are encountered time and again in their dictations. They can then apply this newfound knowledge the next time they are listening to a read-aloud by chiming in with the words they know or by assisting parents with punctuation or spelling during a subsequent dictation activity.

The Power of Connecting Reading and Writing

Reading and writing have been called reciprocal processes, meaning that the more you do one, the more you are able to do the other. This holds true for many of us. We know that the more we read, the better we are at writing, and the more we write, the more we attend to spelling, punctuation, and the fine nuances of how words are put together. This process of writing helps us recognize letter patterns and words in our future reading. And so it continues: by reading we improve our writing, and by writing we become better readers. Although many people believe that learning to read precedes the ability to learn to write, some researchers and educators, such as Donald Graves in his book *A Fresh*

Look at Writing, have found this not to be the case. Many preschool children may not be able to read yet, but they still make beginning attempts at writing. They enthusiastically write their names. They inquire how to spell "I love you," and then happily add it to every note sent to grandma and grandpa. It is not uncommon to see a young child pull out paper and scribble a note that includes random letters and symbols in an attempt to write like Mommy and Daddy. Heather, like many preschoolers, was extremely motivated to write words that had special meaning to her. These included, *Mommy, Daddy, Justin* (her best friend's name), and *Heather's Room* (to keep out little brother, Zack).

In classrooms and at home, writing can serve as an avenue for reflection, a time for someone to make sense of what he is reading, studying, thinking, or feeling. Writing on a particular topic in school forces us to think about and examine that topic more closely. What do we really understand about a specific content area, be it literature, science, social studies, or math? How has an event in our lives affected our mood or thought process? When we write about something, we have a chance to examine our knowledge base and translate what we've learned. This can be true for our children too. When we extend the read-aloud experience with writing, our children have time to make connections with the text, add to their prior knowledge, and experiment with new information.

Once children have heard numerous quality texts, they will have the foundation for embarking on their own writing endeavors. Parents can help build this bridge by using the LEA activity. A good place to begin is with a book your child has heard read aloud again and again. Consider *Brown Bear, Brown Bear, What Do You See?* Since so many children love this book, it can serve as the perfect foundation for writing their own version. We can ask our child to help create a new page for the book or even expand this page into a whole new book to read together. We may start by incorporating our child's name into a page with a format that mirrors the book. "Little Zack, Little Zack, what do you see?" And then Zack could help fill in this line any way he chooses. He may decide to have you write, "I see Mommy looking at me," or he may decide to imitate the format of the book more completely and add color words. For example, "I see a yellow dog named Simba looking at me." The pattern could continue with Simba seeing something. Perhaps a black and orange cat across the street looking at him.

Another way to extend the writing from *Brown Bear, Brown Bear, What Do You See?* is by using a firsthand experience from the family, such as a vacation or important event. If the family takes a trip to the beach, for example, you may want to create a book about this.

> Red crab, red crab, what do you see? I see a white sea star looking at me.
>
> White sea star, white sea star, what do you see? I see a blue fish looking at me.
>
> Blue fish, blue fish, what do you see? I see a black mollusk looking at me.

This way the child has a real experience from which to inspire his writing. You may choose also to personify objects and create a silly book about a Christmas tree that sees a present that sees a stocking by the chimney, and so on. Consider other holidays or family traditions to create new books, too. Chanukah, their birthday, or a trip to the farm provides great motivation for writing adventures. Have fun! Table 11 presents additional ideas for incorporating writing into the read-aloud experience from a variety of wonderful books.

Table 11. Ideas for Using Books as a Springboard to Writing

Title and Author	Brief Synopsis	Writing Activity
Click, Clack, Moo: Cows That Type by Doreen Cronin	Since Farmer Brown cannot understand the language of Moo, the cows must resort to using a typewriter to demand electric blankets for the cold nights on the farm.	If our dog or cat (or other household pet) could type, it would demand. . . .

table 11 continued on next page

Table 11 continued

Title and Author	Brief Synopsis	Writing Activity
Quick as a Cricket by Audrey Wood	Using rhyme and a series of comparisons (similes) the author describes all the different parts of a little boy. Among other things, he is slow like a snail, happy like a lark, and as wild as a chimp.	Help your child create her own simile about herself and then paint a picture to accompany it. "Amanda is as silly as a clown. Sophia is as beautiful as a butterfly. I am as loud as thunder."
If I Were a Tree by Dar Hosta	Listeners are treated to a melodic tribute to different types of trees throughout the four seasons. Information about trees and photosynthesis is provided at the end.	Encourage your child to finish the sentence, "If I were a tree, I would . . ." Ask her what she might see, feel, or do, or what kind of tree she would be. (Consider writing this on recycled paper just like the author.)
The Important Book by Margaret Wise Brown	The important thing about this book is that it helps us look more closely at how special and beautiful ordinary things are. The author uses rhythm and repetition to describe a daisy, apple, wind, rain, and even a child.	Children can use the format from the book to tell about one (or more!) important thing(s) about themselves. "The important thing about me is _____." Or they can make the sentence about a family member or friend.
Diary of a Worm by Doreen Cronin	A young earthworm chronicles the life of his family in this hilarious tale told in the form of the worm's diary. In it, we learn about the upside and downside of being a worm.	Keep your own worm diary. Fill a glass jar with dirt, add an earthworm, sprinkle with water. Record real observations or make up your own silly adventures.
If You Give a Mouse a Cookie By Laura Numeroff	When a little boy gives a mouse a cookie, it leads to a series of hilarious events.	If we had a mouse for a pet and gave him a cookie, what do you think would happen? The mouse would . . .

table 11 continued on next page

Title and Author	Brief Synopsis	Writing Activity
Cloudy with a Chance of Meatballs by Judi Barrett	There's no need for grocery stores in the town of Chewandswallow, where it rains soup and snows mashed potatoes. Eating is a breeze until the weather suddenly changes for the worse.	Ask your child to think about his favorite foods and then complete the sentence, "If it could rain any food, I would want our neighborhood to be sprinkled with. . . ."
Alexander and the Terrible, Horrible, No Good, Very Bad Day by Judith Viorst	Waking up with gum in his hair, being smushed in the car on the way to school, a lunch without dessert, and a cavity are some of the terrible, horrible, no good, very bad (but quite hilarious for the reader) things that happen to Alexander.	Your child may create his own fantasy of what would constitute a terrible and silly day for him or a friend. "It was a bad day when _____ happened."

Selecting Texts for Language Experience Approach

Some texts lend themselves more readily to a follow-up writing activity. Any book that spontaneously sparks discussion from your child could serve as a viable candidate for LEA. If a child is already talking about the book, it is easy for a parent to simply suggest that he write down one or more of the great ideas that have been shared. This is a natural and non-threatening way to bridge to dictation. "You have thought of some really great ideas related to the book we just read. I think they are so impressive that I want to write one of them down. Can you tell me one thing you consider particularly important that I should write on this piece of paper? And then if you want you can draw a picture to go with it. I think we should put it on the refrigerator for Mom to see when she gets home from work."

Look for books on topics of interest to your preschooler. If your child loves dinosaurs, he will no doubt have much to say about the topic. In this way, the text can serve to access the child's background knowledge and ignite verbal interaction. Once a child is talking, a parent can have paper and pencil ready to record the dictation.

When selecting books that serve as springboards for writing, consider those that provide numerous ideas that children may draw upon. *If the Dinosaurs Came Back*, cited earlier, supports preschoolers' writing by offering new ideas on nearly every page. Because of the repetitive pattern of the text, children are more comfortable with verbalizing their own sentences about what would happen if the dinosaurs were alive today. They have heard the rhythm inherent with this type of predictable text and are eager to extend that rhythm with the support of a parent. I also look for books that house exceptional illustrations so that the listener is stimulated and perhaps more excited to add to the text. Captivating pictures can inspire children to think imaginatively and then more confidently verbalize their thoughts. A picture really can be worth a thousand words.

Writing on Their Own

Some children are ready to write on their own. If your child chooses to try to write a sentence or story, support them through the process. Remember that early attempts at writing do not have to be perfect. At this stage of development, the ideas are more important than the exact spelling and punctuation. Depending on the developmental level, as well as the confidence level of your child, encourage him to sound out and approximate the spelling of words. Do not insist that every word be spelled correctly. Praise the letters he does get right. "Great job. You heard the *d* sound at the beginning of the word dinosaur, so you began the word with *d*. I see that you also wrote an *n* and an *s*, because you heard those sounds in the word also. Wow. You're becoming such a good speller." If your child wants you to help him spell each word correctly, feel free to do so, or consider telling him that we are just writing the sounds we hear at this point. Then reinforce all the sounds he heard in each word. "Wow. You heard a lot of sounds. Good spellers listen carefully for the sounds in words and often write all the sounds they hear." However, be mindful of not getting so bogged down with the tedious spelling and writing of each word. This could create frustration for the child and lead him to consider writing a laborious task.

I think it's also important to continue to take dictation for a child even after he has begun to write on his own. This continues to be a powerful way to show our child the close relationship between reading and writing. Transcribing dictation provides parents opportunities to model correct writing skills, letter formation, and punctuation marks. It also can help shift the focus back on the great ideas the child has shared rather than simply highlighting the mechanics of his own writing. Either way, be supportive of all aspects of the writing process. Applaud creative ideas. Praise beginning attempts at writing, and reinforce the different parts of writing that your child is doing correctly. Write on!

CHAPTER 20

Model What Magnificent Readers Do: The Think-Aloud Strategy

If I were a tree,
I would have conversations with
the sky . . .
and the sun . . .
and the stars . . .
and the moon.
If I were a tree,
I would wave to you
whenever
the wind blows.
How would it be
if you were a tree?

In the book *If I Were a Tree*, author Dar Hosta celebrates the importance of trees throughout the seasons and in our daily lives. She uses
a simple poetic text and gorgeous collage illustrations to take an ordinary object and bring it to "life." We see the power of trees to bear fruit,
provide shade, befriend all creatures, and make the earth more beautiful. Throughout the book the author invites the reader to think, "how

would it be if *you* were a tree?" This question creates an interactive format that helps the reader think more clearly about what he hears and reflect upon it. It provides the perfect venue for parents to stop and help their child discuss the story, its application to his life, and to use his imagination to creatively become a tree. "What kind of tree would you be? Why? Where would you want to put your roots down? How would you help the environment? Whom would you want to live in your branches?"

Ideally, our children would initiate meaningful conversations related to the books we read aloud. They would question, wonder, and discuss. They would predict and make connections to prior experiences. However, interacting with texts to assist in our understanding of them is a learned skill. Instead of feeling the need to ask questions, some children have become accustomed to listening and letting the story unfold, having the answers eventually provided for them. Others may naturally have questions during the read-aloud process, but they may have difficulty verbalizing them. It can be helpful for parents to model our own thought processes as we attempt to gain meaning from the written word. We can *show* our children how active readers approach text by thinking out loud in the midst of reading to them.

The Think-Aloud is a strategy in which parents verbalize what they are thinking as they read, illuminating the inner conversations readers have with the text during the reading process. Most parents are proficient and fluent readers who automatically, if not somewhat subconsciously, predict, clarify, visualize, summarize, and make connections while reading. These are all skills and strategies that good readers use to assist with comprehension. However, many young children experience reading as a passive process that involves only listening. They are often pleasantly surprised to see that parents question and wonder and do not have all the answers either.

The purpose of periodically demonstrating Think-Alouds with our preschool child is to help lay the foundation of what good readers do. A list of some of the things that all good readers do within the reading process and an explanation of each is provided in Table 12 on the next page.

Table 12. What Good Readers Do

Activate Prior Knowledge	None of us comes to a text void of prior knowledge. Good readers combine what they already know with the words from the text to help them fully understand it. Our prior experience with feelings, places, people, things and events is accessed when we read something related to it. Without active engagement with prior knowledge, it would be nearly impossible to comprehend text.
Make Personal Connections	Good readers are constantly identifying with characters, settings, or places in stories. They recognize certain authors and make connections to societal and global issues. **Text to self**—Good readers connect the text to their own experiences or background knowledge. They identify with the thoughts or feelings of the characters in the story, or relate to the events taking place. **Text to text**—Good readers cannot help but compare works by the same author or something they have previously read on a similar topic. **Text to world**—Good readers relate the text to societal and global issues.
Predict	Proficient readers are active readers who predict before they even begin reading a story. They use any information available (title, front cover illustration, awareness of author) to help set a focus for the story and help understand it. Throughout the reading process, numerous predictions are made as to what will happen next and why. Predicting lays a foundation for understanding the text. Once the story begins, a reader has an opportunity to "search" for information in the text to either verify the prediction or contradict it, thus assisting them in being an active reader who is thinking about the text.
Visualize	Active readers create pictures in their minds from the words on the page. This is why the best authors select words and phrases so carefully as to create a visual image for the reader. Even with the illustrations provided in many picture books, skilled readers listen closely to the words and form their own movie from them. We envision the characters, setting, and events that are taking place. We see the images of sadness, joy, and love. We go beyond the pictures provided and create a unique visual that brings the reading to life.

table 12 continued on next page

Ask Questions	Since comprehending requires active reading, proficient readers ask questions throughout the story or text and then search for clues to the answers. Our curiosity focuses our reading. *What* will the story be about? *When* will the wolf learn his lesson? *Where* will the wolf go next? *Why* don't all the pigs make their homes out of brick? *How* will it end? Children are often surprised that good readers (like their parents) have questions when they read. They think of parents as the keepers of the answers. It is eye-opening for them to see that all readers question. Instead of merely decoding the words on the page, active readers seek to understand the text. They do this by interacting with it. They wonder, pause to clarify things that don't make sense, and probe deeper.
Clarify	When active readers come across a vocabulary word that is unfamiliar or a phrase or sentence they do not understand, they pause and think. They implement strategies to figure out its meaning. They may read on to see if some of the other context provides clues to its meaning. Or perhaps they reread the sentence, giving them time to think about it and fully access any prior knowledge. They may even ask someone else what it means. Unlike passive readers who may merely focus on decoding the text, good readers know when something does not make sense. They seek to clarify and search the text for any clues that will help decipher the meaning.
Summarize	Good readers pause periodically and briefly summarize what has taken place thus far in the story. They are monitoring their understanding of the reading. If a proficient reader can give a summary of the events thus far, they know they are comprehending the text. If they cannot, they will generally stop at that point and implement strategies to fix the break in comprehension. They may reread the text or look at the illustrations for clues. This helps them focus the remainder of the reading. "Let's see. So far in the story, Little Red Riding Hood has left her house with a basket of cookies. She is taking the cookies to her grandmother's. The wolf has approached her and inquired about her journey. I wonder what will happen next."

By overtly stating what takes place in our minds as we read, parents teach their children how to behave like proficient readers. When we think aloud, our children literally hear the detailed process that reading entails. Good readers continually monitor their reading to make sure they are comprehending it. They ask questions based on their background knowledge and the information provided in the text.

- Does the story make sense so far?
- Do I have any predictions about what the story will be about or what will happen next?
- Am I making connections from the story to my own life?
- Have I ever felt the same way as a character in the story?
- Do I have questions?
- Can I visualize or picture what is happening in the story?
- Have I learned any new information from the text that I'm reading?
- Am I able to tell someone else what I just read or summarize the story?
- Do I understand that word or phrase?
- Am I doing what good readers do?

By modeling our own reading process, it is hoped that our children will begin to understand that reading is complex and multilayered. This can spark our children to also begin to interact with the books we are reading to them. It gives them permission to say out loud if something strikes them, makes them question, or reminds them of a personal experience. When they have opportunities to practice the thinking process that good readers use, they are on their way to becoming proficient independent readers themselves. Children who are accustomed to interacting with text begin to take risks and ask their own questions about plot, characters, and vocabulary. Questions that require simple confirmation from the parent or more open-ended questions that require critical thinking provide insight into the comprehension process of the child. These interactions with the text show that your child is beginning to recognize that proficient reading consists of active involvement with the text in order to understand it. Otherwise, readers are merely decoding the words on the page. There is no real reading without meaning. Louise Rosenblatt, a pioneer in reading theory and the teaching of literature, suggests that each of us brings our own meaning to the text based on our background knowledge, experience, and culture.[1] Children who are actively engaged in the text do not wait for the book to provide all the answers. They implement higher-order skills as they begin to predict what will happen next and clarify misunderstandings by thinking through clues from the story, as well as information they have gained from other stories, other discussions, and other interactions.

How to Implement the Think-Aloud Strategy

Although it is important not to artificially interrupt the natural cadence of the book, parents can look for authentic places to model the think-aloud process. We can periodically wonder aloud. In the midst of reading David Kirk's *Miss Spider's Tea Party*, the story of a lonely spider who hasn't any friends, we can verbalize our thoughts. "Miss Spider seems so sad because all the insects are afraid she is going to eat them. I wonder if she will find a friend before the book ends?" We can pick up a new book, read the title and predict the plot. "*Bear Snores On*. I see the bear sleeping with all sorts of animals near him. I wonder if he's hibernating. I think the other animals are his friends, and I predict that maybe they are going to wake him up. I can't wait to read and find out what happens." We can stop partway through *The Tale of Peter Rabbit* and summarize what we've read thus far without interrupting the power and beauty of the story. "Let's see. Peter's mom told him not to go into Mr. McGregor's garden, but he went anyway. Now he's lost and in big trouble. He seems so scared. Poor little Peter. I wonder if he'll be able to find his way back home again. Let's read some more, shall we?"

When we employ the think-aloud procedure, we pause before, during, or after the read-aloud experience to verbalize thoughts and questions. It is helpful if you adjust the tone of your voice so that your child can more easily distinguish when you are *reading* from when you are *thinking aloud*. In Table 13, I have recorded some think-alouds that illustrate what is stated in the text, what the parent says, and the direct connection to what good readers do. Notice that the think-alouds are taken

Table 13. Think-Aloud Examples

Parent Reads	Parent Thinks (Aloud)	What Parent Is Modeling/Demonstrating
(Reads title) *Hedgie's Surprise*	Hey. This book is by Jan Brett. I remember another book we really liked, The Gingerbread Baby. This is written by the same author, Jan Brett. I wonder if it will be just as good.	**Connection** (text to text) The parent makes a connection to another title by the same author to access prior knowledge. It also assists the child in building a bank of titles for this particular author.
(Reads title) *Hedgie's Surprise*	Hedgie? I wonder who Hedgie is. I'm looking at the picture on the front cover. I see a rooster and a . . . wait a minute. That's a hedgehog! Oh! I think it's going to be about a hedgehog whose name is probably Hedgie. I wonder if he, or maybe she, is friends with the rooster. Let's read and see.	**Prediction**—The parent demonstrates how good readers are active readers who predict before they even begin reading a story. They use any information available (in this case, the cover illustration and the title), to help set a focus for the story and help understand it. Once predicting begins, a reader has an opportunity to "search" for information in the text to either verify the prediction or contradict it.
Reads first page (The author introduces one of the characters, a little Tomten)	Little Tomten. I've never heard of a Tomten. Let's see. On the opposite page there is a picture of an old woman, a cat, and someone who looks a little like a boy but has pointy ears. Hmmm. This book must be a fantasy because there's no such thing as a Tomten. I guess this is an imaginary tale. How fun. I want to see if they give us more information about this Tomten.	**Clarify** - (Vocabulary) The parent shows how good readers stop to question unfamiliar vocabulary. They use other information provided in the text to assist them with meaning.

table 13 continued on next page

Firefly Mountain

Summary—A young girl waits patiently for the hot afternoon to end so that she and her family can experience the magic of a firefly mountain.

Parent Reads	Parent Thinks (Aloud)	What Parent Is Modeling/Demonstrating
"An orange ball of a sun dipped down behind the orchard, painting the sky pink and red behind it."	I can picture this in my mind. The sun is like a giant ball of orange, and it is setting. The sky is so beautiful at this time in the evening. It is pink and red. I've seen the sky look just like this. You've seen it too. Remember? You even painted a red and pink sky with a little bit of orange in one of your pictures. The writer is helping us really imagine what it looks like.	**Visualization** The parent is helping the child understand that many authors use sensory words to help the reader picture what is taking place in the story. By visualizing the place and events in the story, the reader is better able to understand the text.

Miss Spider's Tea Party

Summary—Miss Spider desperately wants to make friends with the other insects and have them over for cakes and tea. However, everyone is too afraid of her and dashes away in "mortal dread." It is not until a moth is caught in the rain and unable to fly that Miss Spider gets the opportunity to show her kindness and pure intentions.

Parent Reads	Parent Thinks (Aloud)	What Parent Is Modeling/Demonstrating
The parent reads a few pages of the text that talk about various insects coming near the main character's house, but they are frightened away because she is a spider.	Oh . . . no one wants to come to Miss Spider's house for tea. All the insects who fly by are afraid of her and they go away. They don't want to be her friend. She's lonely.	Summarize The parent is demonstrating how readers periodically pause and reflect on what has taken place so far in the text. They briefly summarize the story up

Table 13 continued

Parent Reads	Parent Thinks (Aloud)	What Parent Is Modeling/Demonstrating
		to the point where they have stopped reading. This helps make sense of the story and helps focus the remaining reading. If the reader was unable to adequately summarize the story, they could go back and reread or look at the illustration to assist them, rather than waiting until the end of story.

from several texts, demonstrating that different parts of stories lend themselves more readily to predicting, questioning, and reflecting. I firmly believe that parents should only use the think-aloud strategy intermittently, being ever mindful to not interrupt the flow of the story and the child's enjoyment of hearing it in its entirety. Parents can model and support their children's understanding of the strategy and help them think critically about the text, make connections, and ask questions. But this should never impede the richness of the story as a whole.

Balancing Reading and the Think-Aloud

The potential to detract from the enjoyment of the read-aloud experience with too much "talk and interruption" was made very clear to me by a friend of mine who is a kindergarten teacher. Megan was telling me about how she had prepared a wonderful lesson to help her young students become proficient readers. As she was reading aloud, she was stopping and asking them to predict what would happen next. When they volunteered suggestions, she followed with additional probing to help them justify their answers. She also paused periodically and thought aloud to help students begin to hear what proficient readers do to gain meaning with text. In the midst of what she thought was a model lesson, a student shyly spoke up and asked if the teacher could please just finish the story so they could find out what happened. Megan noted that several other students simultaneously nodded at his request. She chuckled to herself, realizing that while trying to demonstrate the process of interacting with text, she had inadvertently taken away from the pleasure of the story. She agreed to "just read it" and made a mental note to place the reading of the story as a whole first and foremost. She would still sometimes insert questions and think-alouds, but would be more mindful of placing a priority on relaying the beauty of the author's message.

Taking the First Step

As you embark on the think-aloud process, refer once again to Table 12 at the beginning of this chapter to help you focus on what good readers do. The more you explore your own metacognition (the process of thinking about how you are reading), I am confident that you will become more aware of the reading strategies you implement without even being conscious of doing so. You will begin to recognize that you do, indeed, weave through the strategies that good readers use. You predict, question, clarify, and summarize. This newfound awareness will help you find authentic times to pause during the read-aloud experience and *show* your child your process. Consider some of the sentence and question starters in table 14 on the following page to assist you in your think-aloud endeavors.

You may use these sentence starters as a springboard to your own interaction with text. As you model this strategy, your child will hopefully begin to ask his own questions and be inspired to think critically about the books being read.

Table 14. Think-Aloud Starters

What Good Readers Do	Sentence and Question Starters
Predict	I think _____ will happen next because _____ . I predict _____ .
Connect	This reminds me of _____ . This author also wrote _____ . I already know _____ about this topic.
Question	Who? What? When? Where? Why? How? I'm wondering _____ . What else can I learn from this text?
Clarify	This doesn't make sense. Let me reread it. I am not familiar with this word. I think it might mean _____. This part is confusing to me.
Summarize	So far the story has been about _____ . I know that _____ happened at the beginning of the book. Then _____ happened. Now I wonder what will happen next. The story was about _____ .
Visualize	I can picture this. I can see this in my mind. This looks like _____ to me.

Part D

More Ways to Promote Early Literacy

CHAPTER 21

Living in a Literate Home: Books, Books Everywhere

So please, oh please, we beg, we pray,
Go throw your TV set away,
And in its place you can install
A lovely bookshelf on the wall.

Surrounding Your Child with Books

Unlike Roald Dahl in the above quote from *Charlie and the Chocolate Factory*, I am not actually suggesting that everyone throw their televisions away. Although . . . one can't help but imagine how different our world would be if we were to do this. On a more serious—and realistic—note, perhaps we should refocus our view of how our children should be entertained. If we have televisions in nearly every room but do not have books in these same rooms, what message are we sending about our priorities? Parents *show* children what is valued. We show our children that we value *them* when we sit beside them and give our undivided attention, when we listen *to* them and talk *with* them. Parents show that they value the written word for learning, growing, exploring, and entertaining every time we visit the library or bookstore and select a book or magazine to read. We offer a profound message about how important books are to our daily lives when we have baskets and boxes and shelves filled with them. We let our children know how special they are every time we pull them close and share a wonderful book together. So, let's get closer. Let's snuggle with our children. Let's pull up the comforter and discover the world of books with them. This is what we value. This is what matters. This is the gift that will change their lives forever.

Create an environment where books are easily accessible for your child to read on his own, share with a friend or loved one, and revisit again and again. We have books in nearly every room in our home. There is a basket of books next to the comfy glider, a box of books next to Heather's bed, books lining our shelves in the den and living room and office. We even have books in each of the bathrooms and bring some with us in the car. Many adults like to read the paper first thing in the morning, reaping the benefits of a cup of coffee, waking up with the morning news at their fingertips. Others find themselves staring at the cereal boxes, hoping to gain some insight into the nutritional value of the morning meal. The point is, meals can be the perfect time to begin a tradition of reading in the home. We can place a box of books near the kitchen table so children can join in on the morning reading routine. I am not suggesting that reading time replace family get-together time or that interacting with one's family isn't valuable. I believe strongly in the idea of families sitting together, informally sharing the day, and becoming connected through this process. I am simply stating that the reality for many of us is that we are trying to balance so many things, and that rather than reading the paper in silence in front of our children, we could invite them into the tradition. We could provide them options at breakfast or while we're clearing the dishes or when we get caught by a phone call. Let us teach our children to know the enjoyment of reading. Knowledge is power. Books are a wondrous way to provide this power.

With long commutes for many of us, it is becoming more and more common to have DVD players mounted in cars for children to watch while we drive. There are also portable players that keep the children entertained on a plane ride and nearly everywhere else they have a moment to spare. Although I recognize that these devices are very convenient and can serve a very specific purpose, I suggest (strongly) that parents consider using books instead of technology to fill the quiet times of the day. We can put books in the car, bring books on the plane, and have books available throughout the house for children to pick up anytime and just about anywhere. Yes, it seems that some children are easily bored and want to be constantly entertained. However, entertainment can take on a variety of forms. Why not turn off the electrical power and turn on the power of books to promote literacy, foster imagination, create critical thinkers, and lay the foundation for lifelong learning?

When I was a principal, there were children's books on the shelves in my office. I was showing the students and the teachers what I believed, what I valued, how important literacy is. I shared books with children, teachers, and parents. I remember even the school librarian coming into my office, scanning the shelves, looking for new books to order for classroom check-out. Keep books within reach of your children and encourage them to read with you, to you, and to their friends.

Modeling the Love of Books

Children at the preschool stage of development love to imitate the behaviors of their parents. They pretend to mow the lawn, shave their whiskers, play "mommy," fix the car, cook, and talk on the phone. We cannot help but laugh when we see our sons and daughters replicating our mannerisms and the family sayings. Parents know the power of modeling appropriate grammar, saying "please" and "thank you," brushing teeth, and having healthy eating habits. It makes sense that reading in front of our children sends a strong message about what we value. Parents who spend time reading the paper, poring over magazines, sifting through novels, and meticulously following step-by-step directions for assembling toys set an example for children about what we find pleasurable, intriguing, informational, and practical. The children who see their parents read and are read to will often pick up books and "pretend read" by themselves. They will use the common language of books as they retell the story, turn the pages, and finally close the book in satisfaction. Preschoolers who come from a home where reading is valued will often ask, "What does this say?" "Will you read this to me?" They begin pointing to words on toy packages, cereal boxes, and road signs because they now understand that letters carry meaning. They have begun the journey of learning to read through their natural curiosity about the messages that surround them.

In addition to making visible our reading, I think it is important to also *show* its value. What I mean by this is to make public just how the reading has impacted us. When Grandmother Dottie comes over to our house, Heather often requests that she read her stories before bedtime. I remember once when she was reading aloud *Yummers!*, a story by James Marshall about Emily the pig, who decides to take a walk with her turtle friend to lose weight. Unfortunately, Emily spends more time stopping to get food than walking and winds up with a stomachache. Grandmother obviously found the story so silly that she began giggling and then laughing through most of the book. I could hear her stopping and providing side comments about her own diet battles. Without even knowing it, Grandmother was showing Heather how enjoyable and personally connecting books can be.

When I taught elementary school, I set aside a certain amount of time each day for children to read to themselves. During Sustained Silent Reading (SSR), I, too, read. I did not use this time as an opportunity to grade papers, finish next week's lesson plans, or take a break. Instead, I recognized the importance of modeling the behavior that I talked, preached, and promoted. I firmly believed (and still do) that instilling the love of reading was the most important activity that teachers can provide their students. Therefore, not only did I read "silently" when my students were expected to do the same, I periodically reacted out loud to what I was reading. When something authentically struck me as humorous, I laughed. When I was caught up in the drama of the book, I closed the chapter after silent reading had stopped and said to the students, "I'm so worried about Peanut (the dog in the book). I hope he gets saved." After reading from a professional journal, I would sometimes tell my students about an interesting fact I had just learned regarding teaching or students or the writing process. Or I might even tell them that I did not get much out of the article I had just read, but that I would read more later and maybe it would prove more informative. I was revealing the truth about reading. Not all of it provided pleasure or valuable insight, but since most did, I was willing to continue my pursuit and not give up.

It was no surprise that my students began asking me about the plot of the stories I was reading during SSR. I had piqued their curiosity through my authentic reactions to books. When our silent reading time was completed each day, I purposely placed the book I had been reading on the chalk rim in front of the class. Undoubtedly, when students had completed other work throughout the day or on subsequent SSR times, they would rush to pick up this book and read it themselves. It was also no surprise that during the next school book sale or trip to the library, numerous students requested the book that I had been reading. As they read it in subsequent weeks, they, too, shared their feelings. We created our own impromptu book club. The power of modeling book behavior before, during, and after reading was contagious. I also noticed that some of the students started laughing out loud while reading their own literature selections. They gasped at things that scared them and even cried at the things that made them sad or moved them. Afterward, we started having discussions and students wound up giving "book talks" that enticed others to read the same titles. In our classroom community, books and other forms of print were read, discussed, and shared just as superior literature often is within our society.

The Present of Books

We have always been very fortunate in our home. Santa Claus and the Easter Bunny have clearly recognized the power of books. On Christmas or Easter morning we have seen some of the best literature slipped under the tree, placed in our stockings, or left in an Easter basket. Grandma and Grandpa often give books for special occasions as well. The "gifts that keep on giving" are the magazine subscriptions that Heather and Zack's grandmother has bought for them. Each month we look forward to the latest editions of *Ladybug, Your Big Backyard*, and *Animal Baby*. We save them and revisit the information and stories they provide.

One of my good friends, Becky, prides herself on giving thematic presents that are fun, valuable, and yes, even educational. When Heather turned three, Becky mailed a "ladybug package." After hurriedly opening it, Heather uncovered a large, fluffy, and snuggly stuffed ladybug to take to bed and gently squeeze at night. There was also a science kit with the life cycle stages of the ladybug, models of the egg, larva, pupa, and the ladybug itself, so Heather could explore these and put them in order and we could talk about each. Becky tied the gift together with *The Very Lazy Ladybug*, a brightly illustrated book about a ladybug that refuses to learn to fly. In this humorous tale, the lazy ladybug decides to hitch a ride on several different animals. However, this does not prove comfortable for her and she is finally thrown into the air when she's atop an elephant who sneezes. With this unfortunate event, the lazy ladybug is forced to learn to fly. Heather, Mike, and I appreciated the cleverness of connecting a little bit of science with a great story and something fun and cuddly to hold. It is gifts like this that reinforce the pleasure of books for our children.

I admit that I have used the idea of themed gifts to spread the love of books to many. After all, the literacy revolution begins with one. Let us, quite literally, "spread the word" about books. When one of Heather's friends had a fourth birthday party and we were told that she loved playing dress-up, we bought jewelry, a princess crown, pretty necklaces and high heels. We added Jane O'Connor's *Fancy Nancy* to connect all the gifts together and make pretending even more fun. Nancy is a witty, endearing little girl frocked in lace, ribbons and tiaras, who is just trying to add a bit of flair to her everyday life. She speaks "fancy" language, substituting the word fuchsia for purple, plume for feather, and stupendous for great. Nancy even manages to teach her extravagant way of life to her otherwise ordinary family. This book is a must have for every little girl who loves the "finer things in life." *Fancy Nancy* helped create a distinctively unique gift for Heather's little friend.

I have found numerous opportunities to give books as presents. In addition to the traditional gifts of a blanket, stuffed animal, or layette, new moms are often pleasantly surprised when they receive a book to read aloud to the new arrival. Some of my favorite books for baby showers include *On the Night You Were Born, Snug in Mama's Arms*, and *Time for Bed*. All are lyrical and have beautiful and soothing illustrations to help calm both baby and new parents.

It is sometimes very easy to create a noteworthy gift just by adding items revolving around a particular theme. For example, if you have found a wonderful story about horses, look for horse stickers or perhaps a journal or notebook with a horse on the cover, and then add a pencil with horses on it. This way, the child can read, write, and play with items all about horses. I like to start with the book and then add items to it. However, if you have found the perfect shorts outfit with ducks on it, look for a darling ducky book to round it out. (How about *Make Way for Ducklings* by Robert McClosky?) I came across a sweet little porcelain tea set with ladybugs painted on each piece. It made an ideal gift for one of Heather's friends, but needed the perfect book to top it off. I chose *Miss Spider's Tea Party*, envisioning little girls being read to and then enjoying a nice cup of tea together. You can add clothing, a beach towel, a stuffed animal, or any other fun items you find based on a theme of choice. I think that plush puppets make a great complement to wonderful literature. These can ignite a child's imagination and invite them to retell the story using the puppet, or they can become one of the characters, re-enacting the events from the book. For more ideas on themed presents for preschoolers centered around a quality literature selection, refer to Table 15. I have included both narrative and informational texts under the "Great Book" column to give you more choices based on what you know about the child.

Table 15. Themed Gifts Centered Around a Quality Book

Theme	Great Books	Other Fun Items to Extend the Theme
Dinosaur	*How Do Dinosaurs Say Good Night?* by Jane Yolen	• Choose from the multitude of dinosaur themed toys, puzzles, or stuffed animals available based on the specific personality and developmental level of the child.
Pig	*If You Give a Pig a Pancake* by Laura Numeroff	• Wooden farm • A plush pig, some pancake mix and syrup

table 15 continued on next page

Theme	Great Books	Other Fun Items to Extend the Theme
Firefighter	*Even Firefighters Hug Their Moms* by Christine Kole MacLean *Fire! Fire!* by Gail Gibbons	• Toy fire truck • Firefighter hat
Elephant	*Emma Kate* by Patricia Polacco *I've Got an Elephant* by Anne Ginkel	• Friendship necklace • Elephant stuffed animal • Tickets to the zoo
Whale	*Whales Passing* by Eve Bunting	• Tickets to the aquarium • Whale watching tour
Soccer	*My Soccer Book* by Gail Gibbons	• Soccer whistle • Soccer ball, soccer clothes
Frog	*Growing Frogs* by Vivian French	• Aquarium with a tadpole • Frog food
Ant	*Two Bad Ants* By Chris Van Allsburg	• Ant farm • Magnifying glass to get a closer look
Jungle	*Rumble in the Jungle* by Giles Andreae	• Plastic jungle animals • "Wild" animal cookies • Child's favorite music on compact disc • Safari hat
Pirate	*How I Became a Pirate* by Melinda Long	• Pirate sword (Many toy stores carry plastic ones that you can fill with air.) • Pirate eye patch • Pirate ship
Puppy	*The Puppy Who Wanted a Boy* by Jane Thayer	• If your family is ready for the responsibility of a real dog, get one. If not, stick with a stuffed animal. (They're pretty cuddly too!)

table 15 continued on next page

Table 15 continued

Theme	Great Books	Other Fun Items to Extend the Theme
Letters of the Alphabet	*The Alphabet Tree* by Leo Lionni *Chicka Chicka Boom Boom* by Bill Martin Jr.	• Wooden alphabet blocks or foam, plastic, or magnetic letters
Kitten	*Violet Comes to Stay* by Melanie Cecka	• Gift certificate to a children's bookstore
Bat	*Stellaluna* by Janell Cannon	• Bat and bird puppet
Fairy	*Good Night, Fairies* by Kathleen Hague	• Fairy wand • Fairy wings • A fairy garden starter kit (flower pot, moss, and a tiny fairy to invite friends)
Construction	*B is for Bulldozer: A Construction Alphabet* by June Sobel	• A big truck
Polar Bear	*Polar Bear Night* by Laura Thompson	• Tickets to the zoo • Snow cone making machine

I am thrilled to see that it is not just Mike and me who are sending messages to our children about the enjoyment that books can bring. Heather and Zack see that important people in their lives other than parents get excited about the joy that can be associated with reading a wonderful book. Books serve as perfect presents because each new page is a surprise, one that excites, delights, and invites the reader back time and again.

The Importance of a Library Card

Take your child to get his own library card and celebrate this monumental occasion. Talk to him about the great privileges this new card affords. Then, make a conscious effort to bring him to the library often and be sure to use his card when checking out books. Make it clear to your child that this is a significant event and entitles him to a whole new world of reading opportunities. This is empowering to a child and serves as a message about how important books are in our lives.

The Borrowing Book Exchange

Consider starting your own "Borrowing Book Exchange" with a friend. Since busy parents may have trouble fitting in a weekly trip to the library or bookstore, capitalize on the book selections of your friend or neighbor. When my friend, Paula, and I were involved in a weekly "mommy and me" class with our younger children, I overheard her mention a book she thought was wonderful that involved the changing seasons and apples. Our class instructor had filled the fall morning with storytelling and songs about apples, harvests, and the changes in the trees that take place throughout the different seasons of the year. The event culminated with the children coring and peeling apples, and then, of course, feasting on the fruits of their labor. The theme from class had reminded Paula of a delightful book. Since I was not familiar with the book, my curiosity was sparked. I inquired about Paula's book and asked her if she could bring it next week when we met again. I reiterated that I was always looking for new and exceptional literature.

The anticipation of being able to share an unfamiliar and wonderful book with Heather and Zack gave me an idea. I emailed Paula and asked if she would be interested in participating in a book exchange in which we borrowed books from one another. I figured we could share some fabulous literature with our children without needing to buy it or try to locate it at the library. I thought this could prove exciting on many levels. We could capitalize on the other person's treasure trove of books and share our own. Perhaps we would discover that we had some of the same titles in our home libraries, thus reinforcing how special the books were. Since Heather and Zack were of similar ages to her children, Julia and Audrey, it would be interesting to involve them in the book selection process. This could serve to empower our children since the parents would be consulting them about what they felt were great books on our shelves. Paula and I could ask them why the particular text stood out as special among the others. Thus, we would be showing them firsthand how much we valued their opinion and assessment of books. What a great way to bridge children into looking critically at texts.

Once you start a book exchange, you may elect to ask friends to peruse their homes for books on specific topics. When Heather and I were planning to create a fairy garden, I asked several of my friends if they had any great fairy books that we could read aloud to provide us more information about fairies as well as set the mood and add to the excitement of our imaginative project. You do not, however, have to narrow the criteria in any way. Since I have spent so much time reading and evaluating child and adolescent literature, I was curious to see what Paula and her family viewed as wonderful. I thought it would be valuable to learn from her choices and gather different opinions. In the email I sent to her, I suggested that we did not need to set any particular parameters on book selections. The only criteria needed to be that we considered the book special in some way. It could be sweet, quiet, sentimental, have beautiful illustrations, include vivid language, or just capture our attention. The range of books needed to strike us in some way, whether they evoked a calming feeling in us, were melodic, reassuring, cheery, or fabulously quirky and funny. The goal was to pore over our collections of books and select the best to share with our friends.

Needless to say, Paula thought this a fabulous idea. Over the next several weeks, we exchanged books and were delighted to share these with our children. When we met the following week, we gave each other a quick review of our children's reactions (and our own) to the readalouds. Paula and I discovered that some of the books enticed us to want to buy our own copy. Not surprisingly, we also found that some of the books were not as popular for the other family as they were for our own. This was a great avenue to explore what we liked in literature and what did not work for us as a family. This process provided our children another opportunity to look critically at and evaluate literature. I loved the process of trying hard to select books that Paula would not already have and I greatly enjoyed the fact that she obviously worked to do the same. I would highly recommend the Book Borrowing Exchange to all. Give it a try. You have nothing to lose!

Beginning the Literate Life

I hope that you now have a heightened awareness of creating a literate home. This involves much more than merely reading aloud to our children. We need to surround them with books, make reading a priority in our lives, and share the value of the written word. Living a literate life means instilling a love of exploring and learning and creating from texts. Take your child to the bookstore. Take him to the library. Fill your shelves at home with books. Tell him about what you're reading and make public your reactions to newspaper and magazine articles. Discuss fiction and nonfiction. Memorize poems together. Fill his world with all that is literate. Think books.

CHAPTER 22

Other Ways to Reinforce Literacy Development

The love of learning, the sequestered nooks, and all the sweet serenity of books.

—Henry Wadsworth Longfellow

Other Ways to Assist in Learning the ABCs

In addition to using alphabet books and other quality literature selections involving letters and sounds, parents can use other tools to teach and reinforce the alphabet. Although I do not feel it is necessary for most preschoolers and other emergent readers to be drilled with flashcards to learn their alphabet, there are numerous ways to expose our children to these skills. We know that many children (and adults too) learn best when the setting is natural, supportive, and even has an element of fun. Seize the opportunity to expose your child to the letters in creative and playful ways. Consider some of the following ideas.

Alphabet Blocks

When we sit with our preschooler and build towers, farms, or places for dolls to sleep, we can use alphabet blocks and name the letters. We can think out loud as we carefully select the right building block for the miniature garage. "Let's see. I'm looking for a block with an *R* on it. I thought I saw it just a minute ago. Is this it? Yes, there's the *R*." Or we can make a direct connection to the sound of the letter. "I need a block whose letter makes the *ffffff* sound, as in *ffffeather*. Can you help me find it?" In this way, we don't quiz our child or pressure him. Instead, we play and interact, while still reinforcing letter names and their sounds.

Shaving Cream Fun

Many children love to get their hands in things, feel the texture, play, and even make a mess. Use a jelly roll pan, or something else with an edge on it, and spray shaving cream in it. Then, smooth it out and invite your child to write the letters and say the corresponding sounds. Children love to literally get their hands into the alphabet. Using kinesthetic activities like this one helps many children more easily remember how the letters are formed because they are actively involved in the process of making them. You may also opt to do this in the bathtub. Spray the shaving cream on the bathtub tile, smooth it, and encourage your child to write the letter of a particular sound you provide. Then, wash it down the drain and finish the bath. So fun and easy cleanup!

Rice, Salt, and Sand

Another activity in which your child can feel and manipulate the letters is pouring salt or rice into a pan and having your child form the letters in it with his index finger. It is helpful if he says the letters as he creates them so that the brain can associate the name with the visual symbol. Saying the sound as he writes it is also important for learning to read, write, and spell. The next time you are at the beach or the park, sit down with your child and model writing a few of the alphabet letters in the sand. Make it a game and keep it fun for your child. You may wish to start with the first letter of your child's name. It is not necessary to go in alphabetical order, either. It is beneficial for a child to recognize and be able to form each letter out of order. This shows a real working knowledge of letters because the child has not just memorized the alphabet song.

Magnetic Letters

Magnetic letters are so versatile. They can be placed on the refrigerator, a magnetic easel, white board, or even on a cookie sheet. I like to write simple little messages to family members and then read them aloud at breakfast. "I love you, Heather and Zack." "Our children are the best!" I think it is also fun to periodically list the name of a food that we need to get at the grocery store or write the name of an upcoming family activity such as *soccer* or *picnic*. Since all of these words have significance in their lives, our children are motivated to look more closely at the letters and make connections to the words and sentences. Through repeated exposure to certain words our children will begin to recognize them and hopefully make connections to the read-aloud experience.

Alphabet Foam Letters

Why not toss some foam alphabet letters into the tub during bath time? Children love to play and imagine while scrubbing and splashing. They wet the letters and "glue" them to the bath tiles, inquiring, "What does this spell?" Of course, so often it doesn't spell anything, but we can talk about the individual letters and their sounds as we shampoo and rinse. We can join in by creating words in the tub for our children or ask them to help us find the letter *t* to spell *tub*. "Where's the first letter of your name? Can you pull out a letter and tell me the sound it makes or a word that begins with that letter?" Periodically draw attention to the letters, but keep it a friendly game. Listen closely to the feedback from your child. If he is not having fun, go back to scrubbing behind the ears and save the alphabet learning for another time or venue.

More Alphabet Fun

I have found alphabet puzzles and alphabet tiles and alphabet cookies. Consider eating your way through some of the alphabet as you and your child enjoy a glass of milk together. Stay true to the idea of always making learning enjoyable for our preschoolers, and stay clear of forcing or pressuring them to learn more and learn it right now. Surround your children with great books and opportunities to see and manipulate letters in creative and innovative ways. When they are cognitively and emotionally ready, they will learn. I promise.

Phonemic Awareness
Sing, Sing a Song
So many children's songs have rhythm and rhyme that will assist our child in gaining phonemic awareness. "Down by the Bay" emphasizes rhyme and invites active participation from our child, making it a fun and non-threatening way to teach and reinforce this key preliteracy skill. Strategically pause at the end of a line in the song and see if your child can fill in the rhyme. "Did you ever see a pig wearing a ___ [wig]? Down by the bay." In addition to songs that rhyme, there are many that specifically play with language and invite our children to apply their own variations. "Willoughby Wallaby Woo," for instance, is a silly song about an elephant who takes turns sitting on different children. However, the first sound in the child's name is substituted with the *W* sound. So instead of Heather, it becomes Weather, and Wack replaces Zack. The song becomes interactive as children try to guess the real name of the child and sing it. I also like the classic song, "The Name Game," because it requires the singer and listener to manipulate a person's name in ridiculous but hilarious ways, focusing once again on the initial sound.

Happy Birthday to You!
Our children can experiment with language by singing the Happy Birthday song and substituting the first consonant. Most children are familiar with the words and tune to "Happy Birthday to You," so this can serve as a springboard to playing with sounds. Instead of singing the original version of the song, change the first sound of each word to match the first sound of your child's name. For example, using Zack's name, the song would sound like this:

> Zappy zirthday zoo zoo.
> Zappy zirthday zoo zoo.
> Zappy zirthday zear Zack.
> Zappy zirthday zoo zoo.

Children love to hear the focus of the entire song shift to the beginning of their name and relish in the silly sounds made. Notice that most of the "words" that have been created are not real words at all. It is not necessary to use conventional language when we are experimenting with sounds in an effort to focus on phonemic awareness. Our goal is to help our children become comfortable with manipulating sounds within the English language so they will understand that these sounds are separate parts that comprise words.

Tongue Twisters

Read and recite, if you can, all those silly tongue twisters we have heard throughout our lives.

> Peter Piper picked a peck of pickled peppers;
> A peck of pickled peppers Peter Piper picked;
> If Peter Piper picked a peck of pickled peppers,
> Where's the peck of pickled peppers Peter Piper picked?

Encourage your child to chime in with you, but don't be surprised if he has a difficult time doing so. Do not be too concerned if your child is unable to perform this skill. After all, many of us still get caught up in the absurdity of the sounds strung together. Since phonemic awareness is an auditory skill, he will benefit from *hearing* you say the words. Read them aloud and then laugh with your child. Have fun exploring the silly world of sounds.

Take a Vacation

Each new learning experience we provide our children increases their background knowledge, better preparing them for reading and writing activities, as well as everything in school. When we visit science museums as a family, we show our children that we value knowledge. We model our own curiosity about how the world works and fuel their curiosity as well. History museums help build a perspective of different times and different cultures. These help our children begin to compare and contrast life now with life during a different period of time. Comparing and contrasting are higher-order skills that can be fostered through this inviting experience. Art museums get our children thinking about how the world around us can be interpreted in a variety of ways, and thus contribute to their own creative outlook. They also provide children a view of different aesthetics, much like children's books can. When we highlight art, our children will no doubt begin to build their own criteria for likes and dislikes. They will come to appreciate certain styles more than others. Visits to the zoo or the aquarium spark inquisitiveness and are places where children can learn by seeing and exploring, as opposed to simply trying to learn by hearing about something. These are the experiences that children will remember.

As I suggested earlier, when we have more than one experience with a particular topic, our knowledge base expands. Therefore, if you are planning a trip to a farm, a nature preserve, or even another country, find books that provide background information on these topics. In this way, you are laying a foundation for focused learning once you arrive at your destination, which will make the trip more valuable and meaningful.

We know that children learn by doing. Learning makes more sense when children see it, touch it, experiment, and hold it in their hands. "Field trips" with the family prominently contribute to a child's knowledge base, thus adding to the "file folders" that exist inside our brain. Each adventure that we plan for our child serves as a way to help him with future reading and writing endeavors. As has been pointed out in different chapters throughout this book (for example, chapter 2, "Build Background Knowledge," and chapter 18, "Make the Most of Reading Aloud with Multiple Intelligences"), having varied experiences with a certain subject contributes to depth and breadth of knowledge. After all, we can never have too much knowledge. As children are expected to read unfamiliar texts in the future and eloquently transcribe their thoughts onto paper, their past experiences will positively contribute to these. They will have heard many more words than those children who have had limited exposure to outside resources. Children with a great deal of background knowledge will therefore be able to use these thick file folders to recognize a word in print or conjure up the best way of saying something in writing.

Electronic Media for Literacy Instruction

In addition to reading to your child, surrounding him with great books, and helping him interact with text in a meaningful and productive way, you may choose to use various forms of electronic media to assist in supporting literacy development. Some parents have found that the use of technology can be very motivating for their child and therefore use computer programs to entice him or her into literacy. Although we do not want to replace the read-aloud experience, parents may choose to use electronic media to support different aspects of literacy learning. Computer programs and websites can become part of a larger effort to prepare our children for success in reading and writing. Since the games offer immediate reinforcement of phonics or other skills, children's learning can be instantly supported. I think it goes without saying that, in my opinion, these programs do not and cannot replace the valuable impact that reading aloud with our child does. However, they may provide other benefits and can help prepare our children for growing up in a technologically driven society.

Parents may choose to investigate electronic books to assist their child in reading independently. The advantage of this type of book is that children can listen to the text being read to them and they can follow along. Many such programs highlight each word as it is being read aloud so that children can more easily track the text. These electronic packages often include second language versions of the texts and instructional games centered around reinforcing key literacy skills. CD-ROMs, websites, and computer programs are available to support literacy development. Common topics include alphabet letters and sounds and creating new words by adding a beginning to "word families" such as *cat, sat, pat,* and *mat* from the *-at* ending. Other programs emphasize rhyming skills, sight word recognition, phonics, word study, vocabulary, writing skills, or comprehension. They may have interactive elements in which a child clicks on a particular object and watches it become animated.

I am not going to endorse or recommend any specific computer programs or websites to parents, but I do suggest that, as you preview them, keep in mind the goals of literacy for your child. Is the program age and developmentally appropriate? The layout should be pleasing to look at and appealing to a young child. It can be colorful and fun but should not be distracting. For example, if the program is very noisy or busy or cluttered, this may overwhelm some children. It should keep your child's attention without being confusing. Make sure that the type is large enough and clear enough to be followed by your child. "Fancy" letters can be hard to read. Consider the amount of parental involvement the program requires. Is it intended to be navigated independently by the child, or does it require the parent to explain directions or even sit with the child and work through each page? Perhaps most importantly, parents should consider the overall benefits of the program. If the skills being addressed through the electronic media are easily covered in a more hands-on or face-to-face way, try to do so. After all, we know that such interactions with parents and peers have the potential to affect the whole child, personally, socially, and cognitively. There is no media available that can replace a warm hug from someone we love.

If you choose to include electronic media in your child's overall literacy development program and wish to help him become computer literate for a variety of reasons, be sure that the programs you select assist with this endeavor. As with anything we read or use with our child to support his learning, the material should not be too complicated or outside the child's zone of proximal development. If it is entirely too difficult for the preschooler, he may become frustrated and later associate other electronic media with this negative experience. Choose wisely and monitor closely.

Let's Talk About Television

It is no surprise that I believe that books offer a unique experience that no other media can replicate. With this in mind, Mike and I limit the amount of time our children view television, as well as closely monitor the selections that we do find acceptable. However, I do not consider myself an extremist when it comes to television. Admittedly, there are occasions when I want to check out the latest home decorating show, and Mike likes to keep up with his sports teams. There are some times, also, when Heather watches television. As my mother always told me, "Moderation is the key to everything in life." This usually seems to work for food and I think it can also work for television.

The key to television viewing is for parents to be mindful of the purpose it is serving. While most parents can understand the need to keep a child occupied while they cook dinner or need to entertain a sick child, we must weigh this with our global goals for him. So many television programs and DVDs are filled with action, chase scenes, and a great amount of violence. If we think like a young child, we can see how many of these shows and videos can be frightening. Even if the story is wrapped up neatly in the end, good triumphs over evil, and they all live happily ever after, it can contain negative, scary images that leave an imprint on our child's brain. We know that the preschool stage of development is a period of rapid brain growth and is ripe for learning. Therefore, parents have an added burden to use this time to expose our children to the wonders and beauty of life. So much of television fills our child's brain with nonsense, pointless banter, and advertisements for things we do not want to buy. We could, instead, use this key time of brain growth to foster a love of learning and exploring. Obviously, there is some television that is more educational than others. Public television, of course, works hard to air programs that can help with reading and writing development, as well as character education. However, I do not think we always have to turn to public or educational television when selecting something for our child to watch. Consider programming that caters to the inquisitive mind of a preschooler. Any show that explores animals, plants, and the world around us is usually liked by young children, and can be very beneficial as well.

It is especially important to try to have our children view television programming with as little commercial interruption as possible. Commercials are rarely educational (and that's being kind) and can provide our child a skewed impression of what is valued and important in his life. Unfortunately, most of the networks that cater to "children's programming" are the very ones that are saturated with commercials for anything and everything our child probably does not need.

Evaluate your purpose in allowing your child to watch television. Do everything in moderation. In other words, it is OK to put a limit on the amount of time in front of any electronic "box." Think like a child whose brain is at a key period of development. Monitor closely. And, when in doubt, pick up a book instead.

CHAPTER 23

Building Bridges to
Independent Reading

Once you learn to read, you will be forever free.
—FREDERICK DOUGLASS

In Roger Duvoisin's *Petunia*, the main character is a silly goose who takes a stroll in the meadow where she discovers a book. She recalls hearing that someone is very wise if they own a book. So Petunia decides to carry the book with her wherever she goes, confident that she now has wisdom. However, when the other animals begin to turn to her for advice based on her newfound ability from the book, one mishap after another occurs until finally she puts everyone in extreme danger. Petunia discovers a box, clearly labeled with the word FIRECRACKERS, and misreads the label as CANDIES. It is not until all the animals are wounded, bruised, burned, and suffering that she sees the writing inside the book and begins to understand the power of being able to read.

Petunia has not yet unlocked the secret code of letters and words housed in books. She comes to understand that without the ability to read, she does not possess wisdom. Some young children, too, are ready to embark on the journey of independent reading. Parents may wonder how to support this process and take their child to the next level of learning. First, it is most important to remember that quality books should still be read aloud to children and that reading independently does not replace this valuable experience. Reading aloud serves as a powerful model of the fluency of reading. Fluency refers to the appropriate speed and rhythm with which we read to gain optimum comprehension. Listening comprehension is often higher than oral reading comprehension. Thus, it is important for children to be read to at a higher level to gain new vocabulary and continue to expand their comprehension skills. Besides, nothing can replace snuggling closely next to Mom or Dad, languishing in the familiarity of their voice, and listening to a wonderful book. For all the reasons mentioned throughout this book, reading aloud continues to prove beneficial to our children on so many levels.

I would also like to caution parents against pushing their children or forcing them to read before they are ready, either cognitively or emotionally. Earlier and faster does not always mean better. If children are pushed too hard instead of encouraged and supported, they may forever associate reading with something unpleasant. Be mindful that it is only if we find reading enjoyable that we will choose to do it. While it is true that we do not want our children to fall behind, please remember that the read-aloud experience provides many key pre-literacy skills that children will transfer to independent reading and writing when they are ready.

For those children who are enthusiastic to uncover the reading code, there are several steps and particular types of texts that parents can use to support this process. Most importantly, celebrate each attempt by your child and hurdle that is overcome. Praise any approximations they make to what is written in the book. "You said *man* instead of *men*. They are both very close and I can see how you got them confused. The vowels are different. Good job. Keep going." Or perhaps, "The word in the book is *gate* and you read *door*. They are very similar in meaning, aren't they? That shows that you are reading to gain meaning from the text. Did you know that this is the most important aspect of reading? To gain meaning? Nice focus on comprehension. Now, let's just make sure we also look closely at the letters in the words. This way we will see that the word *gate* could not be *door* because they don't even begin the same way. I can't wait for you to read more to me." At the same time, please do not be too quick to correct your child. In fact, many children will automatically associate any correction directly with criticism. Instead, if your child says a different word than the one provided in the text, give her a minute to process this. Do not jump to tell her the correct word or even redirect her to it in the text. If, after a moment, she does not correct herself, let her read to the end of the sentence. Often, she will realize that the entire sentence does not make sense because the one word was not read correctly. Many children will go back at this time and reread the entire sentence, filling in the right word. If your child does not self-correct, consider asking, "Did that make sense? Can you read it again and let's see if it makes sense?" This is what good, proficient readers do. When we make an error in reading, we may not catch it right away. However, once we read on and gain the context of the sentence as a whole, our brain (which is checking for meaning) will signal to us that collectively the words did not make sense. Therefore, we need to read the sentence in its entirety again, this time plugging in the correct word.

Conversely, if your child is struggling with the words on the page and is showing signs of frustration, the text may be too difficult for her. In this case, do not insist she sound it out or try again and again. Remember, she is just learning. Learning can only take place if it is at the child's instructional level, the level where she is developmentally ready to take in and understand the information. If it is outside her zone of proximal development (ZPD), it is frustrating for the child and she needs additional support with the text and possible intervention. If the child is not ready for that particular text or an individual word, go ahead and read it to her. Then invite her to read the entire sentence again with you. Use your judgment in determining if you should go back to reading aloud the text or read it together or simply abandon it and try something different another time.

Once your child begins reading to you or by herself, give her a big hug and let her read, read, read. Provide her many selections of books that will support the developmental stage of emergent reading. These are typically texts that emphasize sight words, decodable words, controlled vocabulary, and repetitive phrases. Libraries and bookstores usually have a special section of early readers for children embarking on independent reading. They are leveled for easy selection by the parent. Begin with the level 1 books and see how comfortable your child is with these texts and then proceed to level 2 if he or she is ready.

Predictable Texts

One of the first things that parents can do to encourage independent reading is to share predictable books. As was mentioned in chapter 8, "Play with Predictable Texts," these help scaffold children to independent reading by including rhythm, rhyme, sequencing, and other structures that help young readers anticipate what is coming next. In this way, children gain confidence in their own reading ability and can chime in with words, phrases, and sentences. As your child begins to show more initiative with reading on her own, invite her to read larger portions of the text in predictable books. The books should be ones that you have read numerous times already to your child, so the predictability is strong. Now is the perfect time for you to point to and track the words on the page. It is also a wonderful opportunity for you to encourage your child to take over this process on her own. This will assist her in understanding the direct connection between written and spoken language, an important piece of the reading process.

You may also consider inviting your child to read the other type of predictable texts that may not necessarily have wonderful vocabulary or a great story. These predictable texts were discussed in chapter 8 as well and were contrasted with quality read-aloud books. As your child seems ready to emerge into reading by him or herself, locate books that control the text by limiting word choice. Although these books may not be great for reading aloud, they provide support for early readers and help them on this new endeavor. In the next two sections of this chapter I will discuss two specific types of predictable texts that can assist children emerging into reading on their own. These are Sight Word Texts and Decodable Texts. Some books for early readers will combine both these elements. Sit beside your child as he or she reads to you, and make note of their areas of strength and what type of texts prove challenging. Some children begin to quickly recognize sight words and can readily transfer this knowledge to independent reading, while others seem better at sounding out (decoding) words. Support your child by praising her strengths and giving her many texts where she can be successful, and then bridge her slowly into the type of texts that are more difficult.

Sight Word Texts

Look at the Cakes
I see one red cake.
I see two brown cakes.
I see three yellow cakes.
I see four blue cakes.
Come and eat some cakes with me!

The above text is predictable because of its repetitive pattern and its use of common sight words, including number and color words. Sight words are the most common words in print and therefore must be recognized instantly in order to create fluency in reading. Sight words, sometimes called the Dolch Word List, comprise more than half of all words used in English books, magazines, and newspapers. This list contains 220 words, including *and, the, come, does, can, play, said*, and *look*. (A complete Dolch Word List for preschool through grade three is included in Appendix 2 on page 306.) If children struggle with the words that occur so frequently in print, this will slow down their reading, making it choppy, and could make them unable to understand the text. Therefore, it is essential for children to be able to quickly identify these sight words.

Texts that center around sight words repeat the most common words over and over again, helping children memorize them and later recognize them with automaticity. Although these types of texts are usually controlled and constrained because they are often limited primarily to the words on the list, they can certainly serve the purpose of bridging children to reading on their own. Children gain confidence in their reading ability because they later have numerous opportunities to see and recognize sight words in nearly every text presented to them. Many texts that support sight word learning will have illustrations that provide strong visual clues to assist the reader as well. These clues help children to be successful readers, but also teach them the important skill of looking all over the page for support of meaning. Some parents and teachers wonder if they should use flash cards to teach sight words. Although this can be effective for some older children, it is often more meaningful, and definitely more fun and rewarding, to read the words in context. Try to find books that allow your child to be a "real reader" while she learns sight words. This can help with learning the most common words in print, but even more importantly, it can support a child's self confidence in her ability to truly be an independent reader.

Decodable Texts

Pat's Hat
Pat was a fat cat.
Pat the fat cat had a hat.
Pat the cat sat on her hat.
Pat made the hat flat.
Pat was a sad cat.
The fat cat has a flat hat.
Poor Pat the cat!

Decodable texts like *Pat's Hat* provide children opportunities to look closely at phonetic patterns within words and practice applying these patterns. The words *Pat, cat, sat, sad, hat,* and *flat* all contain the short *a* sound and can be easily decoded by sounding them out, letter by letter. There is a direct one-to-one correspondence from each letter to each sound. Often decodable texts will focus on a specific vowel sound (short *a, e,* or *i,* for example) providing emergent readers practice with this sound within many different words.

Additionally, many of the words from *Pat's Hat* contain the -*at* word pattern. This is powerful for children to discover, because research tells us that the brain is a pattern-seeking device. It is constantly searching for patterns in words, numbers, and the world around us. The more patterns in words that we can point out to our children, the easier it is for them to understand, learn, remember, and then apply to future reading endeavors. By decoding and reading numerous words that contain the same pattern, it is hoped that children will have time to practice it, develop fluency, and recognize it in similar words they may encounter such as *bat, sat, gnat, splat, mat*, and *rat*. Not only does this strategy help our children learn the *-at* pattern (also known as the *-at* family), it teaches them how to learn. The more opportunities our children have to find and use patterns, the more it will reinforce the idea of looking for patterns in all of their reading and writing. We are helping train our child's brain to become a pattern seeker. I like to broach this subject with a child by telling them that their brain is a word detective. It is constantly looking for groups of letters to put together to make a pattern.

Once our brain knows how to read and decode groups of letters, rather than only individual letters, fluency of reading rapidly improves. The child no longer sees, sounds out, then blends back together *c-a-t, cat*. Instead, the brain recognizes the "chunk" of letters as one entity, *-at*. The child simply has to add the beginning letter or letters to the ending pattern, making reading more fluent. Contrast the difference of sounding out the individual letters in the words below and simply sounding out the beginning and adding the ending chunk to it.

c-a-t vs. c-at

f-r-o-g vs. f-r-og

sh-o-p vs. sh-op

Examples of other patterns common in decodable texts which reinforce the word detective in all emergent readers are listed in Table 16 on the opposite page.

Carefully Selecting Decodable Texts

I must caution parents not to select decodable texts that merely focus on a certain sound or a group of letters at the expense of meaning. The predictable texts that repeat endings or groups of letters in a way that is void of making sense are the books I put back

Table 16. Patterns in Words

Pattern	Examples of Words Containing the Pattern
op	bop, cop, hop, mop, pop, top, chop, crop, drop, flop, plop, shop, stop
ad	bad, dad, fad, had, lad, mad, pad, sad, tad, brad, glad
an	ban, can, fan, man, pan, ran, tan, van, plan, scan, than
ice	dice, lice, mice, nice, rice, price, slice, spice, twice
ay	day, gay, hay, may, pay, say, ray, way, clay, gray, play, pray, stay
et	bet, get, jet, let, met, net, pet, set, wet, yet, fret, whet
og	bog, fog, hog, jog, log, clog, frog, smog
ug	bug, dug, hug, jug, lug, mug, pug, rug, tug, chug, plug, slug, snug
um	bum, gum, hum, rum, sum, yum, plum, scum
un	bun, fun, gun, nun, run, sun, shun, spun, stun
ush	bush, hush, lush, mush, rush, blush, crush, flush, plush, slush

on the shelf. I remember volunteering in a kindergarten classroom and working with a small group of children on reading development. I had a few moments to prepare and review the text prior to beginning the lesson. Leafing through it, I saw that it had characters named Tank, Ink, and Plunk. I am fairly certain that the children had never heard names like these before. The author tried desperately to weave words with the *-nk* ending into the "plot." Words like *thank, stunk, bank, skunk,* and *kerplunk* were haphazardly put together in an awkward attempt to create some sort of story. It was no surprise that the children had great difficulty reading the text. They stammered and stumbled. They became confused trying to figure out if "ink" was a character or a thing or something that was used to write on paper. Although the text afforded the children numerous opportunities to practice the *-ink, -ank,* and *-unk* endings, it was devoid of meaning. Because it did not flow or sound like natural language (after all, we do not speak to one another using as many similar endings as we can create), the children became easily distracted and lost track of where they were in the text. Although some would consider this book decodable, it was in no way predictable, and therefore it was a poor candidate for an independent reader. At one point in the lesson, I simply asked the children if they could tell me anything about the book we were reading. All looked at me with blank stares. I decided that it was time to abandon the book and look for something more appropriate for these early readers. If a book serves merely as a tongue twister, it is probably not a good candidate for learning how to read independently. Therefore, search for books that can repeat and reinforce a controlled phonics element without leaving the reader completely confused.

Limitations of Sight Word and Decodable Texts

In real books, children and adults do not encounter controlled texts with specific word families or repetitive use of sight words. Texts like *Look at the Cakes* and *Pat's Hat* serve a valuable but very limited purpose. They help children with two key aspects of reading, sounding out or decoding words and providing opportunities to read and recognize common sight words. However, neither of these "books" replicates natural or fluent speech. They provide extra practice in certain skill areas. Yet, this is not enough to bridge our children to independent reading. It is important that we consistently reinforce what real books sound and look like. As we continue to read aloud quality texts, our children will hear beautiful, playful, expressive language and will see exceptional, breathtaking, and eye-catching illustrations. These are the two components that make up real books. Therefore, parents may use sight word based or phonetically controlled texts, but should do so sparingly and for only a limited time during reading development. These texts should be balanced or even outweighed with the read-aloud experience. Many wonderful authors have artfully employed these key pre-literacy skills while still maintaining authentic language and a sense of story. Search for books that contain sight words and assist children with practicing their decoding skills but still are enjoyable to read.

Chapter Books

What an exciting point in a child's life when he or she begins reading chapter books! For those children who are truly ready for the next big step into reading, carefully select chapter books that they will enjoy enough to keep them hooked on books. Just because a book is labeled as an early reader does not mean that it needs to be simple or boring. There are many texts available that contain rich language, a real plot, and characters that are multidimensional. Consider early readers such as the Frog and Toad series by Arnold Lobel and the Little Bear series by Else Holmelund Minarik and Maurice Sendak. Children love books that are endearing and funny, so I am always drawn to those that have a humorous element. Chapter books for early readers usually have short sentences and short chapters, and while they strategically weave repetitive sight words into them, they will also always maintain fluency of language. A wonderful example of a series of books that do just this is Cynthia Rylant's Mr. Putter & Tabby series. A bumbling yet endearing elderly man and his faithful cat seem always to be in the midst of one silly thing after another. The complementary illustrations comically capture the feelings and expressions of the characters and add to the overall appeal of the stories. The Mr. Putter & Tabby books are perfect for the developing reader, who will giggle through the stories and will feel a true sense of satisfaction after completing each one. Look for other chapter books that provide our young readers with the structure and scaffolding they need in the midst of a wonderful, creative story.

CHAPTER 24

A Final Note

Preparing the Soil, Planting the Seed, and Tending the Garden

Children are made readers on the laps of their parents.
—EMILIE BUCHWALD

In Edith Pattou's book *Mrs. Spitzer's Garden*, the author cleverly uses a garden metaphor to pay homage to wonderful teachers everywhere. At the end of each summer, the principal of Tremont Elementary School gives Mrs. Spitzer, a kindergarten teacher, a packet of seeds. She carefully prepares the soil and tenderly plants the seeds. She looks after the sprouts with love and patience to ensure the beautiful growth of each individual flower. Mrs. Spitzer recognizes the various needs of the separate plants, and she works hard to accommodate and support them so that each may grow to its full potential, blooming bright and strong beneath the shining sun. Some are slow to sprout, taking their time to grow leaves and a flower bud. Others are wild, seeming to find their own special place to grow in the garden, while still others need extra attention sometimes. But at the end of the year, the different colored flowers that have taken on numerous shapes are happy and beautiful. Although Mrs. Spitzer's job is done, the plants will continue to grow, becoming more sturdy and secure with each new season. They have been given the best foundation that any plant could ask for. The soil was rich and fertile and the gardener kept a watchful eye upon them as they began to sprout and then became who they were meant to be. Although each seed went its own separate way and at its own pace, Mrs. Spitzer loved each one just the same. She trusted the process of growing differently, knowing that eventually each would bloom perfectly in its own way.

Mrs. Spitzer is the proverbial teacher who "tends" her garden of students. She clearly recognizes that nurturing is the most important thing to motivate students to grow and become strong and stay focused on moving forward. In this case, the flowers strive to reach toward the warmth of the sun. In the case of our children, we know that the right teacher can help them reach toward the next challenge and forever be lifelong learners.

Since I firmly believe that parents are a child's first teachers, and perhaps the most important teachers throughout their lives, we need to be mindful of creating the best garden we can. Parents must first carefully prepare the soil. This is accomplished each time we gather a pillow or a comfortable blanket and sit beside our child and read. We fertilize the soil by providing our child key preliteracy skills that will help her sprout and grow. By reading books, we lay a strong foundation of background knowledge, concepts about how print works, and phonemic awareness, all tools that will help our child form strong roots before breaking through the earth, ready for everything it has to offer. We plant the seeds of learning and growing each time we read aloud a wonderful book. Quality books serve as the food and water and sun through their use of exceptional language, clever and creative stories, and beautiful artwork. Each of these nutrients fills our child's mind with great ideas for future writing and builds background knowledge for success in future reading.

When we keep a watchful eye over our child and guide her to more extensive texts and ask higher level questions, we are stretching her and helping her reach for the sun. Think-alouds provide the lattice work and guide the plant, our child, in the right direction. Important, too, is that parents know when to slow down and not overwhelm. After all, too much plant food, given too soon, can be detrimental to a plant. Pushing a child before she is ready can kill her love for reading, learning, and growing. It is for these reasons that I have tried to provide parents a variety of choices for interacting with and extending powerful texts. The best gardeners refer to gardening books for knowledge and support, but they also rely on their own instincts and what they know and can see in the flowers in front of them. I hope that you have found this book a valuable reference to continue to tend your own beautiful flower. Parents, like wonderful gardeners, must look to their children to guide them in how to support their learning. We must find the right balance of nutrients and love and just let our child be who she was meant to be. Trust that it is not doing something faster or more strongly that always produces the best flowers. Do not worry about competing with the other flowers in the neighborhood, or school, or anywhere else. Remember that no two flowers are alike, but all are beautiful in their own right. Know deeply that love, nurturing, support, praise, and a wonderful book are everything your child needs to set roots deep in the earth, sprout strong and healthy leaves, and bloom brightly to her full potential.

I hope that you will take the ideas in this book and use them to help plant your own seed and watch it grow. I hope this book will serve as a source of different strategies to try in order to help your child become a successful reader, writer, and learner. Sit closely beside your seedling and hold it gently. Use the "gardening tools" of questions and think-alouds to promote a stronger and brighter plant. Feed her lots of great food in the form of luscious language and interesting information. Try different types of nutrients to assure that her diet is well-rounded. Sprinkle her with poetry and sometimes pour on informational texts. Drizzle predictable books and then trickle in a chapter book here and there. Soak your precious flower with silly and heartwarming and thought-provoking books of all kinds. But whatever types of books you choose, make sure they are nothing but the best. After all, doesn't your child deserve only the finest fuel to help her blossom?

Just as gardeners know that the seedling is vulnerable and must therefore receive the greatest attention, so, too, parents must focus on the child when she is very young. We must make every effort to secure our child's foundation for a lifetime of learning and growing. With the best books by your side there is no doubt that your child will later reap the benefits that you are now sowing. She will become strong, and, whatever flower she turns out to be, she will be colorful, bright, beautiful . . . perfect. Plant your individual seed and let's create a society that forms a literate and happy garden.

Part E

Booklists, Appendixes,
Notes, and References

BOOKLISTS

Affective Domain

Anastas, Margaret, *A Hug for You* (New York: HarperCollins, 2005). A baby duckling sees the many reasons that hugs are given. They can cheer you up, chase monsters away, comfort you, and commend you when you write your own name. But the best hug of all is the one the duckling gives to his parent at the end of the story. Gentle and serene pastels complement the rhythmic text.

Anastas, Margaret, *Mommy's Best Kisses* (New York: HarperCollins, 2003). Many different animal mothers are shown kissing their babies on the neck, the tummy, and their cute little toes. The last illustration shows a human mother and child. Quiet rhythmic text is made even more soothing with gentle, muted watercolor illustrations.

Braun, Sebastien, *I Love My Daddy* (New York: HarperCollins, 2004). Baby Bear Cub describes all the activities he shares with his father in the forest throughout the day. His daddy wakes him, plays with him, and cuddles with him. An extremely simple text is complemented by calming illustrations in shades of gold and brown. This is a beautiful book to invite more discussion between father and child about all the things they do together and how much they love each other.

Brown, Margaret Wise, *The Runaway Bunny* (New York and London: Harper, 1942). A young bunny decides to run away. His mother reassures him that no matter where he goes or what he becomes, she will always be there to bring him back. A rhythmic text that includes sweet bunny banter offers children a reminder of their safety and security with us. Soft pastel illustrations help set the loving tone of the book.

Cusimano, Maryann K., *You Are My I Love You* (New York: Philomel Books, 2001). The loving bond between mother and child is expressed in this sweet and gentle book. Rhyming text is combined with beautiful watercolor illustrations to create a warm reminder of the deep connection between a parent and a child.

Dotlich, Rebecca Kai, *Mama Loves* (New York: HarperCollins, 2004). Young piglets describe all the things their mother likes to do. Each ends with the fact that her favorite things are done with them. She rides bikes with them, listens intently to them, and reads stories to them. This sweet book focuses on the love between a mother and her children. The text is lyrical and is perfectly mirrored by soft and beautiful watercolor illustrations.

Fox, Mem, *Time for Bed* (San Diego: Red Wagon Books/Harcourt Brace, 1997). Rhymed couplets compose a melodic rhythm in this bedtime story. Parents of various mammals, reptiles, birds, and fish bid their children good night. Jane Dyer's gentle watercolors endearingly portray animal parents cuddling with their children and create a sense of warmth and safety for everyone falling asleep.

Fox, Mem, *Sleepy Bears* (San Diego: Harcourt Brace, 1999). As winter approaches, six not-so-sleepy bears snuggle into bed to hear Mother Bear sing a special lullaby. Individualized rhymes are created for each bear's fantasies of swashbuckling pirates, daring trapeze artists, or regal queens. The rhythmic text and fanciful illustrations combine to create a beautiful bedtime story that embodies the love between parent and child.

Frasier, Debra, *On the Day You Were Born* (San Diego: Harcourt Brace Jovanovich, 1991). The reader is offered a celebration of the birth of any child. The sun, moon, ocean, trees, air, animals, and people all prepare for the special beginning of life. This is a wonderful reinforcement of how much our child is deeply loved. It is a beautiful and poetic affirmation of the connections between people, animals, the earth, and the universe.

Grambling, Lois G., *Daddy Will Be There* (New York: Greenwillow Books, 1998). The special relationship between a little girl and her father is highlighted in this sweet book. Wherever she goes and whatever she does, she knows her daddy will be right there. Simple text and soft illustrations make clear the comforting bond between parent and child.

Hague, Kathleen, *Good Night, Fairies* (New York: SeaStar Books, 2002). After wondering how fairies spend their days and nights, Mother invites the child to hop into bed and snuggle beneath the covers. She explains how fairies hang the stars, care for lost toys, read bedtime stories to the animals, paint the tiny wings of insects, and welcome children into dreamland. This gentle nighttime tale of magical creatures is beautifully illustrated in intricate detail. Children will delight in trying to count the 321 fairies depicted in this enchanting book.

Hindley, Judy, *Sleepy Places* (Cambridge, MA: Candlewick Press, 2006). The reader is invited to explore all the snuggly places for children and other sleepy creatures to take a nap. A rabbit is shown in its burrow, a frog in the "ooze of a pond," a bee in the center of a rose, and a cat curled up around a hat. Children envision themselves sleeping atop a turtle in the ocean or upside down with the bats in the roof. The soft pencil and watercolor illustrations in mauves and creams and delicate blues depict the animals and humans snoozing with smiles on their faces. This is a sweet and whimsical book to gently lull our precious little ones to sleep.

Kanevsky, Polly, *Sleepy Boy* (New York: Atheneum Books for Young Readers, 2006). The gorgeous sepia-toned watercolor and charcoal illustrations will take your breath away. A father gently coaxes his son to go to sleep. He lies down beside him, kisses the boy's head, and strokes his cheek, but the boy will not sleep. He vividly remembers his earlier trip to the zoo and thinks about a lion and her cub. Both the father and son and the mother and cub are mirrored in each scene, creating a dreamlike quality to the story. The book is gentle, quiet, and simply beautiful.

Kern, Norris, *I Love You with All My Heart* (San Francisco: Chronicle Books, 1998). Polo the polar bear asks his friends how their mothers love them. In this sweet story with a question-and-answer format, he learns that each mother loves her child in a unique way. As his own mother explains all the ways she loves him, Polo falls soundly asleep with her paws tenderly wrapped around him.

Kindermans, Martine, *You and Me* (New York: Philomel Books, 2006). A goose and gosling travel together around the globe. As they walk on a beach, climb a mountain, cross prairies, and weather heat and cold, the child is reminded, "no matter where we go I will always love you so." The minimal text combined with soft artwork of pinks, lavenders, corals, and yellows creates a beautiful and comforting reminder of the bond between parent and child.

Long, Sylvia, *Hush Little Baby* (San Francisco: Chronicle Books, 1997). In this retelling of a traditional lullaby, a mother rabbit introduces her child to the wonders of the natural world. As the evening shadows fall, mother and child observe a hummingbird flying, a cricket calling, and the harvest moon drifting through the sky. The familiar rhythm and realistic watercolors work together to warmly depict the peacefulness of a child's bedtime.

Medearis, Angela Shelf, *Snug in Mama's Arms* (Columbus, Ohio: Gingham Dog Press, 2004). Soft earth-toned paintings add to the quiet and comfort as mothers and fathers everywhere gently tuck their children into bed. With soothing and poetic text, animals and people from around the globe bid good night to their loved ones. Serene depictions of different parents holding their child create a sense of love and safety, making this the perfect read-aloud just before bedtime.

Melmed, Laura Krauss, *I Love You as Much . . .* (New York: Lothrop, Lee & Shepard, 1993). This poetic picture book personifies the love between mother and child with exquisite portraits of animals and their offspring. The soothing couplets used to define each mother's testament of love form a sweet and beautiful lullaby.

McBratney, Sam, *Guess How Much I Love You* (Cambridge, MA: Candlewick Press, 1995). In this tender tale of the love shared between father and son, Little Nutbrown Hare illustrates his affection for Big Nutbrown Hare by declaring "I love you as high as I can reach." Although Big Nutbrown Hare can outreach and outjump his son, Little Nutbrown Hare's love proves to be immeasurable. The soft greens and browns of the watercolors warmly capture this beautiful and playful relationship.

McBratney, Sam, *You're All My Favorites* (Cambridge, MA: Candlewick Press, 2004). Feeling insecure, each of the three bears in the family wonders how it can be Mommy and Daddy's favorite. The parents explain how each bear is special and how their love for them is unconditional. This reassuring tale reminds our children that each one of them is unique and has a special place in a parent's heart.

Pow, Tom, *Tell Me One Thing, Dad* (Cambridge, MA: Candlewick Press, 2004). Molly is trying to avoid bedtime by asking her dad what he knows about dinosaurs, polar bears, and crocodiles. He provides some informative answers and some silly answers, but he always ends with the fact that parents love their babies. When Dad asks Molly what she knows about him, she confidently states that he loves his baby. This book affirms the deep love between a father and daughter.

Root, Phyllis, *Ten Sleepy Sheep* (Cambridge, MA: Candlewick Press, 2004). In this countdown to bedtime tale, ten little lambs are not quite ready to go to sleep. When Momma calls, they kick up their heels and play some more. However, one by one, they tire and nod off peacefully. Soothing verses with repeated sounds and rhymes are complemented by dreamy acrylic and pastel illustrations. This is a perfect story to entice your child to snuggle beneath the covers.

Ross, Michael Elsohn, *Snug as a Bug* (San Francisco: Chronicle Books, 2004). Insects and slugs and worms all nestle down for slumber in their favorite bed. Whether inside a rose, atop a leaf, or under a rock, all are cozy as bugs in a rug. Darling illustrations showcase various insects in pajamas and nightgowns ready for a good night's sleep. Lyrical verse will have all little ones calm and snoozing before you know it.

Schertle, Alice, *When the Moon Is High* (New York: HarperCollins Publishers, 2003). When baby can't sleep, daddy takes him on a moonlit stroll to discover all the animals that are awake in the night. The repetitious and soothing poem helps lull children to sleep with its gentle lyrics and serene illustrations.

Seeger, Pete, *One Grain of Sand* (New York: Little, Brown, 2002). Listeners take a trip to numerous destinations around the globe, observing human and animal families. The poetic language sings as the simple lullaby is read aloud. Rich and luminescent illustrations complement the warm and inviting tone of this perfect bedtime book.

Spinelli, Eileen, *When Mama Comes Home Tonight* (New York: Simon & Schuster Books for Young Readers, 1998). After coming home from work, a mother is reunited with her daughter in this tender rhyming tale. Special time is spent together wishing on stars, sipping tea, reading aloud, hugging, and finally snuggling into bed. Beautiful soft and nostalgic illustrations by Jane Dyer help create a soothing lullaby perfect for bedtime reading.

Tafuri, Nancy, *You Are Special, Little One* (New York: Scholastic Press, 2003). Six animal babies and one young child all ask their parents the same question, "How am I special?" Together Mama and Papa tell each of their little ones the unique qualities that make them special and reassure them that "we will love you forever and ever and always." Adorable watercolor and pencil drawings show each family huddled close together, snuggling one another. This is a beautiful reminder to our children of the unending love we have for them.

Thompson, Lauren, *Polar Bear Night* (New York: Scholastic Press, 2004). A young polar bear embarks on a journey into the night. As she wanders in the arctic cold, she sees many different animals sleeping soundly. At last she witnesses the beauty of stars falling from the sky, illuminating the world around her. She then heads home to the soft, warm fur of her mother. A soothing color palette of pinks, lavenders, and pastel blues add to the gentle mood of this quiet nighttime tale.

Waddell, Martin, *Sleep Tight, Little Bear!* (Cambridge, MA: Candlewick Press, 2005). Little Bear finds the perfect cave and decides to make it his own special house. After receiving permission from Big Bear to camp out overnight, Little Bear tries to snuggle down in bed. But as the sky grows dark and Little Bear becomes lonely, he heads back home for a bedtime story and falls safely asleep in Big Bear's arms. Soft, muted illustrations beautifully complete this story of every child's struggle between independence and the reassurance from a parent.

Wolff, Ferida, *It Is the Wind* (New York: HarperCollins, 2005). A young boy's attempts at sleep are interrupted by the sounds of the night outside his window. His imagination takes him all over the farm trying to discover its source. Through rhythm, repetition, and attention to the sounds of words, the boy (and your own child) is lulled to sleep.

Yolen, Jane, *Baby Bear's Chairs* (Orlando, FL: Gulliver Books/Harcourt, 2005). It's not easy being the baby bear in the family. You do not have the same privileges as the big bears, and you seem to only cause trouble in your own littlest chair. However, snuggling with daddy bear on his lap proves the best chair of all. Gentle rhymes and adorable illustrations make this book the perfect bedtime reminder of a parent's love.

Zuckerman, Linda, *I Will Hold You 'til You Sleep* (New York: Arthur A. Levine Books, 2006). A sweet, sentimental poem takes the reader through the life of a boy, from infancy to adulthood. It offers a beautiful reminder of the importance of love throughout one's life. The illustrations by Jon Muth are captivating and wonderfully extend the text. This is an inspirational book for everyone.

Bibliotherapy

Carlson, Nancy L., *My Best Friend Moved Away* (New York: Viking, 2001). Although this is a simple story, it may help a child deal with the feeling of being lonely. A young girl recounts the good and bad times she had with her best friend who just moved away. The ending offers a ray of hope as her new next-door neighbor comes over to visit with her dog in tow.

Coffelt, Nancy, *Fred Stays with Me!* (New York: Little, Brown, 2007). A young girl shuffles back and forth between the two homes of her divorced parents. Her dog, Fred, is her loyal companion in both places. However, when he begins to wreak havoc on her parents' lives, they say he must go. The girl is adamant: "Fred stays with me!" The parents ultimately find solutions to deal with Fred's behavior issues, and the canine and girl remain constants in each other's lives. Darling illustrations in browns and dashes of red add warmth and charm.

Curtis, Jamie Lee, *Today I Feel Sily & Other Moods That Make My Day* (New York: HarperCollins Publishers, 1998). The author uses singsong rhymes to make it easy to begin talking about the variety of emotions we all experience. A redheaded girl explores thirteen different feelings and moods and how each manifests itself, from silly, joyful, and excited to confused, angry, and grumpy. A mood wheel in the shape of a face is included at the end of the book to allow everyone to explore their own emotions.

Heelan, Jamee Riggio, *Can You Hear a Rainbow?* (Atlanta: Peachtree Publishers, 2002). A ten-year-old boy tells about the many different ways he compensates for being deaf, including using sign language, hearing aids, and lipreading. The reader is provided a glimpse into how he is similar and different from other children who can hear as well as those who are deaf. Computer-generated photographs are superimposed on drawings, creating interesting artwork.

Heelan, Jamee Riggio, *The Making of My Special Hand* (Atlanta: Peachtree Publishers, 1998). Madison is born with only one hand. This book provides a step-by-step description of how a special prosthesis is made for her. Although it may be too detailed for some younger children, parents can provide additional explanation if needed to support their understanding. Different kinds of helper hands are discussed as well. The text is combined with delightful and unique artwork that makes the book very inviting.

Heelan, Jamee Riggio, *Rolling Along* (Atlanta: Peachtree Publishers, 2000). Taylor, a young boy with cerebral palsy, describes some of his daily activities and compares them to his twin brother, Tyler. Tyler can run and jump and skip, but Taylor must use a walker or wheelchair. Although he experiences many frustrations (drinking fountains that are too high, stairs, and heavy doors), we see that Taylor can do many of the same things as his brother and other children. A positive tone is created both with the text and the illustrations.

Greive, Bradley Trevor, *The Blue Day Book for Kids: A Lesson in Cheering Yourself Up* (Kansas City, MO: Andrews McMeel, 2005). Black-and-white photographs of various animals show expressive faces that demonstrate a range of emotions. The adorable, silly, and clever poses serve to open up a dialogue about one's own feelings and ways of dealing with them.

Henkes, Kevin, *Chrysanthemum* (New York: Greenwillow Books, 1991). Chrysanthemum loves her name. That is, until she enters kindergarten and is teased by her classmates. She struggles with her identity until finally recognizing that she truly is special and unique. Her loving family helps Chrysanthemum bloom in this "absolutely perfect" story about self-esteem and self-confidence.

Henkes, Kevin, *Wemberly Worried* (New York: Greenwillow Books, 2000). Wemberly worries about everything. Big things. Little things. And everything in between. Her biggest worry comes, though, when she is about to go to nursery school. Latching on to her worn rabbit doll, Petal, Wemberly finds a kindred spirit in Jewel. They become fast friends. Her worrying does not disappear, but perhaps it becomes more manageable. Expressive and detailed illustrations add charm to this perfect book for worrywarts of all ages.

Huneck, Stephen, *Sally Goes to the Vet* (New York: Harry N. Abrams, 2004). When Sally the dog trips over a tree trunk she is rushed to the veterinarian hospital. She needs X-rays and a shot, and she is sent home with medicine to take. She tells her feline friend all about her ordeal, but includes a helpful way to cope with scary situations. When receiving her shot, the vet tells her to think a happy thought. (Sally visualizes a strawberry ice cream cone.) This tender story speckled with a sense of humor will reassure children about their pet's visit to the vet and perhaps even their own trip to the doctor.

Keats, Ezra Jack, *Peter's Chair* (New York: Harper & Row, 1967). Peter is having a very difficult time adjusting to the fact that his new baby sister is getting all his old toys. He takes the last blue chair from his furniture that is now being painted pink and runs away from home. However, he learns a valuable lesson about growing up and sharing his parents' attention. Many new older siblings will relate to this sweet and sensitively told story.

L'Engle, Madeleine, *The Other Dog* (New York: SeaStar Books, 2001). When a new "dog" enters the household, Touché is extremely irritated and cannot imagine why his master and mistress would do such a thing. Exceptional language is used to tell the tale of one pooch learning to get used to, and then even *like*, the baby who has joined the family. Darling illustrations add perfectly to the humor.

Lester, Helen, *A Porcupine Named Fluffy* (Boston: Houghton Mifflin, 1986). Fluffy the porcupine tries desperately to live up to his name. He covers himself completely in cotton balls, which doesn't help. When whipped cream doesn't work and eating marshmallows or soaking in the tub for forty-five minutes don't help either, Fluffy is discouraged. He meets a rhino who pokes (no pun intended) fun at him until the rhino is forced to reveal his own ridiculous name, Hippo. The two find this hysterical and become fast friends, realizing there are some things we just cannot change about ourselves and that's okay.

Maclachlan, Patricia, *Through Grandpa's Eyes* (New York: Harper & Row, 1980). The love between John and his grandpa is showcased in this beautifully written and illustrated book. Grandpa is blind and John wonders how he can do all the things he does. Grandpa shares his "secret," and the boy learns about relying on all the other senses.

Mayer, Mercer, *There's an Alligator Under My Bed*. (New York: Dial Books for Young Readers, 1987). When no one believes he has an alligator under his bed, a boy decides to take matters into his own hands. He cleverly creates a trail of food leading from his bedroom to the garage. When at last the alligator has made his way through the house and the boy has him trapped, a funny message is left for the boy's dad. Children will be empowered to think of their own solutions to problems after hearing this creative tale.

Mayer, Mercer, *There's a Nightmare in My Closet* (New York: Dial Press, 1968). A little boy is sure there is a nightmare in his closet after the lights go out. He shuts the closet door and cowers under the sheets. One night he decides to confront the nightmare and puts on his fatigues and gets ready for battle. However, when the nightmare does, indeed, appear, the boy discovers that it is not nearly as scary as he had thought. A wonderful message about confronting our fears is presented with humor.

Penn, Audrey, *The Kissing Hand* (Washington, DC: Child Welfare League of America, 1993). On Chester Raccoon's first night of school, he admits to his mother that he is scared and would much rather remain in the warmth and coziness of his own home. Mrs. Raccoon reassures him with a time-honored secret called the Kissing Hand. Kissing the middle of his palm, she explains that whenever he is lonely, he can press his hand to his cheek and the kiss will rush to his heart to remind him of her love.

Penn, Audrey, *A Pocket Full of Kisses* (Washington, DC: Child & Family Press, 2006). Chester Raccoon is struggling with the fact that he has a little brother who plays with his toys and pulls his tail. When he sees his mother give a special Kissing Hand to Ronny, he is brokenhearted. But Mrs. Raccoon reassures him that she will never, ever run out of Kissing Hands. Then she gives him a special kiss to keep in his pocket.

Rylant, Cynthia, *Cat Heaven* (New York: Blue Sky Press, 1997). When cats cross Rainbow Bridge into cat heaven, God is there to attend to their every need. They receive cat wings so they will never worry about getting stuck in a tree. There are lots of toys, angel laps in which to cuddle, full bowls of food, and pastures for frolicking. This sweet and sensitive book offers comfort and a little humor to anyone mourning a pet. The rhyming text is wonderfully complemented by primitive, childlike art.

Rylant, Cynthia, *Dog Heaven* (New York: Blue Sky Press, 1995). Rylant tenderly and beautifully deals with the emotional topic of the death of a pet. God doesn't give dogs wings when they go to heaven because he knows that what they love best is running. Instead he gives them fields and fields and fields. Heaven has angel children, biscuits shaped like cats, fluffy cloud beds, and lots of petting hands. A beautiful visual is provided of what it is like for our favorite canine once they reach heaven. It will help children (of all ages) be comforted as they deal with their loss.

Sendak, Maurice, *Where the Wild Things Are* (New York: Harper & Row, 1963). When Max is sent to his room without supper for being mischievous, a forest grows and the wildness continues. He heads out on a boat and is gone for weeks, maybe a year, staying with the Wild Things. He tames them and they proclaim him the wildest, scariest of them all and make him king. As children grapple with their own anger, this book offers a way to channel this emotion through imagination and the love of a parent.

Stuve-Bodeen, Stephanie, *We'll Paint the Octopus Red* (Bethesda, MD: Woodbine House, 1998). Although initially unhappy about the prospect of having a new baby in the house, six-year-old Emma begins to imagine a million things she can do with Isaac. When her father comes home from the hospital sad because the baby has Down syndrome, Emma worries that everything she imagined cannot come true. After careful thought, they see that he will be able to do all the things on the list; it just may take him more time or require more patience from them. This wonderful book provides positive messages of acceptance and helping others. It includes an appendix with questions and answers for children.

Thompson, Colin, *Unknown* (New York: Walker & Company, 2000). The little dog in the last cage is routinely overlooked by the humans who visit the shelter. She is too shy to bark and cowers in the back, unnoticed, scared, and shivering. But when a fire breaks out in the middle of the night, it is Unknown who gets help, saving all the animals. Because of her newfound notoriety, she and several others from the shelter are adopted. While this makes Unknown happy, the story ends with her suggesting the tables be turned and the dogs get to select the humans they wanted from cages.

Waber, Bernard, *Ira Sleeps Over* (Boston: Houghton Mifflin, 1972). It is Ira's very first sleepover and he is quite excited. However, his older sister tells him that Reggie will make fun of him because Ira sleeps with a teddy bear named Tah Tah. Ira has never slept without his bear but doesn't want Reggie to think he's a baby. A sweet and reassuring message is provided in this book, which tackles the topic of the anxiety that often accompanies a child's first sleepover.

Willis, Jeanne, *Susan Laughs* (New York: Henry Holt, 2000). Susan laughs, swims, paints, dances, swings, and throws "just like me, just like you." She experiences a range of emotions including fear and anger. It is not until the very end of the book that it is revealed that Susan is in a wheelchair. The simple rhyming phrases focus on the redhead's abilities rather than what she cannot do. Common experiences of all young children are shared, helping everyone realize that Susan is just like everyone else in so many ways.

Wilson, Karma, *Mama Always Comes Home* (New York: HarperCollins, 2005). This is a gentle and soothing book for any child who may be experiencing separation anxiety. A variety of animal moms are shown leaving their offspring for a brief period and then returning. Each beautifully written rhyming verse ends with the refrain, "Mama always comes home." The last page features a human mother reassuring her child of her return. The illustrations are soft and reflective of the comforting tone.

Woloson, Eliza, *My Friend Isabelle* (Bethesda, MD: Woodbine House, 2003). Isabelle and Charlie are good friends. They like doing many things together. This simple book compares the differences and similarities of two special children, one who has Down syndrome and one who does not. It invites discussion about inclusion, acceptance, and what truly defines friendship.

Chapter Books

Atwater, Richard, and Florence Atwater, *Mr. Popper's Penguins* (Boston: Little, Brown and Co., 1938). Mr. Popper has always dreamed of exploring the North and South Pole. His life takes a sudden crazy turn when he receives a package with a penguin inside. He keeps the penguin in the icebox, but before you know it, he has twelve penguins. In order to pay for all the hungry beaks that now inhabit his household, Mr. Popper and his penguins form a show and go on tour. Lots of silly adventures and mishaps ensue, making this story a delight for children and parents.

Catling, Patrick Skene, *The Chocolate Touch* (New York: Morrow, 1952). John Midas loves chocolate more than anything. When he finds an unusual coin and wanders into a unique candy shop, he unknowingly buys a piece of magic chocolate. John's wish is granted, and everything that touches his lips turns to sweet, yummy chocolate. However, things don't turn out as sweetly as John had envisioned, and he learns a valuable lesson about thinking of others instead of himself.

Cleary, Beverly, *The Mouse and the Motorcycle* (New York: Morrow, 1965). Ralph the Mouse has always wanted to explore beyond his knothole in the hotel, and when Keith and his family move in, he has his chance. Ralph is caught by Keith as he unsuccessfully tries to take the boy's toy motorcycle. However, Keith understands the need to want to explore, so he gladly shares his vehicle with Ralph. Then lots of fun adventures happen for both mouse and boy.

Cleary, Beverly, *Socks* (New York: Morrow, 1973). In this enchanting book told from the point of view of Socks the Cat, we learn about his adoption by a lovely couple and his eventual fall from grace when a baby joins the family. Hilarious mishaps and misunderstandings fill Socks's life, until finally everyone finds their own special place in the family.

Dahl, Roald, *Charlie and the Chocolate Factory* (New York: Knopf, 1964). For the first time in history the famous candy maker Willy Wonka plans to open up his factory to five lucky children. Charlie Bucket hopes to get one of the elusive golden tickets to gain entrance into this mysterious and fantastic place. Valuable life lessons are learned by all who enter the gates.

Lowry, Lois, *Gooney Bird Greene* (Boston: Houghton Mifflin, 2002). Gooney Bird Greene is an eccentric second grader who only tells stories that are "absolutely true." Her stories include a flying carpet, driving from China, diamond earrings from a prince in a palace, and directing a symphony orchestra. Through creative wordplay, the classmates and teacher find out that the stories really are true. Gooney does a wonderful job of spinning a fantastic tale while helping the class understand the key features of any good story. Delightful in its own right, this book gives sound advice for all aspiring storytellers and writers. Consider also the other titles in this series, *Gooney Bird and the Room Mother* and *Gooney the Fabulous*.

White, E. B., *Charlotte's Web* (New York: Harper, 1952). Wilbur, a little pig, is befriended by Charlotte, a spider who lives in the rafters above his pen. One day he finds out the destiny of pigs on a farm and is terribly frightened. Charlotte is determined to save him by writing messages about him in her web for all the town to see. This is a beautiful story of friendship and self-sacrifice.

White, E. B., *Stuart Little* (New York and London: Harper & Brothers, 1945). The Little family is quite surprised when their second child turns out to be a mouse, but they gratefully accept him into their family. Stuart is loved by all except for Snowbell, the cat. The reader is taken on numerous adventures with the sophisticated little mouse and begins to see the world from a whole new perspective. This is an endearing tale of friendship and courage that is both funny and touching.

Concept Books

Alphabet—Sound/Letter Recognition

Fleming, Denise, *Alphabet Under Construction* (New York: Henry Holt, 2002). Mouse is working hard to create the alphabet. Full-page vibrant illustrations of each uppercase letter directly correspond to an alliterative phrase. Mouse "levels the L, measures the M, nails the N," and finally "zips the Z."

Gag, Wanda, *The ABC Bunny* (New York: Coward McCann, 1933). A bunny finds its way home by scampering through the alphabet. Detailed black-and-white pencil drawings create a soft touch. The rhythmical text begs to be sung and revisited again and again.

Hosta, Dar, *I Love the Alphabet* (Flemington, NJ: Brown Dog Books, 2004). Each upper- and lowercase letter is prominently displayed in bright color and is accompanied by a clever rhyme. The inviting cut-paper collages that show a multitude of animals romping through the alphabet are full of life and simply gorgeous.

Kirk, David, *Miss Spider's ABC* (New York: Scholastic Press/Callaway, 1998). Oversized letters of the alphabet are set directly next to the alliterative text, helping children associate each with its respective sound. A darling story about all the insects preparing for Miss Spider's surprise birthday party is told through clever rhyme. Kirk's signature bright and vivid oil paintings will surely grab a child's attention.

Lionni, Leo, *The Alphabet Tree* (New York: Pantheon, 1968). In this parable, the letters of the alphabet are tossed and torn in a windstorm, only to realize that they gain strength by banding together, strategically forming words and then sentences. In the end, the letters create an important message about peace.

MacDonald, Suse, *Alphabatics* (New York: Aladdin Books, 1992). Each letter of the alphabet is transformed step by step into an object it represents. The capital *A* is turned upside down, its point rounded a bit until it becomes an Ark. The *b* is cleverly blown until finally the hole in the middle forms a balloon and floats away. The metamorphosis of the alphabet encourages creative thinking as children focus on the shapes and accompanying sounds of letters. The artwork is simple, bright, and cheerful, inviting children back again and again.

Martin, Bill, Jr., and John Archambault, *Chicka Chicka Boom Boom* (New York: Simon & Schuster Books for Young Readers, 1989). The lowercase alphabet races each other up a coconut tree until there is too much weight and all the letters come crashing down. Luckily, the uppercase "mamas and papas" are there to help mend the letters after their big fall. Not only does this book clearly label and illustrate each of the lowercase letters, it offers a lively rhyming text that holds the attention of preschoolers and their parents too.

McDonnell, Flora, *Flora McDonnell's ABC* (Cambridge, MA: Candlewick Press, 1997). Splashy colors and humor are combined in this fabulous alphabet book that helps draw a preschooler's attention to the letters and their corresponding sounds. Each letter is boldly written in upper- and lowercase and is accompanied by a bright illustration that exemplifies it.

Paratore, Colleen, *26 Big Things Small Hands Do* (Minneapolis, MN: Free Spirit Publishing, 2004). The author presents twenty-six ways children can help make our world a better place. Clearly written upper- and lowercase letters are accompanied by a sentence describing something that even the youngest of children can do for themselves, others, and the earth. Among these, they can explore, feed, question, recycle, and volunteer.

Polacco, Patricia, *G Is for Goat* (New York: Philomel Books, 2003). Bouncy rhymes tell all about goats on a farm in this adorable alphabet book. Polacco's signature watercolor and pencil illustrations show a barefoot peasant shepherd girl interacting with the lovable goats.

Sobel, June, *B Is for Bulldozer: A Construction ABC* (San Diego: Harcourt, 2003). Two children and other curious onlookers watch outside a chain-link fence as a busy construction site evolves over time. But what could the workers be building? From A in Asphalt to the final Z in Z-o-o-m! for the roller coaster, children will be surprised to see the completed amusement park. Brightly colored capital letters stand out on each page and are intertwined in the simple lines of the text. This book is a wonderful way to teach the alphabet while in the midst of a clever story.

Wallace, Nancy Elizabeth, *Alphabet House* (New York: Marshall Cavendish, 2005). After introducing a rabbit family that lives in Alphabet House, each page of this book features a letter in upper- and lowercase. There are numerous opportunities to count and name objects that begin with a given letter. In the *Dd* room, we see a dog, duck, diamonds, door, dragon, drum, dinosaur, dollhouse, and much more. Can you find them all? Luckily, the author provides an answer key at the back. Cut-paper illustrations give the pages a 3-D effect, welcoming children into this special house.

Wildsmith, Brian, *ABC* (Brookfield, CT: Millbrook Press, 1995). Magnificent paintings set this alphabet book apart from others. The author uses recognizable objects that preschoolers can easily identify (apple, butterfly, cat, dog, elephant) and associate with each letter of the alphabet, helping to reinforce the sound-symbol connection.

Counting/Numbers

Andreason, Dan, *The Baker's Dozen* (New York: Henry Holt, 2007). This counting book is a tasty treat for all! A plump and enthusiastic baker begins at 5:00 a.m. to make one éclair and ends at 7:00 that same morning with twelve small cupcakes. He is just in time to open the doors for the thirteen customers (a baker's dozen) waiting eagerly outside. Retro-style oil paintings appealingly display the mouth-watering variety of cakes, strudels, cookies, and pastries.

Beaton, Claire, *One Moose, Twenty Mice* (Cambridge, MA: Barefoot Books, 2006). This counting book begins with one moose and ends with twenty white mice. It includes a repetitive question, asking, "Where is the orange cat?" Children will delight in finding the "hidden" cat as well as counting all the animals on the pages. Unique felt artwork is decorated with beads and buttons and rickrack.

Dillon, Leo, and Diane Dillon, *Mother Goose: Numbers on the Loose* (Orlando, FL: Harcourt, 2007). Familiar and lesser-known Mother Goose rhymes involving numbers are showcased in this wonderful collection. Vibrant illustrations extend the playful tone and mischievous action of the numbers as they dance, skip, laugh, and even hide through the rhymes.

Fleming, Denise, *Count!* (New York: Henry Holt, 1992). Children have a wonderful time counting such animals as toucans, gnus, worms, and butterflies as they appear to wiggle and leap and fly off the pages. The numbers 1 through 10, as well as 20, 30, 40, and 50, are covered in this exceptionally illustrated book filled with bright purples, oranges, and pinks. Each number is clearly written, along with the word in English and slashes to represent the quantity of creatures. Eye-catching and fun!

Jay, Alison, *1-2-3: A Child's First Counting Book* (New York: Dutton Children's Books, 2007). While reading, a little girl falls asleep and is whisked away to fairy tale land on the wings of the goose that laid the golden egg. Numbers one through ten and back again are introduced within the context of children's favorite fairy tales and nursery rhymes. For the observant reader and listener, there are many things to count on every page. Faded colors and geometric shapes are finished with a crackly glaze, creating a unique art form to enchant all who pick up the book.

Colors

Baker, Alan, *White Rabbit's Color Book* (New York: Kingfisher Books, 1994). Curious White Rabbit decides to jump into a can of yellow paint. He proceeds to several other colors, hopping in and out, showering at last and then trying some more. While in the midst of his fun, he discovers how to create new colors by mixing primary ones. Finally, he emerges as a beautiful chocolate brown bunny who hops away quite satisfied with his new look.

Ehlert, Lois, *Planting a Rainbow* (San Diego: Harcourt Brace Jovanovich, 1988). A mother and child plant seeds that become a rainbow garden. Vibrant colors depict the yearlong gardening process. A unique feature of the book is six increasingly wider pages that show all the flowers of each color of the rainbow. A visual delight!

Hoban, Tana, *Is It Red? Is It Yellow? Is It Blue?* (New York: Greenwillow Books, 1978). Exceptional photographs highlight the colors of everyday objects. The wordless book showcases the colors of the city with multi-ethnic children running and romping about.

Jonas, Ann, *Color Dance* (New York Greenwillow Books, 1989). Children carrying large colored scarves dance through the pages of the book. As scarves merge, they create new colors. Red and blue mix together to create purple. Bright colors invite children in for a closer look at how primary colors can mix to create secondary colors.

McMillan, Bruce, *Growing Colors* (New York: Lothrop, Lee & Shepard Books, 1988). Photographs of fruits and vegetables showcase the beauty of colors in nature. A small picture shows the plant growing and a large one focuses on a closeup of the produce. The color word is clearly written in bold type in the appropriate shade, reinforcing the connection between the hue and its name. Intense colors make for an inviting look into nature, food, and colors.

Thong, Roseanne, *Red Is a Dragon* (San Francisco: Chronicle Books, 2001). Using rhyming couplets that center around different colors, this book provides a peek into the Chinese American culture. We see red dragons, melons, and lychees, as well as orange crabs, yellow incense sticks and taxis, pink peonies, and white dumplings. Deep and rich illustrations are reflective of the intricate patterns in Chinese paintings and fabrics.

Walsh, Ellen Stoll, *Mouse Paint* (San Diego: Harcourt Brace Jovanovich, 1989). Three white mice atop a white sheet of paper cleverly camouflage themselves from a cat. Once they discover three jars of paint, one red, one yellow, one blue, a colorful adventure begins. Dipping toes and tails into more than one jar creates exciting new color combinations. Cut-paper collage illustrations add to the whimsy of this cute little tail—I mean, *tale*—that serves as a great reinforcement of colors.

Yolen, Jane, *How Do Dinosaurs Learn Their Colors?* (New York: Blue Sky Press, 2006). Color words are woven into a simple text about dinosaurs that replicate the actions and expressions of people. Darling illustrations of dinosaurs drawing, painting, and playing add to the hilarity of the book. We see a red fire truck under a bed, a purple towel left on the floor, a green sign on a door, and so much more.

Opposites

Falconer, Ian, *Olivia's Opposites* (New York: Atheneum Books for Young Readers, 2002). Children who love Olivia will rejoice in this simple but silly book about opposites. In true Olivia fashion, word pairs such as long and short and loud and quiet are shown with flair and humor.

Fox, Mem, *Where Is the Green Sheep?* (Orlando, FL: Harcourt, 2004). The humorous tale follows the antics of various sheep throughout the day. There are sheep taking baths, sheep dancing, sheep skiing, scared sheep, and brave sheep. But where is the green sheep? The simple text reinforces concepts such as colors and comparisons (near, far, up, down). In the end, we get a glimpse of where the green sheep has been hiding all along. Preschoolers will quickly pick up on the repetition and rhyme and will enjoy the bright illustrations that clearly detail the expressions and personalities of the woolly sheep.

Hoban, Tana, *Exactly the Opposite* (New York: Greenwillow Books, 1990). Using a striking collection of photographs of people, animals, and objects, opposites are showcased in this wordless book. The picture pairs cleverly invite open-ended discussion among all viewers. Looking at the cover, for example, one may see shoes that are tied and untied, but they are also neat and messy, new and old, big and little. This is a wonderful concept book that will entertain child and parent.

Shapes
Baker, Alan, *Brown Rabbit's Shape Book* (New York: Kingfisher Books, 1994). Brown Rabbit opens a square box and discovers five balloons that take on various shapes.

Hoban, Tana, *Shapes, Shapes, Shapes* (New York: Greenwillow Books, 1986). Tana Hoban invites children to look closely at ordinary objects, such as a lunch box, and find all the different shaped items in each photograph. Common shapes are covered, such as circle, square, and triangle, as well as more obscure concepts, such as trapezoid, hexagon, and parallelogram.

Thong, Roseanne, *Round Is a Mooncake* (San Francisco: Chronicle Books, 2000). In this lyrical picture book, a little girl's neighborhood becomes a celebration of shapes and Chinese culture. She explores her surroundings and ponders the figures she sees, pointing out objects that are universally known as well as those that are culturally specific—like a round moon cake, a square box of dim sum, and rectangular inking stones. As the little girl makes her own discoveries, she invites audiences to reflect on the wonderful shapes existing in their own lives.

Diversity
Bae, Hyun-Joo, *New Clothes for New Year's Day* (La Jolla, CA: Kane/Miller Book Publishers, Inc., 2007). We witness the elaborate process as a little Korean girl dresses up to welcome the new year. The text and artwork create a story that many girls will relate to and find delightful. Additionally, though, all audiences are provided a great deal of information about the Korean culture.

Bradby, Marie, *Momma, Where Are You From?* (New York: Orchard Books, 2000). In this gorgeously illustrated book, an African-American mother reminisces about her own childhood growing up in a small town around the 1940s or 1950s. Although the book makes note of the inequalities that existed, the main focus is on the love of family and a close-knit neighborhood. The poetic text creates a strong image of being connected to one's family.

Bridges, Shirin Yim, *Ruby's Wish* (San Francisco: Chronicle Books, 2002). In this true story that takes place in China at the turn of the century, a little girl named Ruby comes from a very wealthy family. She is strong, determined, and loves learning. Her greatest wish is to go to university, but only boys are allowed to do so. The patriarch of the house breaks from tradition to provide Ruby her dream. A wonderful story is portrayed about respect for culture, family, and oneself.

Bunting, Eve, *Flower Garden* (San Diego: Harcourt Brace Jovanovich, 1994). An African American father and daughter plan a special gift for mother's birthday. They walk the city streets to get flowering plants, soil, and a window box, and then they take the bus back to their apartment to assemble everything for the big surprise. Rich and gorgeous paintings add depth to the beautiful rhyming verse and portray the closeness of the loving family.

Cooper, Ilene, *The Golden Rule* (New York: Abrams Books for Young Readers, 2007). A grandfather explains to his grandson the meaning of the Golden Rule. He points out its universality and tells how many religions and cultures have their own variations, including Christianity, Judaism, Islam, and the Shawnee Tribe. The boy wonders what kind of world it would be if everyone followed this simple rule. Grandfather provides hope to the boy by explaining that "it begins with you." This thought-provoking book is gorgeously illustrated and serves as a reminder that each of us plays a part in making the world a better place.

Cole, Heidi, and Nancy Vogl, *Am I a Color Too?* (Bellevue, WA: Illumination Arts, 2005). An interracial boy wonders why people focus on the color of one's skin rather than on the person inside. He recognizes that regardless of color, all people feel, dream, sing, and dance. He concludes that he is not a color at all but a human being like everyone else. Gorgeous illustrations capture the beauty of colors in all people.

Chinn, Karen, *Sam and the Lucky Money* (New York: Lee & Low Books, 1995). Sam and his mother head to Chinatown to celebrate Chinese New Year. Sam has four dollars of New Year's money, but he becomes disappointed when he realizes it is not enough for him to buy anything he wants. However, when he accidentally steps on the bare foot of a homeless man, he begins to think differently about his lucky money. Universal themes of compassion and gratefulness are artfully expressed through text and illustrations.

Compestine, Ying Chang, *The Runaway Rice Cake* (New York: Simon & Schuster Books for Young Readers, 2001). The Chang family has only enough flour for one rice cake to celebrate the Chinese New Year. However, just as the cake is done cooking, it comes to life and pops out of the pan. The family chases it through the village, until it bumps into an old woman, knocking her down. When the family realizes that the woman has not eaten for days, the youngest son offers her the rice cake. Their compassion and generosity are later rewarded by the Kitchen God and the people of the village.

Demi, *One Grain of Rice* (New York: Scholastic Press, 1997). In this Indian folk-tale, a clever girl named Rani outsmarts a selfish raja. When offered a reward for a kind deed, she asks for only one grain of rice doubled each day for thirty days. When at last the thirty days have come, the amount of rice adds up to enough to feed her starving village.

Demi, *The Empty Pot* (New York: Henry Holt, 1990). The Chinese emperor needs to choose a successor to the throne. He gives each child in the land a flower seed and tells them that whoever grows the best flower in a year's time will be the successor. Ping hangs his head in shame when he must present his empty pot to the emperor. Lessons about the importance of truth and doing your best are clearly portrayed in this simple but beautiful story.

De Paola, Tomie, *The Legend of the Bluebonnet* (New York: Putnam, 1983). The legend states that an orphaned Comanche girl sacrifices her only doll in order to end the drought that is devastating her village. Because of this, the rains come and beautiful bluebonnet flowers (the color of her doll) cover the state of Texas. They are still there today, as a reminder of her unselfish and loving act.

De Paola, Tomie, *The Legend of the Indian Paintbrush* (New York: Putnam, 1988). Little Gopher is unable to do many of the things that other boys his age can do. However, when he goes to the hills to think about becoming a man, he has a dream vision. He realizes his true calling in life and becomes an artist. He covers the hillside with beautiful flowers the colors of the sun-set and is renamed for his talent, He-Who-Brought-the-Sunset-to-the-Earth. This legend has a wonderful message about being true to oneself.

Dorros, Arthur, *Abuela* (New York: Dutton Children's Books, 1991). While feed-ing birds in the park, Rosalba imagines what it would be like to fly. She and her *abuela* (the Spanish word for grandma) embark on a wondrous adven-ture over New York. They soar above factories and trains, the Statue of Lib-erty, a harbor, airport, and local market. The author seamlessly integrates Spanish phrases into the simple English text, adding to the uniqueness of the book. Vivid and detailed illustrations resemble folk art and perfectly complement the multicultural tale.

Duncan, Alice Faye, *Honey Baby Sugar Child* (New York: Simon & Schuster Books for Young Readers, 2005). The love between a mother and her child is celebrated. Text and exquisite oil paintings mirror one another in this beautiful tribute to mother and son hugging, playing, dancing, and napping together. African American dialect is included in the rhythmic text, creating a singsong quality that begs to be read aloud.

Fox, Mem, *Whoever You Are* (San Diego: Harcourt Brace, 1997). The author simply and beautifully reminds all of us that no matter who we are, the color of our skin, the home where we live, the type of school we attend, we are more alike than different. We all have hearts that are the same. We smile, laugh, cry, hurt, and bleed like everyone else. We experience love and joy as others do. Captivating illustrations bordered in gold and jewels showcase children from all over the world.

Friedman, Ina R., *How My Parents Learned to Eat* (Boston: Houghton Mifflin, 1984). A little girl recounts how her Japanese mother and American father met. The book celebrates the similarities and differences among cultures.

Greenfield, Eloise, *Honey I Love* (New York: Crowell, 1978). A young African American girl tells about all the simple things that she dearly loves. She loves the way her cousin from the South talks. She loves jumping in a pool on a hot day and taking a family ride. She loves playing and laughing and kissing her mother's soft, warm arm. This rhythmic poem is a beautiful reminder to appreciate all that life has to offer.

Hoffman, Mary, *Amazing Grace* (New York: Dial Books for Young Readers, 1991). Grace won't let her race or gender stand in the way of her goal of being Peter Pan in her class play. Although she is discouraged by her classmates, the strong love and support of her family remind her that she can do anything she imagines.

Ho, Minfong, *Peek! A Thai Hide-and-Seek* (Cambridge, MA: Candlewick, 2004). Highlighting a cultural twist on the familiar childhood game, father and daughter play "Jut-Ay." The little girl cleverly hides throughout a lush jungle. When she's finally found by her father, we see the glee in the little girl's face. Rhymed verses and onomatopoeia give a singsong quality to the text, which is complemented by strong, colorful illustrations of indigenous animals in Thailand.

Holwitz, Peter, *Scribbleville* (New York: Philomel Books, 2005). All the people and things in Scribbleville are squiggly and wiggly. When a strange man who is "straight as a stick" comes to town and builds a square house with a pointed roof, people are astounded. They fear that others like him will one day move in. But when a scribbly woman befriends him, she explains that although he is odd on the outside that is not where she looks. A child finally helps bring the town together by making a drawing with both scrib-

bles and straight lines. The bouncy, rhyming text makes the ideas of acceptance and the celebration of differences very accessible for children.

Joosse, Barbara M., *Mama, Do You Love Me?* (San Francisco: Chronicle Books,
1991). A daughter poses outlandish reasons why her mother may not love
her. The mother is always honest, replying that she might be angry or upset,
but that she will love her daughter no matter what. The joyous bond between mother and daughter is reflected in both words and illustrations.
Beautiful scenes of Alaska are reflected in each page spread. The Inuit
mother and daughter are depicted in radiant oranges, reds, and cheery patterns, replicating the warmth of their snuggles and embraces.

Joosse, Barbara M., *Papa, Do You Love Me?* San Francisco: Chronicle Books,
2005). A Maasai father reassures his son of his unconditional love for him
in this beautiful book. Brilliant reds, oranges, and golds reflect both the
Serengeti Plain and the warmth of the parent-child relationship. The father
answers his son's questions with poetic words that reference Maasai life.
The book also includes a glossary that elaborates on the concepts
presented.

Katz, Karen, *The Colors of Us* (New York: Henry Holt and Co., 1999). Lena's
mother describes all the different shades of brown present in the skin tones
of their friends and neighbors. She poetically compares them to many delicious foods including cinnamon, French toast, honey, ginger, peaches, and
chocolate. This book celebrates the unique color of each of us.

Keats, Ezra Jack, *The Snowy Day* (New York: Viking Press, 1962). A young boy
awakens to a snow-covered city. He celebrates the magical experience of a
world blanketed in white by making footprints, snow angels, and attempting to save a snowball for another day. Understated illustrations complement this story about seeing the world through the eyes of a child.

Kimmelman, Leslie, *The Runaway Latkes* (Morton Grove, IL: Albert Whitman &
Co., 2000). In the Hanukkah version of the "gingerbread man," three crisp
and brown potato latkes escape the frying pan and head out on a mischievous adventure. A hilarious chase follows with cantor, rabbi, and mayor
joining in. In this rhythmic cumulative tale, the latkes even make an escape
by jumping into an applesauce river. The clever text is complemented by
whimsical illustrations making a fun book for all to enjoy.

Lin, Grace, *Dim Sum for Everyone* (New York: Alfred A. Knopf, 2001). A family
with three daughters arrives at a Chinese restaurant and begins a traditional meal. Carts are wheeled around to the table, and each family member chooses a favorite dish. Then everyone shares. A brief cultural history

of dim sum is provided, as well as detailed illustrations throughout the book that reflect the Chinese culture.

Lin, Grace, *The Ugly Vegetables*. (Watertown, MA: Charlesbridge, 1999). The Chinese American girl is very disappointed that she and her mother are growing "ugly vegetables" when all the neighbors are growing beautiful flowers. However, when they harvest the crops and make an aromatic soup, the neighbors come to join them. An illustrated glossary of the vegetables and their Chinese characters is included. And there's even a recipe for the "ugly" but delicious soup.

Lionni, Leo, *Little Blue and Little Yellow* (New York: McDowell, Obolensky, 1959). A seemingly simple concept book about a yellow blob hugging a blue blob that together becomes a green blob. However, upon closer reflection, one finds themes of diversity, tolerance, friendship, love, and parenting.

Makhijani, Pooja, *Mama's Saris* (New York: Little, Brown, 2007). Since her mother always wears a sari on special occasions, the little girl who narrates the story wants to do the same. It is her seventh birthday and she yearns to be a grown-up. Her mother finally relents and she is adorned in a beautiful blue sari, fancy bangles, and a glittery bindi placed between her eyebrows. This is a delightful celebration of mother-daughter relationships and growing up. The deep, vibrant acrylic paintings in jewel tones reflect the patterns of the saris mentioned throughout the story. A glossary of Hindi words provides helpful background information.

Moreillon, Judi, *Vamos a Leer* (New York: Star Bright Books, 2004). In this Spanish translation of the English book *Read to Me*, a simple poem about the importance of reading to a child is stressed. The rhythmic message is complemented by illustrations of multiethnic children and families reading to one another and themselves.

Morris, Ann, *Loving* (New York: Lothrop, Lee & Shepard Books, 1990). Beautiful photographs showcase people from many different cultures engaged in everyday activities. The focus is on the loving relationship between parent and child. This title in a series of books by the same author and photographer is particularly unique because most of the photographs are taken within the United States, highlighting the breadth of diversity in this country. It is a moving tribute to families everywhere. A glossary contains a miniature of each photograph, the country or location in which it was taken, and a brief description. This book, as well as many others by the same team, provides a wonderful view of the bigger world around us and opens the door to numerous discussions about how we are different and the same as our neighbors all over the world. Other titles by Ann Morris and photographer Ken Heyman: *Bread, Bread, Bread* (1998), *Families* (2000), *Hats, Hats, Hats* (1993), *Houses and Homes* (1995), *Shoes, Shoes, Shoes* (1998), *Tools* (1998), and *Weddings* (1995).

Munsch, Robert N., *Paper Bag Princess* (Buffalo, NY: Discis Knowledge Research, 1993). Elizabeth is a beautiful princess with beautiful clothes and is planning to marry Prince Ronald. Quite unexpectedly, a dragon burns down her castle and takes Ronald captive. Elizabeth outwits the dragon and opens the door to his cave, only to have Ronald declare her a mess and reject her. She counters that he may look like a prince but does not have good manners. Needless to say, they do *not* live together happily ever after.

Parr, Todd, *It's Okay to Be Different* (Boston: Little, Brown, 2001). Brightly colored childlike figures are outlined in black, giving the book a playful feel. The author uses reassuring statements to remind all of us that it really is okay to be different. Without being preachy or overbearing, the book focuses on acceptance of self and of others. This is a powerful message presented in an inviting way for children of all ages.

Parr, Todd, *The Peace Book* (New York: Little, Brown, 2004). The author uses simple text to provide various images of what peace is so that children can better understand this abstract concept. Deep and bright colors, including reds, oranges, and purples, are used to show multiethnic people in various scenes. The book can serve as a great discussion starter with your child about what peace means to each of us.

Park, Linda Sue, *Bee-Bim Bop!* (New York: Clarion Books, 2005). A little girl helps her mother shop and prepare her favorite Korean meal, Bee-bim Bop! Bouncy, rhyming text is enhanced by the repetitive phrase, "Hungry, hungry, hungry for some BEE-BIM BOP!" A recipe for this popular dish is included at the end.

Richmond, Marianne, *Hooray for You* (Minneapolis, MN: Waldman House Press, 2001). This book celebrates different cultures, different physical traits, and other ways that each of us is unique. The bouncy rhyming lines provide a powerful message that will help a child feel confident and proud of who he is. Bold, colorful illustrations resemble fingerpaintings and add to the positive and cheerful tone.

Singer, Marilyn, *Nine O'clock Lullaby* (New York: HarperCollins, 1991). It is 9:00 p.m. in Brooklyn, New York, and a mother begins to read a bedtime story to her child. At that very same moment, a father plays the congas in Puerto Rico, a village draws water from a well in India, an aunt flies like a dragon as she rides her bike in the streets of China, and an Australian family cooks on the "barbie." This rhythmic lullaby provides an awareness of the fifteen different time zones and the different cultures thriving in each.

Siomandes, Lorianne, *My Box of Color* (Honesale, PA: Boyds Mills Press, 1998). This book initially appears to be a concept book about colors. However, upon closer inspection it combines the ideas of colors (reinforcing them) with a much deeper lesson. A series of questions guides the reader into looking differently at the world around us. If I changed the color of a cat, would he still purr and sit in my lap? If the flowers were the same color as trees, would they still feed the bees? If the sun were a different color, would it still be as hot? The pattern is repeated showing common things in very uncommon colors. The intensely bright illustrations will pull the reader in, but it is the thoughtful question at the end that will promote discussion. What if I were a different color, would you still like me?

Soto, Gary, *Too Many Tamales* (New York: Putnam, 1993). When Maria sneakily slips her mother's diamond ring on her finger while kneading the masa for tamales, trouble begins. After losing the ring, she and her cousins decide they must eat all the tamales in order to find it. In this story about close familial relationships and love, we learn the values of telling the truth and forgiveness.

Stuve-Bodeen, Stephanie A., *Elizabeti's Doll* (New York: Lee & Low Books, 1998). A young Tanzanian girl longs for a doll after watching her mother care for her new baby brother. Elizabeti finally settles on a rock, the perfect size and shape to be her special baby. She names her Eva, and just like her mother, she carries her in a kanga cloth, sings her lullabies, and feeds her (although Eva is too polite to burp). When Eva gets lost, no other rock can replace her. She is finally found, brushed off, hugged, and kissed. The gentle and serene story provides a glimpse into another culture but houses the universal themes of love and a child's very real imagination.

Tarpley, Natasha Anastasia, *I Love My Hair!* (Boston: Little, Brown, 2004). An African American girl describes the process of her mother's combing out her hair each night. When she cries in the midst of a particularly tangled spot, her mother tells her how beautiful her hair is. She focuses on the many different styles Keyana can wear and explains the cultural heritage related to her hair. This is a well-written and illustrated book about self-acceptance and celebration of one's uniqueness.

Uegaki, Chieri, *Suki's Kimono* (Tonawanda, NY: Kids Can Press, 2003). On her first day of school, Suki wears her kimono because it reminds her of visits with her grandmother. Suki's sisters and classmates make fun of her. However, when she talks to her class and performs a Japanese dance, her class realizes how unique and special she is. This is a story of a strong and determined little girl who celebrates being different. Japanese words are sprinkled within the context of the story, providing many of us a window into another culture.

Williams, Vera B., *A Chair for My Mother* (New York: Greenwillow Books, 1982). After a devastating fire destroys their home, a little girl, her mother, and her grandmother save coins in a jar for more than a year. Once the jar is full, they buy a beautiful, comfortable chair. The story shows the strength of a family working together against difficult odds. Through bright, primitive illustrations and a touching story, we see the love of a family.

Informational Books

Allen, Judy, *Are You a Butterfly?* (New York: Kingfisher, 2000) Listeners are invited to imagine what it is like to be a butterfly. A conversational and humorous tone is used to provide information and create a balance between facts and readability for preschoolers. Large closeup illustrations of the butterfly throughout its metamorphosis add to the inviting style of the book. The book ends with a final contrast between being a butterfly and a human child. Other books in the series: *Are You an Ant? Are You a Bee? Are You a Dragonfly? Are You a Grasshopper? Are You a Ladybug? Are You a Snail? Are You a Spider?*

De Paola, Tomie, *The Cloud Book* (New York: Holiday House, 1975). This extensive book about clouds is both entertaining and informative. Delightful illustrations add a comedic tone to the text, making it readily accessible to preschoolers. Metaphors are used to compare different types of clouds to cauliflower, sheep, or "thin milk-white sheets," helping all readers more easily remember the information presented. Other books by Tomie De Paola: *The Family Christmas Tree Book*, *The Kids' Cat Book*, *The Popcorn Book*, *The Quicksand Book*.

Gibbons, Gail, *Monarch Butterfly* (New York: Holiday House, 1989). Clinging to a leaf, a tiny egg hatches and out crawls a caterpillar. As the caterpillar transforms into a beautiful Monarch butterfly, details about metamorphosis and the migration of these marvelous creatures is explained. The straightforward language helps to define science terms, and the brightly colored illustrations incorporate diagrams and maps to assist in comprehension, providing an enjoyable and interactive introduction to nonfiction text. Other books by Gail Gibbons: *Apples*, *The Art Box*, *My Baseball Book*,

Emergency! Fire! Fire! Frogs, The Honey Makers, How a House Is Built, The Milk Makers, My Football Book, The Planets, The Post Office Book: Mail and How It Moves, My Soccer Book, Spiders, Trains, and *Weather Words and What They Mean.*

Heller, Ruth, *Chickens Aren't the Only Ones* (New York: Grosset & Dunlap, 1981). The author combines lively prose and beautiful illustrations to provide information about the many animals that lay eggs. Preschoolers are exposed to extensive vocabulary and learn numerous facts about oviparous animals through a lively and entertaining approach. Other books by Ruth Heller: *Animals Born Alive and Well, How to Hide a Butterfly and Other Insects, How to Hide a Crocodile and Other Reptiles, How to Hide a Meadow Frog and Other Amphibians, How to Hide an Octopus and Other Sea Creatures, Plants That Never Bloom,* and *The Reason for a Flower.*

Himmelman, John, *A Ladybug's Life* (New York: Chidlren's Press, 1998). Because of its simple text, this book is a wonderful introduction to nonfiction. The life cycle of the ladybug is recorded and a glossary of terms included for some additional information. The large, colorful illustrations make this book visually inviting.

Let's-Read-and-Find-Out Science Series by HarperCollins: Well-written and very informative, this series covers a wealth of topics for every inquisitive child. Written in an easy-to-read format, the books bridge children into the nonfiction genre through appealing illustrations that range from brightly colored paintings to photographs. Many include hands-on activities or science experiments to engage the child and further extend their knowledge. Most of these require adult supervision or assistance. Stage 1 books introduce and explain basic science concepts. Stage 2 covers more challenging material and includes more detailed text. I have included a list of Stage 1 titles below. Be sure to preview each selection within Stage 2 in order to determine which ones are appropriate for your child's developmental and interest level. See *My Feet; My Hands; I'm Growing!; Animals in Winter; Pop! A Book About Bubbles; Air Is All Around You; The Big Dipper; Is There Life in Outer Space? Baby Whales Drink Milk; How Animal Babies Stay Safe; Where Are the Night Animals? Ducks Don't Get Wet; Fireflies in the Night; From Caterpillar to Butterfly; Starfish; A Nest Full of Eggs; How a Seed Grows; From Seed to Pumpkin; From Tadpole to Frog; What's It Like to Be a Fish? Bugs Are Insects; My Pet Hamster; Big Tracks, Little Tracks: Following Animal Prints; How Many Teeth? Sleep Is for Everyone; Where Do Chicks Come From? Dinosaurs Big and Small; What's Alive?* and *What Lives in a Shell?*

Eye-Openers books by Dorling Kindersley: *Cars, Diggers and Dump Trucks Dinosaurs, Farm Animals, Jungle Animals, Planes, Sea Animals, Trucks,* and *Zoo Animals.*

I Wonder Why Series by Kingfisher: These delightful nonfiction books cater to the younger audience while still including enough facts to keep the reader interested for many years. The easy to understand question and answer format invites listeners to skim, scan, and pick and choose different parts to read and learn. Realistic illustrations, reflective of nonfiction textbooks, are complemented by engaging cartoons. Other nonfiction features include numbered pages, a table of contents, and an index page. Parents, too, may be surprised at all the interesting things they learn about the solar system, animals, the body, and numerous other nonfiction topics. *I Wonder Why I Blink and Other Questions About My Body, I Wonder Why My Tummy Rumbles and Other Questions About My Body, I Wonder Why the Dodo Is Dead and Other Questions About Animals in Danger, I Wonder Why Trees Have Leaves and Other Questions About Plants, I Wonder Why Fish Grew Legs and Other Questions And Prehistoric Life, I Wonder Why Mountains Have Snow On Top and Other Questions About Mountains, I Wonder Why Pine Trees Have Needles and Other Questions About Forests, I Wonder Why Stalactites Hang Down and Other Questions About Caves, I Wonder Why Camels Have Humps and Other Questions About Animals, I Wonder Why the Sea Is Salty and Other Questions About the Oceans, I Wonder Why the Wind Blows and Other Questions About Our Planet, I Wonder Why Columbus Crossed the Ocean and Other Questions About Explorers, I Wonder Why Planes Have Wings and Other Questions About Transportation, I Wonder Why the Telephone Rings and Other Questions About Communication, I Wonder Why Geese Go on Holiday and Other Questions About Birds, I Wonder Why Snakes Shed Their Skin and Other Questions About Reptiles, I Wonder Why Spiders Spin Webs and Other Questions About Creepy Crawlies, I Wonder Why Flutes Have Holes and Other Questions About Music, I Wonder Why the Pyramids Were Built and Other Questions About Egypt, I Wonder Why Stars Twinkle and Other Questions About Space, I Wonder Why Soap Makes Bubbles and Other Questions About Science, I Wonder Why Zippers Have Teeth and Other Questions About Inventions, I Wonder Why Triceratops Had Horns and Other Questions About Dinosaurs, I Wonder Why the Sun Rises and Other Questions About Time and Seasons, I Wonder Why Caterpillars Eat So Much and Other Questions About Life Cycles,* and *I Wonder Why Kangaroos Have Pouches and Other Questions About Baby Animals.*

Read and Wonder Series by Candlewick Press. Each title combines beautiful text with wonderful illustrations to invite young children into the world of nonfiction. Writing styles range from stories to poetry, but all include scientifically accurate information. Preschoolers are eased into expository text with affectionate and amusing writing. Many of the titles include nonfiction features such as indexes, closeup illustrations, diagrams, and explanatory notes. Titles include *My Goose Betsy*, *Bat Loves the Night*, *Big Blue Whale*, *Jody's Beans*, *Growing Frogs*, *A Field Full of Horses*, *Walk with a Wolf*, *Chameleons Are Cool*, *The Emperor's Egg*, *All Pigs Are Beautiful*, *I Love Guinea Pigs*, *Think of an Eel*, and *Gentle Giant Octopus*.

Magazines: *Click* (Carus Publishing) and *Your Big Backyard* (National Wildlife Federation).

Phonemic Awareness

Andreae, Giles, *Giraffes Can't Dance* (New York: Orchard Books, 2001). Gerald the Giraffe is the only animal in Africa not looking forward to the annual jungle dance . . . because he can't dance! It seems to come so naturally to others, but Gerald's long, lanky limbs just can't seem to move to the rhythm. When the entire jungle begins to make fun of Gerald, he sadly leaves, feeling rejected. On the way home, however, he meets a kindhearted cricket, who helps him see that sometimes it takes finding the beat of your own music to learn to dance. *Giraffes Can't Dance* is written in singsong prose that will help draw children's attention to the rhyming scheme and promote phonemic awareness.

Alborough, Jez, *Duck in the Truck* (New York: HarperCollins Publishers, 2000). As Duck is driving home in his truck, he hits a stone in the road and the truck bounces, getting stuck in the mud. Luckily, Frog, Sheep, and Goat come to the rescue. Simple rhyming text will certainly have children chiming in with this funny, but rather messy, story with darling illustrations.

Bayer, Jane, *A My Name Is Alice* (New York: Dial Books for Young Readers, 1984). Using a repetitive jump rope rhythm, the sounds of each letter (phonemic awareness) are connected to their respective symbols (phonics). The author cleverly names a husband-and-wife team, tells where they are from, what they sell, and what type of animal each is. Barbara the Bear and Bob the Baboon are from Brazil and they sell balloons. Children will have a great time hearing the sounds repeated and guessing the different animals, places, and items up for sale.

Brown, Margaret Wise, *Sleepy ABC* (New York: HarperCollins, 1994). The theme of getting ready for bed is used in this rhyming alphabet book. Large upper case letters are accompanied by a short phrase about going to sleep. M is for the Mother who tucks you in. N represents a dark and starry Night. This is a gentle and calming bedtime story that also reinforces the connection between the letters and sounds of the alphabet.

Cleary, Beverly, *The Hullabaloo ABC* (Berkeley, CA: Parnassus Press, 1960). Raucous rhymes and inviting illustrations depict the energetic life taking place in and around a farmhouse. Lively verbs and attention to sound words (kerchoo, hee-haw, quack-quack) make this ABC book a big hit for a noisy read-aloud time.

Cronin, Doreen, *Click, Clack, Quackity Quack: An Alphabetical Adventure* (New York: Atheneum Books for Young Readers, 2005). In this book, phonemic awareness is naturally connected to phonics. Large lowercase gray letters serve as the background to the more prominent illustrations of the hilarious plot. The cows have been busy typing a special note that Duck delivers to all the barnyard friends. Alliterative phrases and sentences are cleverly strung together to unveil the silly tale surrounding a picnic invitation. Animals awake beneath blue blankets. Clickety-clack! Duck dashing, eggs emptying. Flippity-flip!

Edwards, Pamela Duncan, *Clara Caterpillar* (New York: HarperCollins Publishers, 2001). After deciding to finally hatch from her egg, Clara the Caterpillar grows up and eventually turns into "an ordinary cabbage butterfly." Luckily for her more brightly colored friends, she is able to distract a pesky crow looking for lunch. After the others have made a hasty escape, Clara camouflages herself among the flowers in a camellia bush and emerges the heroine. In this clever alliterative tale, the author emphasizes the K sound, and uses exceptional vocabulary that begins with the letter *c*. "Clara climbed, crawled, and capered about, having carefree caterpillar fun."

Fleming, Denise, *In the Small, Small Pond* (New York: H. Holt, 1993). Bouncy, rhythmic text gives celebration to pond life. Unique and exquisite illustrations add the perfect touch.

Fleming, Denise, *In the Tall, Tall Grass* (New York: H. Holt, 1991). Both words and illustrations combine beautifully to reflect the business of life in the tall, tall grass. Bright colorful collages create a unique visual effect.

Hoberman, Mary Ann, *Whose Garden Is It?* (Orlando, FL: Gulliver Books/Harcourt, 2004). When Mrs. McGee and her toddler friend come across a beautiful garden, they wonder whose it is. Everyone from the gardener, rabbit, bee, seeds, rain, and earth claim it as their own. An upbeat rhyming verse introduces the reader to gardening and teaches us that each part of nature adds a piece to the successful outcome. Jane Dyer's intricate and realistic watercolors make the reader feel as though they are participating in Mrs. McGee's stroll.

Hoberman, Mary Ann, *One of Each* (Boston: Little, Brown, 1997). Oliver Tolliver is a canine who has one of everything he needs. What is missing is a friend. With the help of a gray cat named Peggoty Small, Oliver learns how to make his house fit for two and even more! Bright colors and patterns in the illustrations play perfectly off the intelligent rhymes.

Guarino, Deborah, *Is Your Mama a Llama?* (New York: Scholastic, 1989). Lloyd the Llama queries each of his animal friends trying to find out who else has a mama who is a llama. The animals respond in rhythmic fashion by describing their own mothers. Since the author uses natural language that makes sense, children will delight in guessing the name of the animal that appears on the following page of each riddle. Sweet illustrations by Steven Kellogg make the book even more special.

Kirk, David, *Miss Spider's ABC* (New York: Scholastic, Callaway Editions, 1998). Alliterative phrases for each letter of the alphabet are combined to create a silly story. "Bumblebees blow balloons . . . Ladybugs laugh . . . Moths mingle." All the insects are getting ready for the big surprise party for Miss Spider's birthday. With the large uppercase letters prominently displayed on each page of brightly colored insects, preschoolers are assisted in making direct connections between letter names and their corresponding sounds.

Kirk, David, *Miss Spider's Tea Party* (New York: Scholastic: Callaway Editions, 1994). Miss Spider desperately wants to make friends with the other insects and have them over for cakes and tea. However, everyone is too afraid of her and dashes away in "mortal dread." It is not until a moth is caught in the rain and unable to fly that Miss Spider gets the opportunity to show her kindness and pure intentions. She nurses the moth back to health and releases it. When the news travels of her good deed, everyone decides to come for tea and be her friend. The bouncy rhyming verse is accompanied by bold yellows, oranges, greens, and blues that vividly illustrate each insect.

Lear, Edward, and Suse MacDonald, *A Was Once an Apple Pie* (New York: Orchard Books, 2005). Follow the letters of the alphabet using an apple pie theme and you've got a great book. The text focuses on stretching and playing with the sounds of the English language. With bright illustrations that sometimes seem to reach beyond the borders of the text, this version of Lear's classic poem is perfect for young children.

MacLennan, Cathy, *Chicky Chicky Chook Chook* (New York: Boxer Books, 2007). When fluffy chicks, friendly bumblebees, and cuddly kitties get together, you better believe it is a joyous occasion! The animals romp and play and then snuggle and sleep in the "sunny, sunny, hot shine." But a rainstorm awakens them and they get "soggy, groggy, moggy." How will they ever get dry? The infectious beat, replete with the use of onomatopoeia and repetitive sounds, provides children opportunities to hear and play with the English language. Bold, seemingly textured art captures a child's attention and adds to the whimsy of the book.

Martin, Bill, Jr., *"Fire! Fire!" Said Mrs. McGuire* (Orlando, FL: Harcourt, 2006). The familiar nursery rhyme is given new life by Vladimir Radunsky, the illustrator of this publication. A group of bumbling mice live peacefully in a closet until a fire is discovered through the keyhole. A chain of silly events ensues, until finally the commotion is resolved with the discovery of candles on a birthday cake for a party of cats. Clever rhymes keep the tempo moving and provide opportunities for building phonemic awareness.

Most, Bernard, *Cock-a-Doodle-Moo!* (San Diego: Harcourt Brace, 1996). When Rooster gets laryngitis, he is unable to wake all the animals and the farmer. Cow finally steps in to help and makes several close attempts at the early morning signal including, "Mock-a-moodle-mood!" Finally, Rooster coaches him to say something that is not quite right but nonetheless does the trick. Everyone on the farm wakes with a laugh. Clever play with language will help children attend to sounds and become phonemically aware.

Riley, Linnea, *Mouse Mess* (New York: Blue Sky Press, 1997). After the family of humans goes to sleep, Mouse helps himself to a "little snack." This leads to lots of rollicking mischief and a huge mess all over the kitchen. Irresponsible Mouse isn't even apologetic in the end. "These people ought to clean their house," he states, heading off to bed. A simple story with simple rhymes that is just silly enough to have children wanting to hear it again and again.

Root, Phyllis, *One Duck, Stuck* (Cambridge, MA: Candlewick Press, 1998). One duck gets stuck in the muck and needs help. Two splish, splish fish aren't able to help. Three clomp, clomp moose are also unsuccessful. The number of animals trying to help increases incrementally until ten zing, zing dragonflies see what they can do. However, it is not until all the helpers work together that duck is finally "un-stuck." Children will laugh at both the text and illustrations, and they'll relish the inventive sounds and actions made by each animal helper.

Root, Phyllis, *Rattletrap Car* (Cambridge, MA: Candlewick Press, 2001). Each time their rattletrap car breaks down on the way to the lake, the family comes up with a crazy, innovative way to fix it. Using bouncy and rhythmic language, the author provides a hilarious story. Nonsense words, alliteration, and onomatopoeia contribute to the silliness. Fun, fun, fun!

Sendak, Maurice, *Chicken Soup with Rice: A Book of Months* (New York: HarperTrophy, 1991). A little boy describes his adventures and travels for each month of the year, all the while eating chicken soup with rice. Charming rhyming verses will have children chanting and singing.

Seuss, Dr., *Hop on Pop* (New York: Beginner Books, 1963). Clever rhymes accompanied by hilarious illustrations invite children into the world of books. Listeners can chime in with the silly sounds and patterns in words.

Seuss, Dr., *There's a Wocket in My Pocket* (New York: Beginner Books, 1974). In classic Seussian fashion, we are introduced to a number of made-up creatures all around the house. Silly rhymes that contain both real words and made-up ones help stretch a child's imagination while reinforcing key elements of phonemic awareness.

Shaw, Nancy, *Sheep in a Jeep* (Boston: Houghton Mifflin, 1986). Five sheep happily pack into a jeep and head out on a lively road trip. Every turn leads to another hilarious misadventure as the sheep plummet down a steep hill, plunge into a mud puddle, and crash into a tree. The bright-colored pencil drawings of the sheep's expressions enhance the brief, rhyming text, adding to the silliness of the tale.

Slepian, Jan, and Ann Seidler, *The Hungry Thing* (Chicago: Follet Publishing, 1967). A large creature comes into town demanding all sorts of food from the people. However, it is only a little boy who is able to figure out what the Hungry Thing wants to eat. Shmancakes, feetloaf, and hookies turn out to be pancakes, meatloaf, and cookies. This darling and delicious story allows children to hear how sounds in words can be manipulated to form new and silly ones.

Weeks, Sara, *Oh My Gosh, Mrs. McNosh!* (New York: HarperCollins, 2002). When Mrs. McNosh's dog, George, breaks loose during a walk in the park, a series of unfortunate and hilarious events ensues. While chasing him, Mrs. McNosh falls in a lake, crashes into a wedding buffet, and catches a cold. Discouraged, she finally heads home, only to find that George has slipped through the doggie door and is waiting for her, grinning from ear to ear. The text is both repetitive and rhyming, which encourages prediction and participation.

Poetry

Brown, Margaret Wise, *Give Yourself to the Rain* (New York: Margaret K. McElderry Books, 2002). The twenty-four poems in this book were collected posthumously and range from cheery, silly topics to more serene and thoughtful ones. Were Margaret Wise Brown still alive, she may have edited some, but the collection is nonetheless still worthy of a place on your bookshelf. Like so much of her work, these poems capture the experience of being a child.

Dyer, Jane, *Animal Crackers: A Delectable Collection of Pictures, Poems, and Lullabies for the Very Young* (Boston: Little, Brown, 1996). This darling compilation of some of the best traditional, contemporary, and multicultural works is beautifully illustrated with soft watercolors. It will surely be a treasure in every household.

Engelbreit, Mary, *Mary Engelbreit's Mother Goose* (New York: HarperCollins, 2005). A classic collection of Mother Goose rhymes is illustrated in Engelbreit's distinctive and charming style. Only a few rhymes are included on each page spread, making the book uncluttered and perfect for preschoolers.

Hague, Michael, *Animal Poems: A Collection of Poems for Children* (New York: Henry Holt, 2007). This is a wonderful collection of twenty poems about animals. The bright and beautiful illustrations are eye-catching and add a sweet touch.

Hoberman, Mary Ann, *The Llama Who Had No Pajama: 100 Favorite Poems* (San Diego: Harcourt Brace & Co., 1998). A wealth of clever rhymes are centered around all the things children love, from animals to playing. Most important, there is a healthy dose of just plain silliness. Both parent and child will enjoy this collection.

Horton, Joan, *Hippopotamus Stew* (New York: Henry Holt, 2006). Animals are caught in a variety of silly situations in this themed poetry book. The centipede is desperately looking for one hundred pairs of matching shoes. The snake wishes for a built-in zipper to more easily shed his skin. The chameleon is aghast when he dreams that all of his surroundings turn from green to plaid. Twenty-one hilarious poems are sure to keep children entertained.

Katz, Bobbie, *Pocket Poems* (New York: Dutton Children's Books, 2004). More than fifty poems are written by the author or collected by her and compiled in this wonderful volume. The poems are about childhood and silliness and celebrate the ordinary. Children and adults will delight in the variety and wit provided and will no doubt giggle their way through time and again.

Kennedy, Caroline, *A Family of Poems: My Favorite Poetry for Children* (New York: Hyperion/Hyperion Books for Children, 2005). The selections in this wonderful anthology range from silly poems to more serious ones. It is separated into seven categories including About Me, That's So Silly, Adventure, and Bedtime. All of these focus on topics that children love. A sampling of the poets from this collection are Emily Dickinson, Robert Frost, William Blake, Carl Sandburg, Langston Hughes, and e.e. cummings.

Lansky, Bruce, *Mary Had a Little Jam, and Other Silly Rhymes* (New York: Meadowbrook Press, 2004). The author gives many famous nursery rhymes a silly spin. This will definitely have both your child and you laughing out loud at the clever reinvention of classic Mother Goose.

Lewis, J. Patrick, *Doodle Dandies: Poems That Take Shape* (New York: Atheneum Books for Young Readers, 1998). *Doodle Dandies* serves as an excellent introduction to concrete poetry. The lyrical text describes an ordinary thing or tells a story. However, it is the placement of the words themselves that distinguishes this type of poetry. The words in the poem about a skyscraper, for example, come together to form the image of this tall building and are set atop a cloud-filled sky. The book is well designed and will give creative pause to how words can be inventively put together.

Yolen, Jane, and Andrew Fusek, *Here's a Little Poem* (Cambridge, MA: Candlewick Press, 2007). A compilation of wonderful poems by a variety of respected artists (both classic and contemporary) fill this volume. The book is divided into four sections—"Me, Myself, and I," "Who Lives in My House?" "I Go Outside," and "Time for Bed." Charming, whimsical illustrations are a delightful complement to this must-have book.

Predictable Books

Repetition

Brown, Margaret Wise, *The Important Book* (New York: Harper, 1949). The important thing about this book is that it helps us look more closely at how special and beautiful ordinary things are. The author uses rhythm and repetition to describe a daisy, apple, wind, rain, and even a child. Because of its predictable opening and closing line of each page spread, children will likely read along with you.

Carle, Eric, *The Very Busy Spider* (New York: Philomel Books, 1984). A spider spends her day spinning a web. Several animals approach her to ask if she would like to play. However, she does not answer because she is too busy with her job. As night falls, she captures a fly and then takes a rest. The spider web is embossed on each page spread, giving it a 3-D effect and inviting children to touch it. The repetitive phrase about the spider being too busy will have children quickly chiming in.

Carle, Eric, *The Very Lonely Firefly* (New York: Philomel Books, 1995). As the sun sets, a firefly is born. Stretching its wings, it flies off in search of firefly friends. It mistakenly follows other light sources, including a candle, a flashlight, and a lantern. At last it finds just what it has been searching for, and we see numerous fireflies twinkling (with the help of a battery embedded in the book.) The fun surprise ending, along with Carle's signature bright illustrations, make this book a special treat.

Dunrea, Olivier, *Bear Noel* (New York: Farrar, Straus, and Giroux, 2000). A joyful repetitive text follows Bear Noel as he tromps through the snow on Christmas Eve, singing and laughing. He decorates a tree with nuts and seeds and berries and then invites all the animals to gather round and share the feast. For this one night, at least, everyone comes together in peace. A beautiful lyrical text is highlighted with gorgeous illustrations.

Fleming, Denise, *Mama Cat Has Three Kittens* (New York: Henry Holt, 1998). While Fluffy and Skinny spend the day with Mama Cat, Boris lazily naps. The cat family washes and sharpens their claws, walks on a stone wall, and chases leaves, finally tiring. Just as they settle in for their own nap, Boris wakes, stretches, and pounces! Bright collages complement the repetitive and bouncy text.

Fox, Mem, *The Magic Hat* (San Diego: Harcourt, 2002). When a whirling, magical hat blows into the park and lands atop a man's head, he is instantly transformed into a toad. Then the hat is once again lifted by the wind and taken to one person after another, each becoming a different animal. Finally, a wizard arrives and restores everyone to their original selves. He then places the hat on his own head for one last magical twist. Rhymed verses combined with a repetitive phrase keep listeners involved and guessing what will happen next.

Galdone, Paul, *The Little Red Hen* (New York: Seabury Press, 1973). When the little red hen finds a grain of wheat and decides to plant it, she solicits the help of her animal friends. However, they are very lazy, leaving her to plant the seed, tend the wheat, take it to the mill to be ground into flour, and even bake the cake without the help from anyone. In the end, the other animals learn a valuable lesson about assisting with the chores when the little red hen is rewarded by eating the cake all by herself.

Guarino, Deborah, *Is Your Mama a Llama?* (New York: Scholastic, 1989). Lloyd the Llama approaches his animal friends asking if their mamas are llamas. Each replies in turn with lively rhyming text describing the unique characteristics of their own species. Darling illustrations by Steven Kellogg serve as the perfect addition to this rhythmic romp.

Martin, Bill, Jr., *Brown Bear, Brown Bear, What Do You See?* (New York: Holt, Rinehart and Winston, 1967). Each colored animal (yellow duck, blue horse, green frog, etc.) is asked what it sees. The popular repetitive text is perfect for children emerging into reading. Easily identifiable animals are brightly colored, creating an inviting book.

Miranda, Anne, *To Market, to Market* (San Diego: Harcourt Brace, 1997). In this adaptation of the traditional nursery rhyme, the elderly woman returns again and again to the market to get a pig, a hen, a trout, a lamb, and many more. However, each time she leaves, the other animals wreak havoc at home. The zany tale is made exceptional because of the unique illustrations that perfectly capture the chaos and hilarity. Rhyme, repetition, and incredible artwork make this a crowd pleaser.

Most, Bernard, *If the Dinosaurs Came Back* (New York: Harcourt Brace Jovanovich, 1978). Scaring away robbers, helping firefighters put out fires, and taking swimmers for rides at the beach are just a few of the ways dinosaurs would be of great help if they were to return. Striking black-and-white backgrounds are contrasted with bright, colorful dinosaurs to create unique illustrations that add to the appeal of the story.

Rosen, Michael, *Bear's Day Out* (New York: Bloomsbury Children's Books, 2007). Bear usually spends his days singing to himself and splashing in the waves. However, when the city beckons him, he discovers a bustling, hustling, whooshing world. This, however, overwhelms Bear, and he runs away to a nearby park. There he is rescued by a group of children who take him home, and the newfound friends all sing and splash together. The playful words and repetitive question-and-answer format prompt participation from all listeners.

Rosen, Michael, and Helen Oxenbury, *We're Going on a Bear Hunt* (New York: Margaret K. McElderry Books, 1989). When a father, his four children, and the family dog go on a bear hunt, they encounter a cold river, oozy mud, and a deep, dark forest. Since they can't go over or under each obstacle, they must "splash splosh," "squelch squerch," and tiptoe through them. This delightful version of the familiar chant allows young readers to actively follow along and eventually "read" much of it by themselves.

Spinelli, Eileen, *I Know It's Autumn* (New York: HarperCollins, 2004). A young girl tells about all the sights, sounds, and smells of autumn, including hayrides at night, jack-o'-lanterns with crooked smiles, and watching the Native American storyteller leap and clap around the bonfire. Each rhyming verse begins with the phrase, "I know it's autumn when . . ."

Williams, Sue, *I Went Walking* (San Diego: Harcourt Brace Jovanovich, 1990). When a little boy goes walking through a farm he stumbles upon many different animals. Continuing on his walk, he realizes the animals are in fact following him! Making use of colors, rhymes, repetition, and illustrative hints, this story encourages all listeners to participate in the reading.

Wilson, Karma, *Bear Snores On* (New York: Margaret K. McElderry Books, 2001). One by one the woodland animals escape the unwelcoming weather into Bear's cave, bringing with them food to share. Despite the sounds and smells of a party, the hibernating Bear "snores on." This playful story about friendship is brought to life through vivid language and expressive illustrations. Rhyming and repetition beg listeners to chime in with the light-hearted text.

Rhyme and Rhythm

Andreae, Giles, *Rumble in the Jungle* (Wauwatosa, WI: Little Tiger Press, 1997). We are taken on a playful journey through the jungle to discover the animals there. Rhythmic and silly text tells a little about each of the animals featured. Bright, rich illustrations will capture the attention of preschoolers who will want to hear this book again and again.

Bunting, Eve, *Sunflower House* (San Diego: Harcourt Brace & Co., 1996). A boy plants sunflower seeds in a giant circle and tends the plants as they grow taller than he is. Then he and his friends play all summer in this giant sunflower house. When fall comes and the plants begin to brown, they harvest the seeds, let the birds have some, and save the rest for the following summer when the cycle will begin again. Rhymed couplets tell the story from the perspective of the boy.

Dewdney, Anna, *Llama Llama Red Pajama* (New York: Viking, 2005). The meaning of "llama drama" becomes quite clear when Baby Llama is afraid to go to sleep after his mother kisses him good night and leaves the room. When he calls for her and she does not come back immediately, he begins to "weep and wail," bringing Mama Llama frantically rushing up the stairs. This familiar experience for parents and children will have both audiences smiling and feeling reassured. Rhyming words and natural language encourage young listeners to participate.

Ginkel, Anne, *I've Got an Elephant* (Atlanta, GA: Peachtree Publishers, 2006). The little girl has a special elephant friend. Unfortunately, when she goes to school, it gets lonely and decides to bring home another elephant friend. The pattern continues each time the busy girl has something she must do. When at last there are too many elephants for her to handle, she sends them off to the zoo, but visits often. Will she repeat the pattern with another animal? Fun rhymes and whimsical illustrations add up to a darling book.

Hoberman, Mary Ann, *A House Is a House for Me* (New York: Viking Press, 1978). The author uses rhyme and repetition to tell us all about different kinds of houses for people, animals, and even things. After numerous examples of houses, the reader is invited to start thinking about how just about everything is a house for something. Bookshelves are houses for books. Hives are homes for bees. A mitten's a house for a hand. Can you think of more? Detailed illustrations will have everyone looking closely to find all the homes mentioned in the upbeat text.

Numeroff, Laura, *When Sheep Sleep* (New York: Abrams Books for Young Readers, 2006). Counting sheep is a timeless remedy for sleeplessness. But what do you do when the sheep themselves are sleeping? A tired little girl takes an imaginary adventure to try to count cows in the meadow, pigs in the mud, and even cats on the sofa. However, all are snoring peacefully. The counting finally exhausts her and she falls asleep, bringing the animals around the bed to thoughtfully watch over her. Dreamy, warm illustrations are a delightful complement to this rhyming lullaby.

Wood, Audrey, *Quick as a Cricket* (New York: Child's Play International, 1990). Using rhyme and a series of comparisons (similes) the author describes all the different parts of a little boy, celebrating how special he is. Among other things, he is slow like a snail, happy like a lark, as mean as a shark, and as wild as a chimp. The singsong quality of the text will invite your child to listen carefully and anticipate the next rhyme. Endearing illustrations show the boy with the variety of animals that are used in the similes. When you put these all together, you've got a wonderful celebration of being a child.

Sequential Patterns

Carle, Eric, *The Very Hungry Caterpillar* (New York: Philomel Books, 1979). After an egg hatches, the hungry caterpillar eats his way through a number of yummy foods during the week. This, however, gives him a stomachache, so he selects one last juicy leaf. He then spins his cocoon and finally emerges as a beautiful butterfly. Numbers one through five and the days of the week are included, as well as a repetitive phrase.

Carle, Eric, *A House for Hermit Crab* (Saxonville, MA: Picture Book Studio, 1987). When Hermit Crab outgrows his tiny shell, he searches for a new house. On his quest to decorate his shell, he meets an anemone, sea star, coral, lantern fish, and other friendly sea life. He politely asks each to join him, and they agree, turning his house into a home. When this home becomes too small, Hermit Crab seizes the opportunity to once again be artistic. This beautiful story addresses the challenges of dealing with the inevitable changes in life.

Numeroff, Laura Joffe, *If You Give a Mouse a Cookie* (New York: Harper & Row, 1985). If you give a mouse a cookie, he's going to want some milk. And, of course, he'll need a straw for his milk. So begins the hilarious tale of cause and effect as Mouse demands more and more. This darling story comes full circle, inviting a child to want it read again and again. The repetition and predictability of the pattern of requests leading to more requests will have children reading along with you. Consider also Numeroff's *If You Give a Pig a Pancake*.

Numeroff, Laura Joffe, *If You Take a Mouse to School* (New York: Laura Geringer Books/HarperCollins Publishers, 2002). When the little boy decides to bring Mouse to school, Mouse excitedly takes advantage of all the adventures there. He writes big words, performs a science experiment, builds a "mouse house" with blocks, and much more. The crisp, bright watercolors lightheartedly detail this little charmer's enthusiasm about everything he undertakes and the little boy's indulgent participation.

Cumulative Patterns

Bond, Felicia, *Tumble Bumble* (Arden, NC: Front Street, 1996). In this cumulative tale, ten friends join each other one by one, starting with an ant and ending with a boy. They march together and grab a snack and then all head to bed for a little nap. Cheerful rhymes and adorable illustrations make this counting book fun for everyone.

Brett, Jan, *The Mitten* (New York: Putnam Juvenile, 1989). Once out in the snow, Nicki promptly loses one of his new pure white mittens. A mole takes refuge in the mitten and is soon joined by a rabbit, a hedgehog, an owl, and many other cold little animals. When the whiskers of a tiny mouse tickle the bear, he sneezes and out fly all the furry friends. Nicki finds his enormously stretched out mitten and brings it home to his grandmother to wonder what could have caused this. Gorgeous detailed illustrations complement this wonderful folktale.

Brown, Ken, *The Scarecrow's Hat* (Atlanta, GA: Peachtree Publishers, 2001). Chicken is very interested in Scarecrow's hat, and he agrees to exchange it for a walking stick to hold up his weary arms. Unfortunately, this is something that Chicken doesn't have, but she knows that Badger does. Through a series of trades that satisfy each of the animals she encounters, Chicken finally gets her hat and does something very special with it. Beautiful watercolor illustrations make this book stand out among others.

Burningham, John, *Mr. Gumpy's Outing* (New York: Holt, Rinehart and Winston, 1970). One beautiful morning Mr. Gumpy decides to take a boat ride down the river. Before long, his boat is filled with children, a rabbit, a cat, a dog, a pig, and several other animal friends. When the goat kicks, a chain of unfortunate events ensues, and the boat capsizes, forcing the entire crew to swim to shore. Mild Mr. Gumpy takes it all in stride, serving tea and inviting everyone to come for a ride another day. Repetitive dialogue and cumulative lists of animals make this silly tale easy for preschoolers to follow and enjoy.

Cole, Henry, *Jack's Garden* (New York: Greenwillow Books, 1995). A garden theme is used in this spin-off of the popular rhyme, "This Is the House That Jack Built." In addition to a cumulative story that will support the reading development of preschoolers, it is filled with a wealth of information about the process of gardening. Delightful illustrations provide views of the garden above and below the soil so that everyone can clearly follow the progress from soil preparation, to seeding, to a beautiful garden in full bloom.

Downey, Lynn, *The Flea's Sneeze* (New York: Holt, 2000). All the animals are sleeping peacefully in the barn except for flea. He sniffles and snuffles and then asks for a tissue, but his request goes unanswered. When he sneezes a giant sneeze, he wakes the mouse, who wakes the cat, who in turn wakes the dog, and so on, until everyone is now wide awake. At last a tissue is found, and they all settle back down, but then the hog feels a twitch in his nose. Both the illustrations and the rhyming text are hilarious.

Fleming, Denise, *The First Day of Winter* (New York: Henry Holt, 2005). In this fun spin-off from the famous song "The Twelve Days of Christmas," a snowman is the recipient of many gifts. His best friend provides him one red hat. For nine subsequent days, he is treated to two bright blue mittens, three striped scarves, and so on. As each new item is introduced, all previous gifts are repeated. Unique illustrations show the snowman from a variety of angles and contrast the winter white snow with the colorful decorations received.

Fox, Mem, *Hattie and the Fox* (New York: Bradbury Press, 1986, 1987). The big black hen tries to warn all her animal friends when she repeatedly sees more and more of an unknown predator. The goose, sheep, horse, and cow seem uninterested until the fox finally appears and nearly gets them all. Repetitive lines in the cumulative tale make this a perfect read-aloud.

Fox, Mem, *Shoes from Grandpa* (New York: Orchard Books, 1990). After Grandpa buys Jessie a new pair of shoes, all her relatives decide to add to her wardrobe. Mom buys a skirt and her cousin buys a blouse. Sister, Grandma, aunt, uncle, and brother help complete the feminine ensemble until Jessie politely thanks them but asks for a pair of jeans instead. As each new item is bought for Jessie, the previous items are repeated, creating a cumulative tale that encourages participation from the listener. Children will no doubt laugh at the ending twist to this humorous story.

Galdone, Paul, *The Gingerbread Boy* (New York: Seabury Press, 1975). After being baked up nice and brown, the gingerbread boy escapes. People and animals join the cumulative chase, until finally the gingerbread boy thinks he has eluded all of them. However, he meets his match when a clever fox spies him.

Mayo. Diana, *The House That Jack Built* (Cambridge, MA: Barefoot Books, 2006). Although this rhyme may not yet be familiar to young children, they will no doubt catch on to its repetitive and cumulative verses quickly, engaging them to read along. At a house and surrounding farm, one event sets into motion a series of silly outcomes. The malt is eaten by the rat, who is chased by the cat, who, in turn, is worried by the dog, who is tossed by the cow. The bold illustrations and easy-to-read text make this version perfect for preschoolers embarking on the reading process.

Pearson, Tracy Campbell, *Bob* (New York: Farrar, Straus, Giroux, 2002). Bob the rooster has lived his whole life with chickens and only knows how to cluck. When Henrietta the cat tells him he is supposed to crow, he heads from one animal to another to learn the right sound. Along the way, different farm and countryside animals teach him to meow or woof or ribbet. Luckily, he finally meets Fred, someone who looks a bit like himself, and Bob learns to "cock-a-doodle-do!" When a fox enters the coop, Bob's repertoire of animal noises comes in handy as he scares him away and keeps everyone safe.

Thompson, Lauren, *The Apple Pie That Papa Baked* (New York: Simon & Schuster Books for Young Readers, 2007). The 1940s style nostalgic illustrations perfectly complement this cumulative tale. A small girl discusses the steps taken by papa to make an apple pie, beginning with the end product and then all the way back to the tree that grew the apples, the roots that fed the tree, the rain that watered the roots, and so on. The simple text with carefully chosen descriptors of each contributing factor to the pie will undoubtedly spread a warm, homey feeling to all.

Wilson, Karma, *A Frog in the Bog* (New York: Margaret K. McElderry Books, 2003). A greedy frog overfills his tummy with insects. He begins with one tick, but quickly adds two fleas, three flies, four slugs, and five snails. We watch as he grows bigger and bigger on the outside and are also able to see inside his stomach as the quarters for the insects grow more and more crowded. When the frog is startled by an alligator (that he was unknowingly sitting upon), he screams and out come all the insects in reverse order.

Wood, Audrey, *The Napping House* (San Diego: Harcourt Brace Jovanovich, 1984). Various creatures sequentially pile atop one another and happily slumber. But when a flea jumps on the mouse and bites him, a hilarious chain of events ensues. As the nap unravels, the sun and the world outside awaken. Charming illustrations in hues of blues and greens add to the hilarity of the tale. Preschoolers will have extra fun tracking the animals in each picture.

Wood, Audrey, *Silly Sally* (San Diego: Harcourt Brace Jovanovich, 1992). Silly Sally goes to town, "walking backwards, upside down." On the way she meets various animals who join in on the ridiculous fun, dancing, leaping, and singing. Neddy Buttercup happens by and attempts to "right" them, but instead decides to join in on the adventure. The cumulative story ends with the entire town adopting this new way of travel.

Books from Songs, Chants, and Finger Plays

Cabrera, Jane, *If You're Happy and You Know It* (New York: Holiday House, 2005). A cast of animals demonstrates each of the verses in this book version of the popular song. The monkey claps his hands, the elephant stamps his feet, and the lion roars. Bright, cheery art contrasts well with the large black font used for the text, making the words easy to follow. Children are invited to join in on the words and the motions.

Hillenbrand, Will, *Down by the station* (San Diego: Harcourt Brace, 1999). Toot! Toot! If you've ever wondered what the zoo train does before all the guests arrive, this book provides the answer. It picks up each of the baby animals and brings them to their appropriate place in the zoo. Hilarious illustrations capture the sleepy animals as they wave goodbye to their mommies and daddies and then board the train.

Hort, Lenny, *Seals on the Bus* (New York: Henry Holt, 2000). In this crowd-pleasing spin-off of the song "The Wheels on the Bus," animals quickly fill the vehicle. The seals, "Errp, errp, errp!" The tiger roars. The geese honk, and many other animals join the raucous chorus, until finally the people on the bus yell, "Help! Help! Help!" Children will likely chime in with all the silly animal sounds.

Jones, Carol, *Old MacDonald Had a Farm* (Boston: Houghton Mifflin, 1988, 1989). The detailed illustrations depict a white-bearded farmer happily going about his day doing his chores. A small peephole is included on each spread with part of the next animal peaking through. Listeners are invited to guess what it is and then sing along.

Loesser, Frank, *I Love You! A Bushel & a Peck* (New York: HarperCollins Publishers, 2005). In this rendition of the song made famous in the 1950s musical *Guys and Dolls*, a farmer duck shown in overalls courts his love while busily working on the farm. When he's having trouble sleeping, he calls her in the middle of the night. He shows his affection by skywriting Xs and Os and serenading her. In the end her love is captured, and they drive off in a red wind-up toy convertible. Rosemary Wells includes numerous humorous details in her bright and cheery illustrations. No doubt everyone will be smiling, tapping their feet, and joining in on this infectious song.

Norworth, Jack, *Take Me Out to the Ballgame* (New York: Four Winds Press, 1993). A 1947 World Series game between the Brooklyn Dodgers and the New York Yankees is the backdrop for this book version of the famous song. Bold watercolors work well to portray all the action of America's favorite pastime, from crowds, to Cracker Jacks, to Jackie Robinson, to cheering.

Ormerod, Jan, *If You're Happy and You Know It* (New York: Star Bright Books, 2003). In a lively twist, eight different animals create their own verses to this well-known song. A puppy invites listeners to sing "If you're happy and you know it, wave your tail—swirl, twirl!" An elephant refutes this and suggests flapping your ears. The crocodile wants everyone to snap their teeth. The illustrations show action and energy, creating a cheery tone for each reading.

Raffi, *Baby Beluga* (New York: Crown Publishers, 1997). Darling illustrations show the cuddly little baby whale with his mother, swimming and enjoying the world around them.

Siomades, Lorianne, *The Itsy Bitsy Spider* (Honesdale, PA: Boyds Mills Press, 1999). Bright, engaging illustrations add to this popular finger play. The use of brilliant purples, hot pinks, blues, and yellows grab the attention of the listener. Clever details for the attire of the spider and a friendly butterfly make this version extra special.

Trapani, Iza, *Mary Had a Little Lamb* (Dallas: Whispering Coyote Press, 1998). In this extension of the familiar song, the lamb is strong and independent, deciding to wander around the farm by himself. However, much to his dismay, he encounters one mishap after another. He is knocked down by a horse, drenched by a cow, and butted by a goat. Luckily, Mary rescues him, cleans, kisses, and finally tucks him snuggly into bed. The detailed and beautiful watercolors are exceptional, making this book a treasure.

Quality Books

Aardema, Verna, *Anansi Does the Impossible: An Ashanti Tale* (New York: Atheneum Books for Young Readers, 1997). Anansi, the clever spider, employs the help of his wife, Aso, in this trickster tale. Anansi wants to buy back all the folktales that are now owned by the sky god, but the price is difficult to obtain. He must get a live python, a real fairy, and forty-seven stinging hornets. Children will love finding out how the husband-and-wife spider team work together to play their tricks and get what they want.

Aston, Dianna Hutts, *An Orange in January* (New York: Dial Books for Young Readres, 2007). An everyday object is highlighted, revealing how special it is. The reader is taken on a journey of an orange, from blossom to fruit, to truck and then market. Once purchased, a little boy shares its juicy segments with all his friends on the playground swing. The beautiful, sunny paintings add to the precious tone of this delightful book.

Barrett, Judi *Cloudy with a Chance of Meatballs* (New York: Atheneum, 1978). There's no need for grocery stores in the town of Chewandswallow, where it rains soup and snows mashed potatoes. Eating is a breeze until the weather suddenly changes for the worse. Pancake storms, salt and pepper winds, and tomato tornadoes force the residents to abandon the town. Giant pieces of stale bread are held together with peanut butter to build rafts and sail to a new and exciting land. Preschoolers will delight in this tall tale.

Brett, Jan, *Gingerbread Baby* (New York: Putnam, 1999). Even though the gingerbread boy recipe clearly warns not to peek, Matti can't wait any longer. He opens the oven and out jumps a gingerbread baby. A rollicking chase ensues as townspeople and animals try desperately to catch the Gingerbread

Baby. He outruns, outclimbs, and outwits everyone until finally discovering the perfect home, where he is content to stay. Brett includes intricately detailed drawings of the Swiss countryside as the backdrop for this artistic remake of the traditional tale. Her beautifully rendered illustrations include borders of cookie-shaped cutouts that provide glimpses into upcoming story events.

Brett, Jan, *Hedgie's Surprise* (New York: Putnam, 2000). Henny laments not being able to have a brood of chicks because Tomten, an elf-like creature, steals her freshly laid egg each morning. She finally solicits the help of Hedgie, a friendly hedgehog, who devises a clever plan to outwit the thief. On successive days he substitutes for the egg an acorn, a strawberry, a mushroom, and a potato. Finally, Hedgie himself rolls up into a tight ball and sits in the nest, giving the Tomten a prickly surprise and scaring him away for good. Without the threat to her eggs, Henny gets her wish and hatches five fluffy offspring. Brett's signature illustrations portray each event and the expressions of the characters with meticulous detail.

Brett, Jan, *The Three Snow Bears* (New York: G. P. Putnam's Sons, 2007). In a clever twist on *Goldilocks and the Three Bears,* this version takes place in the Arctic with an Inuit girl named Aloo-ki taking center stage. The three polar bears are out for a walk and curious little Aloo-ki can't resist going into their igloo. Exceptional illustrations will have every child and parent poring over the book for hours.

Bruss, Deborah, *Book! Book! Book!* (New York: Arthur A. Levine Books, 2001). When the children go back to school, the animals are bored and left with nothing to do. They head to town and discover the library where everyone has happy faces. They decide to go in and join the fun. However, the librarian cannot understand their neighs, moos, and baahs. The hen figures out what to do and winds up with three books to take back home. This delightful story depicts the draw of reading as a wonderful way to fill our days and nights with endless possibilities.

Bunting, Eve, *Butterfly House* (New York: Scholastic Press, 1999). A little girl saves a tiny black caterpillar from a jay who was about to make it his lunch. Her grandfather explains that it is a larva that will one day turn into a butterfly. Together, they create a beautiful butterfly home, decorated with flowers and a blue sky. Once the metamorphosis is complete, the Painted Lady is released. When the girl becomes as old as her grandfather, she reminisces and delights in the fact that butterflies (no doubt, the descendants of the one she saved) still come to visit her garden.

Bunting, Eve, *Secret Place* (New York: Clarion Books, 1996). Amid a bustling, concrete-riddled, pollution-filled city, a boy discovers a secret treasure. A small patch of wilderness is home to sparrows, mallards, an egret, ducklings, and even a nocturnal coyote and possum with babies. In his excitement, he wants to tell everyone about this haven, but is warned that some may want to try to change it. He shares the wonder of this beautiful slice of paradise, but decides to keep the location his special secret.

Bunting, Eve, *The Wednesday Surprise* (New York: Clarion Books, 1989) On Wednesday night, Grandma arrives with her big, lumpy bag of books. Anna and she have been planning a surprise, their Wednesday surprise. They spend the night reading story after story in preparation for dad's birthday. When the big day arrives, everyone is indeed surprised. This heartwarming tale about family, love, and literacy has a wonderful twist at the end.

Bunting, Eve, *Whales Passing* (New York: Blue Sky Press, 2003). A young boy and his father stand atop a cliff and watch in awe as a pod of Orcas swim by. The boy wonders aloud if the whales can talk and imagines all the conversations they have about the two humans on the shore. Soft, poetic language and beautiful illustrations combine to perfectly capture this majestic moment.

Cannon, Janell, *Stellaluna* (San Diego: Harcourt Brace Jovanovich, 1993). During an owl attack, a young fruit bat named Stellaluna is knocked out of her mother's loving grasp. Unable to fly, she plunges into a bird's nest and is adopted by the bird family. She is forced to adapt to their ways, eating bugs, staying awake all day, and sleeping all night. Once reunited with her own mother, she acknowledges her natural bat habits but also recognizes that her friendship with the baby birds flourishes despite their differences.

Cecka, Melanie, *Violet Comes to Stay* (New York: Viking Children's Books, 2006). The youngest kitten in the litter is adopted by a plant nursery owner and then by a bakery chef, both with the idea that Violet could kill pesky mice. However, the kitten is returned to her mother by each because she gets into mischief and cannot perform her cat duties. Finally she is adopted by Alice and is given a home in the woman's bookstore. Surprisingly, Alice is grateful that she does not kill a mouse because mice are also God's creatures. The story is a beautiful reminder that God has a special plan for each of us.

Cronin, Doreen, *Click, Clack, Moo: Cows That Type* (New York: Simon & Schuster Books for Young Readers, 2000). When Farmer Brown left the old typewriter in the barn, he never would have guessed that cows could type.

Nevertheless, the resourceful cows type and type all day, sending requests for electric blankets the farmer's way. When he refuses, the cows go on strike: "Sorry. We're closed. No milk today." So Farmer Brown turns to the neutral duck to mediate, but soon discovers that cows are not the only farm animals who can type.

Cronin, Doreen, *Diary of a Worm* (New York: Joanna Cotler Books, 2003). A young earthworm chronicles the life of his family in this hilarious tale. Using a diary format, we learn about the upside and downside of being a worm. Unfortunately he can't chew gum, and his face looks an awful lot like his rear end, but at least he doesn't have to brush his teeth (because worms don't have teeth.) The cartoon-like illustrations complete the hilarity of the story and will have everyone laughing out loud.

Dunrea, Olivier, *It's Snowing* (New York: Farrar, Straus and Giroux, 2002). In a small hut on a remote hill, a mother bundles up her baby in furs and they head outside to share the first snowfall. They smell it, hear it, touch it, and taste it, and then go back inside to snuggle by the cozy fireside. Spare poetic text creates a winter song, and soft, endearing watercolors celebrate this joyous occasion.

Edwards, Richard, *Copy Me, Copycub* (New York: HarperCollins, 1999). A little cub mimics everything his mother does, from splashing through swamps in the spring, picking berries in the summer, to lolloping through trees in the fall. When the first frost comes, the cub becomes tired and wants to sleep. He must work hard to copy his mother through the snow to make it to the safety of their quiet and dry cave, ready for hibernation.

Ehlert, Lois, *Growing Vegetable Soup* (San Diego, CA: Harcourt, 1987, 2004). Intense colored illustrations are used to provide all the information needed to grow and nurture your own garden of vegetables. From seed to tending to picking to cooking pot, this wonderful book even includes a tasty recipe for vegetable soup. Yum!

Ehlert, Lois, *Leaf Man* (Orlando, FL: Harcourt, 2005). A narrator tells us about the Leaf Man who used to live nearby but blew away in the wind. He imagines all the different places it could have gone. Collage art of various leaves form animals and objects on each page, making the book a visual delight. Readers are invited to head outside to search for their own Leaf Man.

Ehlert, Lois, *Red Leaf, Yellow Leaf* (San Diego: Harcourt Brace Jovanovich, 1991). We learn about the life of a maple tree, from tiny seed to young seedling, to full-grown tree with beautiful autumn leaves in shades of red, yellow, gold, and orange. An appendix provides detailed information about trees and leaves. Gorgeous collage illustrations artfully depict the stages of the tree, as well as many varieties of birds and the natural surroundings.

Falconer, Ian, *Olivia* (New York: Atheneum Books for Young Readers, 2000). In the first of a series of books about Olivia, we are introduced to this outlandish little pig. Olivia is like so many children. She is energetic, very particular about her wardrobe, an exceptional castle builder, and frequently wears out her family. She doesn't like naps but does like getting into mischief. A delightfully understated text works perfectly with the simple artwork in mostly black and white, with splashes of red.

Finn, Isobel, *The Very Lazy Ladybug* (Wilton, CT: Tiger Tales, 2001). Spending her days and nights sleeping, the very lazy ladybug has not learned how to fly. When its time to find a more comfortable place to rest, she decides to hitch a ride on the various animals passing by. She soon discovers, however, that the kangaroo likes to jump, the tiger likes to roar, and the monkey likes to swing, making it impossible for her to sleep. The elephant's trunk seems perfect until he sneezes, and the ladybug is flung into the air, being forced to fly.

Fox, Mem, *Wilfrid Gordon McDonald Partridge* (Brooklyn, NY: Kane/Miller Book Publishers, 1984, 1985). A young boy named Wilfrid Gordon McDonald Partridge lives next door to a retirement home and enjoys the company of all the extraordinary people there, like Mrs. Jordan who plays the organ and Mr. Hosking who tells him scary stories. His favorite, though, is Miss Nancy Alison Delacourt Cooper because she has four names just like him. In this tender story about friendship between generations, Wilfred Gordon pursues the meaning of a memory when he learns that Miss Nancy has lost hers. Julie Vivas's offbeat caricature-like watercolors add the perfect touch to this endearing story.

Freeman, Don, *Corduroy* (New York: Viking Press, 1968). A teddy bear named Corduroy anxiously awaits being adopted and taken home like the other toys in the department store. When the mother of a little girl points out a missing button on his green overalls, Corduroy realizes it is gone and determines to find it. After the store closes for the night he embarks on a series of adventures in search of his missing button. Although it is never found, the little girl returns and buys him anyway. At home, she lovingly mends the clothes of her new friend.

Hatkoff, Isabella, *Owen & Mzee* (New York: Scholastic Press, 2006). This is the true story of the remarkable friendship between a baby hippopotamus and a 130-year-old tortoise. After being separated from his group during the 2004 Indonesian tsunami, Owen the Hippo was placed in a sanctuary with several other animals. Here, he found Mzee the Tortoise. The unusual friendship is showcased through photographs of them eating together, snuggling, and resting. The book reminds all of us about the importance of tolerance, love, and hope.

Henderson, Kathy, *And the Good Brown Earth* (Cambridge, MA: Candlewick Press, 2004). Joe and Gram are good friends who like to do things quite differently. When they head down to the vegetable patch in the fall, the two begin a yearlong process of tending a garden. Gram plants seeds in long straight rows. Joe plants lots of seeds too, "Here, there and who-knows-where." With the good brown earth playing its key role in the process, Joe and Gram each grow vegetables in their own way . . . perfect!

Henkes, Kevin, *Kitten's First Full Moon* (New York: Greenwillow Books, 2004). Kitten mistakes her first full moon for a bowl of milk. She attempts to lick it, spring on it, chase it, and climb the tallest tree to reach it. Yet the elusive milk escapes her. Wet, sad, tired, and hungry, Kitten heads home to find that her spirited determination finally pays off.

Henkes, Kevin, *Sheila Rae, the Brave* (New York: Greenwillow Books, 1987). Sheila Rae isn't afraid of anything: not monsters in the closet or cracks in the sidewalks, not even stray dogs! She laughs in the face of danger . . . until she gets lost on the way home from school. Luckily, Sheila's little sister Louisa is there to save the day, proving Sheila is not the only brave one in the family.

Hesse, Karen, *Come On, Rain!* (New York: Scholastic Press, 1999). Tessie and the rest of the urban neighborhood eagerly anticipate a rainstorm on a sweltering hot day. When the deluge of water pours down from the sky, even the parents can't resist romping and splashing and celebrating. Sophisticated and poetic language combine seamlessly with exceptional artwork by Jon Muth to clearly capture the essence of this magnificent event.

Hills, Tad, *Duck and Goose* (New York: Schwartz & Wade Books, 2006). When Duck and Goose discover a brightly spotted sphere, they think it is an egg ready to hatch. Each becomes possessive of the find, and they argue over whose it is and how it will be raised. However, over time they bond and begin discussing how they will interact with their new offspring. When a little bluebird happens along, the true identity of the "egg" is revealed and Duck and Goose waddle off to happily play together. Darling artwork makes this book a real keeper.

Horning, Sandra, *The Giant Hug* (New York: Alfred A. Knopf, 2005). Instead of sending a picture of a hug to his grandmother through the mail, Owen the Pig decides to send the real thing. He hands the clerk at the post office his granny's address, accompanied by a big hug. The loving embrace is passed across the country from postal worker to pilot to driver and is finally delivered to granny. She replies with a warm kiss. While following the hug relay, children will learn about the path a letter takes. Detailed illustrations showing slight embarrassment and joy on the faces of the adults add to the preciousness of the story.

Hosta, Dar, *I Love the Night* (Flemington, NJ: Brown Dog Books, 2003). As each of the nocturnal animals wake from their lazy day, they celebrate the wonders, sounds, and beauty of the darkness. Crickets chirp, fireflies twinkle and the octopus unrolls itself and looks for dinner. In her perfectly perfect tribute to the night, the author uses rhythm and exceptional language with detailed collages to provide us a glimpse into life after dark.

Hosta, Dar, *If I Were a Tree* (Flemington, NJ: Brown Dog Books, 2007). Listeners are provided a melodic tribute to different types of trees throughout the four seasons. Beautiful collage illustrations accompany the poetic text. Information about trees and photosynthesis is provided at the end. The format of the book is vertical, replicating that of a tree, and is printed on 100 percent recycled paper.

Hosta, Dar, *Mavis & Her Marvelous Mooncakes* (Flemington, NJ: Brown Dog Books, 2006). Did you know that the moon is a cake made by a striped orange cat named Miss Mavis Sugar? For fourteen days and nights, she makes more and more shining slices of mooncake. Then her friends and she spend the next fourteen days and nights eating it all up, one slice at a time. Yum! Detailed collage illustrations make this book a special treat. Enjoy!

Inkpen, Deborah, *Harriet* (Hauppauge, NY : Barron's, 1998). When Harriet, a curious little hamster, escapes from her cage, she discovers that the outside world is full of surprises, some of which are not very pleasant. After falling into a murky pond, being rejected by field mice, and chased by a hedgehog, Harriet finally finds the perfect place to take a nap. But will she ever find her way back home?

James, Simon, *Dear Mr. Blueberry* (New York: M. K. McElderry Books: Maxwell Macmillan, 1991). During summer vacation Emily discovers a blue whale in her backyard pond. Excited, she writes a series of letters to her teacher, Mr. Blueberry, inquiring about the best way to care for her new pet. Despite his declarations of the impossibility of a whale living in her pond, he provides details about whales and their habits. Emily is sad when her whale friend decides to be migratory again, but she is grateful to later see him swimming in the ocean.

Keats, Ezra Jack, *A Letter to Amy* (New York: Harper & Row, 1968). Peter wants to invite Amy to his birthday party but is nervous since she will be the only girl. He decides to write her a letter. When his party arrives, his good friend Amy is there, making it an extra special day. The signature blurred collage illustrations provide a wonderful complement to the simple text.

Kellogg, Steven, *Can I Keep Him?* (New York: Dial Press, 1971). Arnold desperately wants a friend with whom to play. After his mother refuses the dog and cat, he imagines bringing home a fawn, a tiger, a snake, a bear cub that fell off the circus train, and a defrosted dinosaur from Alaska. Although he pleads, "Can I keep him?" Mom finds all the reasons each animal cannot stay. In a clever ending twist, Arnold finally meets the perfect friend.

Laminack, Lester, *Saturdays and Teacakes* (Atlanta: Peachtree, 2004). In this gentle, nostalgic memoir of the 1960s, the narrator describes his Saturdays as a boy. Each week he headed through the rural area on his bike to his Mammaw's house. There they shared a special day of talking, doing chores, and making and eating teacakes. Descriptive and sophisticated language is accompanied by art inspired by Norman Rockwell. The book clearly displays the loving bond between a boy and his grandmother.

Lester, Helen, *Tacky the Penguin* (Boston: Houghton Mifflin Co., 1998). There's no tuxedo for this penguin! Tacky, complete with flowered shirt and purple-checkered bowtie, seems at ease with his nonconformist ways. In the end, the neat and poised penguins that live with him are very grateful for his outlandish behavior. By being his unconventional self, Tacky saves everyone from a group of hunters trying to capture the penguins and become rich. This humorous story subtly tells important messages about individuality and acceptance of oneself and others.

Lionni, Leo, *Fish Is Fish* (New York: Pantheon Books, 1970). A tadpole and minnow are inseparable friends until the tadpole becomes a frog and leaves the pond. He returns one day and describes all the extraordinary things he has seen on land, including birds, cows, and humans. Because of minnow's limited experience and background knowledge outside of pond life, he incorrectly pictures each animal looking similar to a fish with the specific details frog states. This is a delightful story about the importance of expanding one's prior knowledge.

Lionni, Leo, *Swimmy* (New York: Pantheon, 1963). Through bravery and determination, a little black fish devises a plan to camouflage his friends and himself to protect them from their natural enemies. The theme of working together is emphasized in both text and illustrations.

Long, Melinda, *How I Became a Pirate* (San Diego: Harcourt, 2003). Aye! Treasure! While in the midst of building a sandcastle at the beach, Jeremy Jacob is invited aboard a pirate ship. Pirate life seems fun at first. You don't have to brush your teeth and you don't have to eat vegetables. However, when night comes, Jeremy misses being tucked in and hearing a story read aloud. Children will gravitate to this silly and adventurous tale complete with zany illustrations to add to the fun! Arr!

McClosky, Robert, *Make Way for Ducklings* (New York: Viking Press, 1941). Mr. and Mrs. Mallard are looking for the perfect spot in Boston to raise their family. They finally settle on a little island near Public Garden because it is safe and near food. This classic tale is sweet and humorous. Children will enjoy all the drama in the life of a duck family and the humanlike feelings these quackers exhibit. This is a treasure that will continue to stand the test of time.

Newman, Marjorie, *Mole and the Baby Bird* (New York: Bloomsbury Children's Books, 2002). If you love something, set it free. Mole finds a hurt and abandoned baby bird and nurses it back to health. When the bird regains his strength and attempts to fly, Mole builds a cage to keep him from leaving. Mole's parents gently remind him that it is not a pet but a wild bird. However, it is not until grandfather takes him to a hilltop to watch the birds soar overhead that Mole realizes he loves his bird enough to release it back to the wild.

O'Connor, Jane, *Fancy Nancy* (New York: HarperCollins, 2006). Nancy is a witty, endearing little girl frocked in lace, ribbons, and tiaras who is just trying to add a bit of flair to her everyday life. She speaks "fancy" language, substituting the word fuchsia for purple, plume for feather, and stupendous for great. Nancy even manages to teach her extravagant way of life to her otherwise ordinary family. When a trip, slip, double flip mishap at the pizzeria makes Nancy yearn for the comfort of home, she is tucked snuggly into bed and realizes that the love of her family is the most glamorous thing of all.

Pattou, Edith, *Mrs. Spitzer's Garden* (San Diego: Harcourt, 2001). At the end of each summer the principal gives Mrs. Spitzer, a kindergarten teacher, a packet of seeds. She tenderly prepares the soil, plants the seeds, and closely watches over them as they sprout and grow. She recognizes that different plants need different things and that each one grows at its own pace. This beautiful metaphor pays homage to all teachers and parents who are, after all, a child's first and perhaps most important teachers. The cheery water-color-and-pen illustrations add many creative details that complete this darling story. Flowers and bugs have delightful little faces of the children they represent. Although young listeners may not understand the metaphor, they will nonetheless find the book delightful.

Pfister, Marcus, *The Rainbow Fish* (New York: North-South Books, 1992). Rainbow Fish is undoubtedly the most beautiful fish in the sea, covered with green, blue, purple, and sparkling silver iridescent scales. The other fish admire his beauty and ask him to share his most prized possession, the scales. Refusing to do so, Rainbow Fish is left all alone without any friends. Upon seeking counsel from the wise octopus, he learns to "give away his beauty" and thus discovers how to be happy. This story reinforces the themes of sharing, friendship, and the value of true beauty on the inside.

Polacco, Patricia, *Emma Kate* (New York: Philomel Books, 2005). Emma Kate and her best friend do almost everything together. They walk to school, swing at recess, read with one another, and even have their tonsils out together. A clever twist at the end of the story will put a smile on everyone's face that has ever had a special imaginary friend. The mostly black-and-white graphite drawings are contrasted sharply with small splashes of color creating unique and captivating illustrations.

Polacco, Patricia, *Thunder Cake* (New York: Philomel Books, 1990). Grandma has the perfect "recipe" to allay her granddaughter's fears of a thunderstorm. As the storm nears, the child helps gather eggs from mean old Nellie Peck Hen, get milk from Kick Cow, creep into the dark shed for chocolate, sugar, and flour, and then gather the secret ingredients. She is rewarded with a cake she helped make just in time for the storm to arrive.

Potter, Beatrix, *The Complete Adventures of Peter Rabbit* (New York: F. Warne, 1982). Mischievous Peter Rabbit doesn't listen to his mother and gets into all sorts of trouble in Mr. McGregor's garden. Children will relate to Peter and his rebellious ways but will also be reminded of the importance of following directions given by a parent. This is a sweet and classic tale to be visited again and again.

Priceman, Marjorie, *How to Make an Apple Pie and See the World* (New York: Dragonfly Books, 1996). When do you get to travel the world to make an apple pie? When the market is closed of course! An adventurous little baker sets off on a whimsical trip around the world, visiting exotic and exciting places, to collect the finest ingredients for her apple pie. She gathers eggs from France, cinnamon from Sri Lanka, sugar from Jamaica, and apples from Vermont. Back home, she quickly whips up the pie and invites friends from all over the globe to share.

Rosenthal, Amy Krouse, *Cookies: Bite-Size Life Lessons* (New York: HarperCollins, 2006). Using the idea of making and eating cookies, the author explains various terms that may otherwise be difficult for children to understand. The traits covered include being cooperative, patient, trustworthy, and compassionate. Lovely watercolor illustrations by Jane Dyer (one of my favorite book artists) show multiethnic children and adorable personified animals interacting with one another over the cookies. Beautiful!

Rosenthal, Amy Krouse, *Little Pea* (San Francisco: Chronicle Books, 2005). Although Little Pea enjoys doing many things, the one thing that he does not like to do is eat candy. This story puts a hilarious twist on the struggle parents have trying to get their children to eat vegetables at dinner. After being told that he must eat five pieces of candy before he can have dessert, Little Pea chokes each one down and is finally rewarded with his favorite treat . . . spinach!

Ryan, Pam Munoz, *There Was No Snow on Christmas Eve* (New York: Hyperion Books for Children, 2005). Two children venture out on a snowy night and begin contrasting the wintry scene with the one that took place in Jerusalem the night Jesus was born. The sparse and lyrical text is masterfully complemented by exceptional watercolor artwork. Together, they emote a calming feeling that pays homage to the birth of Jesus.

Rylant, Cynthia, *The Old Woman Who Named Things* (San Diego: Harcourt Brace, 1996). Since the elderly woman has outlived all of her friends, she decides that the only relationships that were safe were that of inanimate objects. She names her car Betsy, her bed Roxanne, and her chair Fred. However, when a stray dog wanders into her yard and then disappears, she decides to take a risk and invite love back into her life. Quirky artwork adds to this tender tale about giving life another chance.

Rylant, Cynthia, *The Relatives Came* (New York: Bradbury Press, 1985). When the large group of relatives from Virginia come to visit, everything in the house turns upside down, but in a beautiful, fun-loving, memorable way. There's hugging, people sleeping everywhere, snoring, laughter, singing, and eating . . . and eating. The house seems a little too quiet once they leave, but the promise of their returning next summer brings glee.

Sams, Carl R., II, and Jean Stoick, *Stranger in the Woods* (Milford, MI: C. R. Sams II Photography, 2000). Spectacular photographs of real animals set this book apart from other children's books. The forest animals are in a frenzy after a winter snowstorm when they find out that there is a stranger in the woods. Once they discover that the snowman poses no danger, they help themselves to some tasty treats. His carrot nose, nuts for eyes, and hat brim filled with seeds are soon gobbled up. Children hiding behind bushes watch the animals in delight and replenish the food for their visit the next day.

Salley, Coreen, *Why Epossumondas Has No Hair on His Tail* (Orlando, FL: Harcourt, 2004). In this delightful folktale, Epossumondas learns why he and all his relatives no longer have fluffy tails. Mama tells him the story about how his great-great-grandpa talked Rabbit into climbing Bear's persimmon tree. But when grandpa doesn't share enough with Rabbit, Bear is told all about it. A chase ensues and, needless to say, grandpa barely gets out of there. Ever since, no opossum has had hair on its tail. Signature mixed-media illustrations by Janet Stevens increase the hilarity of the book.

Schnur, Steven, *Spring Thaw* (New York: Viking, 2000). The beginning of spring in a rural setting is showcased in this lyrical book. The thaw "begins with a warm wind late at night, sighing through the hemlock trees." In the end, the farmer and his son collect buckets of sap from the maples and revel in the warmth of the sun upon their faces. Although this book does not tell much of a story, it serves to set the mood for spring. The captivating illustrations combined with exquisite language beg to be read again and again.

Sierra, Judy, *Wild About Books* (New York: Knopf, 2004). When librarian Molly McGrew drove her bookmobile into the zoo, the animals were curious and then won over. Each received the perfect book. Giraffes received tall books, crickets got small books, and the otter was given a waterproof book to read. In this rollicking and rhythmic tale, the animals discover all the fun things about books and even open their own Zoobrary.

Stanley, Diane, *Goldie and the Three Bears* (New York: HarperCollins, 2003). Goldie is looking for just the right friend, one that is not too bossy or boring or snobby. When she gets off at the wrong bus stop one day, she happens upon a little house. It will not surprise you that she tries out some peanut butter and jelly sandwiches, three chairs, and three beds. When the bears come home, all is forgiven and she finds a friend to love with all her heart. Darling childlike art adds the perfect touch to this creative version of the familiar tale.

Stevens, Janet, *My Big Dog* (New York: Golden Books, 1999). Merl, a self-proclaimed very special cat, is so upset when an annoying and slobbery golden retriever puppy moves into the house, he decides to look for a new place to live. However, he is unsatisfied with any of the potential owners he meets and learns that there really is no place like home. The now Big Dog, Violet, rescues Merl and they become friends. Splashy colorful illustrations of the animals are juxtaposed with black-and-white photographs of humans, creating a unique and interesting effect in this hilarious and endearing tale.

Stevens, Janet, *Tops and Bottoms* (San Diego: Harcourt Brace, 1995). Desperate after selling their land to pay off a debt to Tortoise, Hare and his family partner up with Bear down the street. In a clever deal about "tops and bottoms" of vegetables, Hare outsmarts snoozing Bear and comes out on top in the end. This trickster tale has roots in European folktales and slave stories and proves that an energetic and hardworking Hare is smarter and more profitable than a rich, lazy Bear.

Thayer, Jane, *The Puppy Who Wanted a Boy* (New York: Morrow, 1958). This story is a clever twist on the familiar scenario about a boy wanting a dog for Christmas. When there are no boys available to give to her puppy, the mother dog suggests he ask other dogs if they would be willing to give up their boy. Unfortunately, none of the dogs are willing to do so. Feeling sad and dejected, Petey the Puppy winds up in front of an orphanage. Here he gets not just one boy, but fifty.

Thomas, Patricia, *Firefly Mountain* (Atlanta: GA: Peachtree, 2007). A young girl waits patiently for the hot afternoon to end in hopes that she and her family can experience the magic of a firefly mountain. At nightfall, they journey to the top of the hill and she stares in awe. Lyrical prose and dark, rich paintings capture the beauty of the night.

Van Allsburg, Chris, *Two Bad Ants* (Boston: Houghton Mifflin, 1988). When a troop of ants discovers sugar crystals to bring back to the queen, two greedy ants decide to stay behind and have their fill. They fall asleep in the sugar bowl, but are dramatically awakened when a large scoop pours them into a hot cup of coffee. The mishaps continue from there. The ants are heated in a toaster, swirled down a garbage disposal, and electrocuted in a wall socket. Thankfully they learn their lesson and decide to conform to their role as dutiful servants of the queen.

Van Allsburg, Chris, *The Polar Express* (Boston: Houghton Mifflin, 1985). As a little boy lies in bed on Christmas Eve, he hears the sound of a train. The conductor invites him aboard the Polar Express bound for the North Pole. He and several other children meet Santa Claus and share a wondrous adventure. Captivating luminescent paintings add to the magical tone that will surely make everyone a true believer.

Van Hitchtum, Nienke, *The Apple Cake* (Edinburgh: Floris Books, 1996). An elderly woman wants to make an apple cake but she only has plums. She sets out with a basketful of the fruit hoping to make a trade. When she comes upon a young woman, she exchanges her plums for a bag of feathers. Through a series of exchanges, she winds up helping many people along her journey. Not surprisingly, an apple tree is eventually found, and a final trade makes it possible for her to bake the delicious treat. This yummy tale reinforces the values of kindness and compassion.

Viorst, Judith, *Alexander and the Terrible, Horrible, No Good, Very Bad Day* (New York: Atheneum, 1972). Waking up with gum in his hair, being smushed in the car on the way to school, a lunch without dessert, and a cavity are some of the terrible, horrible, no good, very bad things that happen to Alexander. As his day continues to unravel with more and more bad luck, he is convinced that moving to Australia will fix everything. When the day finally ends, he is reminded that everyone has bad days, even in Australia.

Yolen, Jane, *How Do Dinosaurs Say Good Night?* (New York: Blue Sky Press, 2000). The dinosaur children in this book don't seem to know the appropriate way to behave before bedtime. Some pout, slam their tails, or even throw their teddy bear all about. Human parents and children alike will relate to the postponing antics of these expressive and lovable dinosaurs. Although the raucous and rhyming beat of this playful tale may invite children to imitate some of the silly dinosaurs, it still serves as a perfect bedtime story. After hearing it, children can't help but slumber with a smile on their faces.

Yolen, Jane, *Owl Moon* (New York: Philomel Books, 1987). The special relationship between a daughter and her father is highlighted in this tale about going owling for the first time. They brave the cold and late night darkness in hopes of getting a glimpse of the Great Horned Owl. The poetic and melodious text is simply beautiful and is enhanced by soft, lush watercolors.

Waddell, Martin, *Room for a Little One: A Christmas Tale* (New York: Margaret K. McElderry Books, 2004). Kind Ox invites one animal after another into the stable for shelter from the cold. Old Dog, Stray Cat, Small Mouse snuggle together as peaceful friends. When Donkey brings Mary and Joseph, all witness the beautiful birth of the most special One of all, Baby Jesus. The acrylic paintings have a magical quality to them as each seems to illuminate from the center. This book is a wonderful addition to holiday collections for every family.

Weaver, Tess, *Opera Cat* (New York: Clarion Books, 2002). Alma the Cat has been practicing her opera singing and longs to head out to the streets of Milan. She is finally given her chance when her owner, Madame SoSo, gets laryngitis. In this hilarious story we see that a special friendship between cat and owner can certainly come in handy.

Wordless Books

Blake, Quentin, *Clown* (New York: H. Holt, 1996). After he is dumped in a garbage bin, a clown doll comes to life, escapes, and works to rescue his toy friends. Readers follow his adventures as he tries to get help for the other dolls. Expressive and detailed watercolor-and-ink illustrations clearly depict all the action taking place. Because of the intricate illustrations that follow each event in the story, the reader is easily able to retell this darling tale.

Briggs, Raymond, *The Snowman* (New York: Random House, 1985). A boy spends his day making a giant snowman. When he has trouble sleeping that night, he heads out to check on the snowman that has now miraculously come to life. The boy gives him a tour of his home, showing him television, running water, and ice cubes. They hold hands outside and take flight high in the sky on a wondrous adventure. Soft and hazy illustrations give the illusion of snow gently falling on each picture frame.

Butterworth, Nick, *Amanda's Butterfly* (New York: Harper Collins Publishers, 1992). Net in hand, Amanda searches for butterflies in her backyard garden. It begins to rain, so she heads for shelter in the toolshed where she discovers a fairy with a broken wing. After several creative attempts, she mends the wing and happily releases the delicate fairy back to nature and freedom.

Day, Alexandra, *Good Dog, Carl* (La Jolla, CA: Green Tiger Press, 1985). Mom leaves the house and puts Carl, the dog, in charge of the baby. Then the mischief begins! Under Carl's watchful eye, the baby slides down a laundry chute, swims in the fish tank, and makes a general mess throughout the house. Luckily, trustworthy Carl cleans everything up just in time for mom to return. Expressive illustrations of Carl make this book a delight! Consider all the Carl sequels in the series and make this pooch your new family friend.

De Paola, Tomie, *Pancakes for Breakfast* (New York: Harcourt Brace Jovanovich, 1978). An elderly woman wakes up early in the morning craving pancakes for breakfast. She goes to great lengths to procure all the necessary ingredients, but her efforts are thwarted by her own cat and dog. Luckily, she smells something yummy coming from the neighbor's house.

Hutchins, Pat, *Changes, Changes* (New York: Macmillan, 1971). Two wooden dolls are perfectly content to live in their house made of various shapes.

That is, until it catches fire. They rearrange the shapes to create a fire engine, but then there is so much water they must design a boat. Children will have fun identifying the various colored shapes that transform to become useful and fun objects.

Hutchins, Pat, *Rosie's Walk* (New York: Macmillan, 1967, 1968). Although the book contains a few words, it still serves as an excellent story starter because there is so much more going on than the text divulges. Rosie, the hen, is out for a stroll, and fox is hot on her trail, hoping to catch a meal. However, clueless Rosie unwittingly creates one obstacle after another for the fox. When at last she safely reaches the coup, it is fox that is bruised and mangled, forcing him to rethink his meal choice.

Mayer, Mercer, *A Boy, a Dog, and a Frog* (New York: Dial Press, 1967). A boy and his dog go for a walk through a swamp. Then they spot a frog and try desperately to catch it. Detailed illustrations perfectly capture the expressions on each of the characters and create a hilarious tale. Consider other titles in this wonderful wordless series including *Frog, Where Are You? Frog on His Own*, and *Frog Goes to Dinner*.

Turkle, Brindon, *Deep in the Forest* (New York: Dutton, 1976). In a clever twist on Goldilocks and the Three Bears, a little bear decides to investigate a house while its three human inhabitants have gone out. Children can guess what comes next as the bear samples porridge and tests chairs and beds for comfort. Expressive illustrations invite hilarious dialogue from anyone who "reads" this wordless book.

Wiesner, David, *Sector 7* (New York: Clarion Books, 1999). On a field trip to the Empire State Building, a young boy makes friends with a jolly cloud. He is whisked away and brought to a secret location where clouds are given their daily weather assignments. After hearing the clouds complain about how boring their shapes are, the artistic little boy creates new blueprints for each and the skies become filled with excitement.

Wiesner, David, *Tuesday* (New York: Clarion Books, 1991). On this particular Tuesday, around eight, frogs from the local swamp are lifted into the air on lily pads. The adventure begins as the amphibians fly to a nearby suburb and wreak hilarious havoc on some unsuspecting humans, a bird, a dog, and a cat. At daybreak, life goes back to normal and the town is left puzzled by the stray lily pads scattered all about.

1 - Pro-Reader	2 - Emerging Reader	3 - Developing Reader
✶ Shows interest in reading ✶ Pretends to read ✶ Chooses books and has favorites ✶ Listens to and responds to literature ✶ Knows some letter names ✶ Holds books and turns pages correctly ✶ Can show beginning and end of book	✶ Uses illustrations to get meaning ✶ Knows some letters and their corresponding sounds ✶ Reads some environmental print ✶ Understands basic concepts about print	✶ Knows most letters and their corresponding sounds ✶ Recognizes simple words ✶ Chooses picture books and simple story books ✶ Retells story in own words ✶ Able to read personally written stories

4 - Beginning Reader	5 - Early Reader	6 - Bridging Reader
✶ Reads a variety of print for comprehension ✶ Begins to read silently ✶ Can retell beginning, middle, and end of story ✶ Independently attempts reading of unknown words using syntactic and visual clues ✶ Attempts to observe punctuation signals when reading aloud	✶ Reads beginning chapter books ✶ Uses a variety of reading strategies ✶ Identifies plot, characters, and events with guidance ✶ Recognizes different types of books (genres) ✶ Reads silently for short periods ✶ Relates reading to personal experiences ✶ Uses punctuation signals and phrasing when reading orally	✶ Reads beginning chapter books ✶ Uses a variety of reading strategies ✶ Identifies plot, characters, and events with guidance ✶ Recognizes different types of books (genres) ✶ Reads silently for short periods ✶ Relates reading to personal experiences ✶ Uses punctuation signals and phrasing when reading aloud

7 - Fluent Reader	8- Proficient Reader	9 - Independent Reader
✶ Reads higher level chapter books ✶ Self-selects, reads, and finishes a variety of materials ✶ Uses references materials independently ✶ Begins to interpret deeper meaning from text and to connect own experience and knowledge ✶ Understands literacy elements and story structure ✶ Participates in guided literacy discussions	✶ Reads and interprets complex young adult literature with guidance ✶ Self-motivated and confident about reading ✶ Identifies author's purpose ✶ Participates in complex literacy discussions	✶ Independently reads and understands a wide variety of sophisticated material ✶ Uses reading as a method to obtain information across subject areas ✶ Evaluates, interprets, and analyzes literary elements ✶ Is aware of moral issues presented in written material

Appendix 2. Dolch Sight Word List

Preprimer	Primer	First	Second	Third
a	all	after	always	about
and	am	again	around	better
away	are	an	because	bring
big	at	any	been	carry
blue	ate	as	before	clean
can	be	ask	best	cut
come	black	by	both	done
down	brown	could	buy	draw
find	but	every	call	drink
for	came	fly	cold	eight
funny	did	from	does	fall
go	do	give	don't	far
help	eat	going	fast	full
hers	four	had	first	got
I	get	has	five	grow
in	good	her	found	hold
is	has	him	gave	hot
it	he	how	goes	hurt
jump	into	just	green	if
little	like	know	its	keep
look	must	let	made	kind
make	new	live	many	laugh
me	no	may	off	light
my	now	of	or	long
not	on	old	pull	much
one	our	once	read	myself
play	out	open	right	never
red	please	over	sing	only
run	pretty	put	sit	own
said	ran	round	sleep	pick
see	ride	some	tell	seven
the	saw	stop	their	shall
three	say	take	these	show
to	she	thank	those	six
two	so	them	upon	small
up	soon	then	us	start
we	that	think	use	ten

Preprimer	Primer	First	Second	Third
yellow	there	walk	very	today
you	they	where	wash	together
	this	when	which	try
	too	why	warm	
	under		wish	
	want		work	
	was		would	
	well		write	
	went		your	
	what			
	white			
	who			
	will			
	with			
	yes			

Appendix 3. Caldecott Medal Winners, 1938–2008

2008: *The Invention of Hugo Cabret* by Brian Selznick

2007: *Flotsam* by David Wiesner

2006: *The Hello, Goodbye Window* written by Norton Juster, illustrated by Chris Raschka

2005: *Kitten's First Full Moon* by Kevin Henkes

2004: *The Man Who Walked Between the Towers* by Mordicai Gerstei

2003: *My Friend Rabbit* by Eric Rohmann

2002: *The Three Pigs* by David Wiesner

2001: *So You Want to Be President?* illustrated by David Small; text by Judith St. George

2000: *Joseph Had a Little Overcoat* by Simms Taback

1999: *Snowflake Bentley*, illustrated by Mary Azarian; text by Jacqueline Briggs Martin

1998: *Rapunzel* by Paul O. Zelinsky

1997: *Golem* by David Wisniewski

1996: *Officer Buckle and Gloria* by Peggy Rathmann

1995: *Smoky Night*, illustrated by David Diaz; text by Eve Bunting

1994: *Grandfather's Journey* by Allen Say; text edited by Walter Lorraine

1993: *Mirette on the High Wire* by Emily Arnold McCully

1992: *Tuesday* by David Wiesner

1991: *Black and White* by David Macaulay

1990: *Lon Po Po: A Red-Riding Hood Story from China* by Ed Young

1989: *Song and Dance Man*, illustrated by Stephen Gammell; text by Karen Ackerman

1988: *Owl Moon*, illustrated by John Schoenherr; text by Jane Yolen

1987: *Hey, Al*, illustrated by Richard Egielski; text by Arthur Yorinks

1986: *The Polar Express* by Chris Van Allsburg

1985: *Saint George and the Dragon*, illustrated by Trina Schart Hyman; text retold by Margaret Hodges

1984: *The Glorious Flight: Across the Channel with Louis Bleriot* by Alice and Martin Provensen

1983: *Shadow*, translated and illustrated by Marcia Brown; original text in French by Blaise Cendrars

1982: *Jumanji* by Chris Van Allsburg

1981: *Fables* by Arnold Lobel

1980: *Ox-Cart Man*, illustrated by Barbara Cooney; text by Donald Hall

1979: *The Girl Who Loved Wild Horses* by Paul Goble

1978: *Noah's Ark* by Peter Spier

1977: *Ashanti to Zulu: African Traditions*, illustrated by Leo and Diane Dillon; text by Margaret Musgrove

1976: *Why Mosquitoes Buzz in People's Ears*, illustrated by Leo and Diane Dillon; text retold by Verna Aardema

1975: *Arrow to the Sun* by Gerald McDermott

1974: *Duffy and the Devil*, illustrated by Margot Zemach; text retold by Harve Zemach

1973: *The Funny Little Woman*, illustrated by Blair Lent; text retold by Arlene Mosel

1972: *One Fine Day*, retold and illustrated by Nonny Hogrogian

1971: *A Story, a Story*, retold and illustrated by Gail E. Haley

1970: *Sylvester and the Magic Pebble* by William Steig

1969: *The Fool of the World and the Flying Ship*, illustrated by Uri Shulevitz; text retold by Arthur Ransome

1968: *Drummer Hoff*, illustrated by Ed Emberley; text adapted by Barbara Emberley

1967: *Sam, Bangs & Moonshine* by Evaline Ness

1966: *Always Room for One More*, illustrated by Nonny Hogrogian; text by Sorche Nic Leodhas [pseudonym Leclair Alger]

1965: *May I Bring a Friend?* illustrated by Beni Montresor; text by Beatrice Schenk de Regniers

1964: *Where the Wild Things Are* by Maurice Sendak

1963: *The Snowy Day* by Ezra Jack Keats

1962: *Once a Mouse*, retold and illustrated by Marcia Brown

1961: *Baboushka and the Three Kings*, illustrated by Nicolas Sidjakov; text by Ruth Robbins

1960: *Nine Days to Christmas*, illustrated by Marie Hall Ets; text by Marie Hall Ets and Aurora Labastida

1959: *Chanticleer and the Fox*, illustrated by Barbara Cooney; text adapted from Chaucer's *Canterbury Tales* by Barbara Cooney

1958: *Time of Wonder* by Robert McCloskey

1957: *A Tree Is Nice*, illustrated by Marc Simont; text by Janice Udry

1956: *Frog Went A-Courtin'*, illustrated by Feodor Rojankovsky; text retold by John Langstaff

1955: *Cinderella, or the Little Glass Slipper*, illustrated by Marcia Brown; text translated from Charles Perrault by Marcia Brown

1954: *Madeline's Rescue* by Ludwig Bemelmans

1953: *The Biggest Bear* by Lynd Ward

1952: *Finders Keepers*, illustrated by Nicolas [pseudonym Nicholas Mordvinoff]; text by Will [pseudonym William Lipkind]

1951: *The Egg Tree* by Katherine Milhous

1950: *Song of the Swallows* by Leo Politi

1949: *The Big Snow* by Berta and Elmer Hader

1948: *White Snow, Bright Snow*, illustrated by Roger Duvoisin; text by Alvin Tresselt

1947: *The Little Island*, illustrated by Leonard Weisgard; text by Golden MacDonald [pseudonym Margaret Wise Brown]

1946: *The Rooster Crows* by Maude Petersham and Miska Petersham

1945: *Prayer for a Child*, illustrated by Elizabeth Orton Jones; text by Rachel Field

1944: *Many Moons*, illustrated by Louis Slobodkin; text by James Thurber

1943: *The Little House* by Virginia Lee Burton

1942: *Make Way for Ducklings* by Robert McCloskey

1941: *They Were Strong and Good* by Robert Lawson

1940: *Abraham Lincoln* by Ingri and Edgar Parin d'Aulaire

1939: *Mei Li* by Thomas Handforth

1938: *Animals of the Bible, A Picture Book*, illustrated by Dorothy P. Lathrop; text selected by Helen Dean Fish

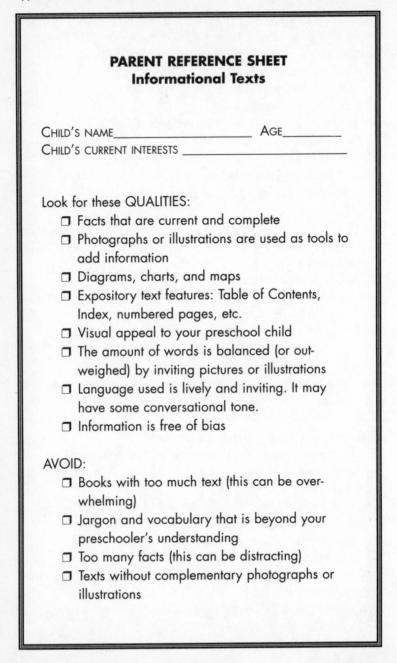

PARENT REFERENCE SHEET
Informational Texts

CHILD'S NAME_____ AGE_____
CHILD'S CURRENT INTERESTS _____

Look for these QUALITIES:
- ❏ Facts that are current and complete
- ❏ Photographs or illustrations are used as tools to add information
- ❏ Diagrams, charts, and maps
- ❏ Expository text features: Table of Contents, Index, numbered pages, etc.
- ❏ Visual appeal to your preschool child
- ❏ The amount of words is balanced (or outweighed) by inviting pictures or illustrations
- ❏ Language used is lively and inviting. It may have some conversational tone.
- ❏ Information is free of bias

AVOID:
- ❏ Books with too much text (this can be overwhelming)
- ❏ Jargon and vocabulary that is beyond your preschooler's understanding
- ❏ Too many facts (this can be distracting)
- ❏ Texts without complementary photographs or illustrations

PARENT REFERENCE SHEET
Diversity

CHILD'S NAME_____AGE_____

Look for these QUALITIES:
- ❏ Serves as a window and/or mirror into a specific culture
- ❏ Universal themes and common values of all people
- ❏ Celebrates the uniqueness of a specific culture
- ❏ Emotional impact
- ❏ Culturally diverse characters portrayed with respect
- ❏ Informs us about the individual differences of others
- ❏ Accurate cultural details
- ❏ Language that is beautiful
- ❏ Exquisite illustrations
- ❏ An interesting story

AVOID:
- ❏ Stereotypes of any kind
- ❏ Books that leave you unaffected

PARENT REFERENCE SHEET
Predictable Text

CHILD'S NAME_____ AGE_____

Look for these QUALITIES:
- ❏ repetitive sentences or phrases
- ❏ interruption in the repetition at some point in the story
- ❏ rhyming
- ❏ sequential patterns
- ❏ cumulative patterns
- ❏ natural language
- ❏ the story has a clear beginning, middle, and end
- ❏ the story can be retold
- ❏ beautifully illustrated books created from your child's favorite songs

AVOID:
- ❏ Strained language
- ❏ Controlled or contrived text
- ❏ Books that focus on sight words
- ❏ Books that focus on decodable words
- ❏ Books that focus on word patterns (for example, at, cat, fat, rat, sat, mat, splat)
- ❏ Books without a real story (if the story cannot be retold, it may not be a good candidate for a read aloud)

PARENT REFERENCE SHEET
Selecting Quality Literature

CHILD'S NAME_____AGE_____

Look for these QUALITIES:
- ❏ Illustrations that are beautiful, captivating, or unique
- ❏ Exquisite and exceptional language
- ❏ A main character to relate to and love
- ❏ An emotional impact; they make you laugh, cry, sing, smile, think, feel
- ❏ A universal theme, be it love, friendship, honesty, or growing up
- ❏ A text that is unique in some way, clever, or offers a surprise or twist for the reader

AVOID:
- ❏ Contrived language and forced dialogue
- ❏ Books with simple words like pretty, nice, good, bad (opt for spicy words and beautiful language)
- ❏ Books that make you think, "So what?" (opt for books with an emotional impact)

NOTES

The Origin of This Book

    1. L. S. Vygotsky, *Thought and Language*.

Chapter 1

    1. Edward J. Dwyer and Evelyn E. Dwyer, "How Teacher Attitudes Influence Reading Achievement," in *Fostering the Love of Reading*, 66–73.

Chapter 4

    1. Mem Fox, *Reading Magic*, 84.

    2. P. E. Bryant et al., "Nursery Rhymes, Phonological Skills and Reading."

    3. K. E. Stanovich, "Romance and Reality."

    4. Michael F. Opitz, *Rhymes and Reasons*.

Chapter 5

    1. Frederick J. Morrsion et al., *Improving Literacy in America*.

    2. Isabel L. Beck, Margaret G. McKeown, and Linda Kucan, *Bringing Words to Life*.

    3. D. P. Hayes and M. G. Ahrens, "Vocabulary Simplification for Children: A Special Case of 'Motherese.'"

    4. Susan Benedict and Lenore Carlisle, *Beyond Words*.

    5. Hayes and Ahrens, "Vocabulary Simplification for Children."

Chapter 6

    1. Carol Lynch-Brown and Carl Tomlinson, *Essentials of Children's Literature*, 76.

    2. Ibid., 3.

Chapter 7

    1. Perry Nodelman and Mavis Reimer, *The Pleasures of Children's Literature*, 3rd ed., 278.

Chapter 10

    1. Rudine Sims Bishop, "Selecting Literature for a Multicultural Curriculum," in *Using Multiethnic Literature in the K–8 Classroom*.

Chapter 14

1. S. Vardell, "A New 'Picture of the World': The NCTE Orbis Pictus Award for Outstanding Nonfiction for Children."

2. R. Palmer and R. Stewart, "Nonfiction Trade Book Use in Primary Grades."

3. R. Doiron, "Using Nonfiction in a Read-Aloud Program: Letting the Facts Speak for Themselves."

Chapter 15

1. Marie Clay, *Becoming Literate*, 181.

Chapter 20

1. Louise Rosenblatt, *Literature as Exploration*.

REFERENCES

Bishop, R. S. 1997. Selecting literature for a multicultural curriculum. In V. J. Harris, ed. *Using multiethnic literature in the K–8 classroom.* Norwood, MA: Christopher-Gordon.

Bryant, P. E., L. Bradley, M. Maclean, and J. Crossland. 1989. Nursery rhymes, phonological skills and reading. *Journal of Child Language* 16:407–28.

Bus, A. G. 2003. Social-emotional requisites for learning to read (in press). In A. van Kleeck, S. A. Stahl, and E. B. Bauer, eds. *On reading books to children: Parents and teachers.* Mahwah, NJ: Erlbaum, 3–15.

Chall, J., V. Jacobs, and L. Baldwin. 1990. *The reading crisis: Why poor children fall behind.* Cambridge, MA: Harvard University Press.

Clay, Marie M. 1991. *Becoming Literate: The Construction of Inner Control,* Portsmouth, NH: Heinemann.

Davey, B. 1983. Think aloud—Modeling the cognitive processes of reading comprehension. *Journal of Reading* 27:44–47.

De Temple, J., and C. Snow. 2003. *Learning words from books.* In A. van Kleeck, S. A. Stahl, and E. B. Bauer, eds. *On reading books to children: Parents and teachers.* Mahwah, NJ: Erlbaum, 16–36.

Doiron, R. 1994. Using nonfiction in a read-aloud program: Letting the facts speak for themselves. *The Reading Teacher* 47:616–24.

Duke, N. 2000. 3.6 minutes per day: The scarcity of informational texts in first grade. *Reading Research Quarterly* 35:202–24.

Dwyer, E. J., and E. E. Dwyer. 1994. How teacher attitudes influence reading achievement. In E. H. Cramer and M. Castle, eds., *Fostering the love of reading: The affective domain in reading education.* Newark, DE: International Reading Association, 66–73.

Fox, M. 2001. *Reading magic: Why reading aloud to our children will change their lives forever.* New York: Harcourt.

Gardner, H. 1983. *Frames of mind.* New York: Basic Books.

Geller, L. G. 1983. Children's rhymes and literacy learning: Making connections. *Language Arts* 60:184–93.

Graves, D. 1994. *A fresh look at writing.* Portsmouth, NH: Heinemann.

Gunderson, L. 1995. *The Monday morning guide to comprehension.* Markham, Ontario: Pippin Publishing.

Harvey, S., and A. Goudvis. 2000. S*trategies that work: Teaching comprehension to enhance understanding.* York, ME: Stenhouse Publishers.

Hayes, D. P., and M. G. Ahrens. 1988. Vocabulary simplification for children: a special case of 'motherese.' *Journal of Child Language* 15:395–410.

Loxterman, J. A., I. L. Beck, and M. G. McKewon. 1994. The effects of thinking aloud during reading on students' comprehension of more or less coherent text. *Reading Research Quarterly* 29:353–68.

Lynch-Brown, C., and C. M. Tomlinson. 2005. *Essentials of children's literature.* Boston, MA: Allyn & Bacon.

Morrsion, F., H. Bachman, and C. Connor. 2005. *Improving literacy in America: Guidelines from research.* New Haven and London: Yale University Press.

Moss, B., S. Leone, and M. Dipillo. 1997. Exploring the literature of fact: Linking reading and writing through information trade books. *Language Arts* 74:418–29.

Nodelman, P., and M. Reimer. 2003. *The pleasures of children's literature.* 3rd ed. New York: Allyn & Bacon.

Opitz, M. 2000. *Rhymes and reasons: Literature and language play for phonological awareness.* Portsmouth, NH: Heinemann.

Palmer, R., and R. Stewart. 2003. Nonfiction trade book use in primary grades. *The Reading Teacher* 57:38–48.

Rosenblatt, L. M. 1983. *Literature as exploration.* New York: Modern Language Association of America.

Snow, C., S. Burns, and P. Griffin, eds. 1998. *Preventing reading difficulties in young children.* Washington, DC: National Academy Press.

Spiegel, D. L. 1994. A portrait of parents of successful readers. In E. H. Cramer and M. Castle, eds., *Fostering the love of reading: The affective domain in reading education.* Newark, DE: International Reading Association, 74–87.

Stanovich, K. E. 1993. Romance and reality. *The Reading Teacher* 47:280–91.

Teale, W. H. 2003. *Reading aloud to young children as a classroom instructional activity: Insights from research and practice.* In A. van Kleeck, S. A. Stahl, and E. B. Bauer, eds., *On reading books to children: Parents and teachers.* Mahwah, NJ: Erlbaum, 114–39.

Vardell, S. 1991. A new "picture of the world": The NCTE Orbis Pictus Award for outstanding nonfiction for children. *Language Arts* 68:474–79.

Vygotsky, L. S. 1986. *Thought and language.* Cambridge, MA: MIT Press.

Your big backyard. 8, no. 11 (November 2004), National Wildlife Federation.

Your big backyard. 9, no. 8 (August 2005), National Wildlife Federation.

PERMISSIONS

Page 45: From *Owl Moon* by Jane Yolen, copyright © 1987 by Jane Yolen, text. Used by permission of Philomel Books, A Division of Penguin Young Readers Group, A Member of Penguin Group (USA) Inc., 345 Hudson Street, New York, NY 10014. All rights reserved.

Page 53: From *Firefly Mountain* written by Patricia Thomas, illustrated by Peter Sylvada, copyright © 2007. Used by permission of Peachtree Publishers, 1700 Chattahoochee Ave., Atlanta, GA, 30318.

Page 53: From *Saturdays and Teacakes*, written by Lester Laminick, illustrated by Chris Soentpiet, copyright © 2004. Used by permission of Peachtree Publishers, 1700 Chattahoochee Ave., Atlanta, GA, 30318.

Page 56: From *The Kissing Hand* by Audrey Penn, copyright © 2006, permission granted by Tanglewood Books.

Page 61: From *Llama, Llama Red Pajama* by Anna Dewdney, copyright © 2005 by Anna Dewdney. Used by permission of Viking Children's Books, A Division of Penguin Young Readers Group, A Member of Penguin Group (USA) Inc., 345 Hudson Street, New York, NY 10014. All rights reserved.

Page 72: From *The Very Lonely Firefly* by Eric Carle, copyright © 1995 by Eric Carle. Used by permission. All rights reserved.

Page 75: Excerpt from *The Magic Hat*, text copyright © 2002 by Mem Fox, reprinted by permission of Harcourt, Inc.

Page 78: From *I've Got an Elephant,* written by Anne Ginkel, illustrated by Janie Bynum, copyright © 2006. Used by permission of Peachtree Publishers, 1700 Chattahoochee Ave., Atlanta, GA, 30318.

Page 79: Excerpt from *The Napping House*, text copyright © 1984 by Audrey Wood, illustrations copyright © 1984 by Don Wood, reprinted by permission of Harcourt, Inc.

Page 85: From *Vamos a Leer,* by Judi Moreillon, copyright © 2004. Used by permission of Star Bright Books, Inc., New York.

Page 87: From *I Love My Hair,* by Natasha Tarpley, copyright © 2001. Used by permission of Little, Brown and Company, Publishers.

Page 88: From *Too Many Tamales*, by Gary Soto, copyright © 1993 by Gary Soto, text. Used by permission of G. P. Putnam's Sons, A Division of Penguin Young Readers Group, A Member of Penguin Group (USA) Inc., 345 Hudson Street, New York, NY 10014. All rights reserved.

Page 89: From *Abuela,* by Arthur Dorros, copyright © 1991 by Arthur Dorros, text. Used by permission of Dutton Children's Books, A Division of Penguin Young Readers Group, A Member of Penguin Group (USA) Inc., 345 Hudson Street, New York, NY 10014. All rights reserved.

SUBJECT INDEX

drama
   adding to the best books, 175
   being dramatic when reading
      aloud, 142, 163
   using to ignite your child's
      imagination, 174–75
   in wordless book, 84
   electronic media for literacy in-
      struction, 224–25
emotional impact
   multiculural literature, 92
   in poetry, 100
   in stories, 55
empathy
   books for understanding
      disabilities and other
      challenges, 157–59
   multicultural literature and, 89,
      97
exceptional language
   an element of quality literature,
      53, 86
   in *I Love My Hair*, 86
   in *I Love the Alphabet*, 102
expository text, 100, 128–32, 137
   booklist, 270
fluency, 3, 24, 74, 229, 232, 234
fourth-grade slump, 130
Gardner, Howard, 164. *See also* multiple intelligences
gender
   dispelling stereotypes, 95–96
illustrations. *See also* artwork
   in alphabet books, 113
      in chapter books, 122
   an element of quality literature,
      51–52, 192, 236
   collage illustrations, 194

complement to text, 61–68,
   70–71, 74, 86, 232
emotional impact of, 55
in *I Love the Night*, 38
in multicultural literature, 87
in nonfiction texts,136
in number books, 114
role of in reading, 23
taking cues from when reading
   aloud, 142
in *The Magic Hat*, 76
in *Tops and Bottoms*, 21
in wordless books, 84
imagery, 18, 100
informational texts, 57, 127–37, 212,
   240. *See also* expository text
   booklist, 270
   parent reference sheet, 310
intrapersonal intelligence, 164
kinesthetic activities, 219
kinesthetic intelligence. *See* bodily-
   kinesthetic intelligence
language experience approach
   (LEA), 183–88, 191
language play, 32, 36–37
Laura Ingalls Wilder Award, 58
library card, 214
linguistic intelligence, 164, 166
logical-mathematical intelligence,
   164, 166–67
lyrical sounds, 32, 99
magnetic letters, 214, 220
metacognition, 203
metaphors, 18, 44–45, 48, 100, 104
mood
   changing intentionally when
      reading aloud, 81, 142

conveyed in literature, 62–63,
65–66
emotions and, 160
establishing when reading
poetry, 107
of your child and influence on
book selection, 140–41
multicultural literature
as a mirror and window, 90–91
categories of, 93
characters in, 88
cultural details of, 88–89
emotional impact of, 92–93
gender, 95–96
religions and values in, 95
selecting, 86, 89–90
universal themes and values,
87–88, 91
multiculturalism as mainstream,
93–94
multiple intelligences, 163–66, 223
music. *See also* books created from
songs
musical intelligence, 164
narrative text, 129, 131
naturalist intelligence, 164, 176
nonfiction. *See* expository text *and*
informational texts
nursery rhymes, 36, 99, 105, 107, 114
patterns in words, 111, 233, 235
personification, 44–45, 48, 104–5
phonemes, 34, 36
phonemic awareness, 3, 29–37,
75–76, 99, 221–22, 239
booklist, 273
phonics, 19, 31, 34–35, 224, 236
picture books
contrasting speech with, 43

created from songs, 79
developing reader and, 305
emotional impact and, 55
myths about, 41
text and, 38, 46, 62, 68
selection of, 51–52, 57–58
universal themes, 56
used to teach opposites, 115
plot
early reader identifies, 305
element in a quality book, 80
interacting with text and, 198
twist or surprise in, 56
poetry, 3, 15–16, 18–19, 57, 98–103,
105–7, 144, 240
booklist, 278
predictable texts, 57, 69–79, 231, 234
booklist, 279
print conventions, 14, 16
prior knowledge, 12–13, 18, 20, 73,
120, 136, 145, 166, 188, 196–97,
200
prose, 16, 19, 126
psychomotor domain, 8
quality books, booklist, 289
quality literature
multicultural literature and,
86–93
parent reference sheet, 313
selection of, 50–60
questions
open-ended, 198
rote, 151
read-aloud experience, 4, 8, 10, 15, 18,
22, 28, 32, 39–40, 47, 50, 71, 80,
89, 98, 142, 146, 163, 165, 167–68,
172, 174, 177, 180, 184, 188–9,
199, 202–3, 220, 224, 229, 236

INDEX OF TITLES AND AUTHORS